D0563906

EDUCATING AN URBAN POPULATION

EDUCATING AN
URBAN POPULATION

Edited by

MARILYN GITTELL

SAGE PUBLICATIONS, INC. / Beverly Hills, California

Sage Publications, Inc., Beverly Hills, California

Library of Congress Catalog Card Number: 67-18421

Standard Book Number: 8039-1001-0 **(C)**
8039-0069-4 **(P)**

SECOND PRINTING

Printed in U.S.A. by
NOBLE OFFSET PRINTERS, INC.
NEW YORK 3, N. Y.
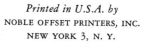

CONTENTS

INTRODUCTION

THE FAILURE OF URBAN SYSTEMS to meet the demands of a changing technology and a changing population results from an inability to readily adjust institutions and public policy. In recognition of this, research and reporting in urban studies has moved from a description of problems to an exploration of the policy process in order to better appreciate how decisions are made and who makes them. These studies, under the general heading of community power analysis, describe the relative responsiveness of urban institutions and leaders to changes in demands and the facility with which demands are converted into policy. Generally, these studies have concluded that functional specialization in decision-making is common to the large urban community. Thus, in each area of policy the groups which concern themselves with a particular function tend to control decisions. This conclusion suggests the importance of more intensive study by social scientists of the policy process in each of the functional areas. It is for this reason that this book is devoted to recent findings in educational research on the urban community.

In the last several decades, social scientists virtually ignored educational institutions and educational policy. Much of the research that has been conducted by professional educators concentrates on programs and techniques with only very recent interest expressed in how educational policy is made and the adaptation of educational institutions to the changes in urban communities. The 1954 decision of the Supreme Court on school integration exposed the schools and the school professionals to more critical scrutiny. The issue aroused the interest of social scientists, and studies of desegregation policy revealed more fundamental problems worthy of analysis. Fortunately, the taboos that surrounded the problems of public education and sealed them off from critical study have given way to more forthright scholarship. Although some material has been published recently, there is an obvious dearth of information available on the more complex problems of urban education. Despite the interest that has been aroused there continues to be a shortage of the kind of research that goes beyond the description of problems to an understanding of the school system as a political and social subsystem.

In the 1960's the pressures for coping with the failure of urban education shifted from pleas for integration and compensatory education to demands for complete restructuring of city school systems and increased community control. The decay of urban education in city school systems throughout the country, and the ineffectiveness of those solutions which have been offered, will persuade larger segments of the community of the need for more fundamental reform of school systems. More and more pressure will be brought to bear on school professionals to relinquish control, particularly because they have been unable to cope with the educational needs of a changing urban population. The crises in public education will lead to increased conflict until there is acceptance of the pressing need for reform. Administrative reforms can only offer temporary relief—even those cities which are responding in this area will find that unless they can again make the public feel a part of the educational process, their administrative reorganization will be unable to resolve the basic school problems. Researchers will be pressed for more intensive analysis of the political and social aspects of the educational process and for more viable solutions to the educational needs of the urban population.

The movement for greater community participation in the policy process in American cities extends beyond school reform to other areas. It represents the hope of a large segment of the

8

population which has been alienated from the institutions of the society. Because education is so integral a part of local government and because it represents such a vital link in the development of the community, it will be a major target of community activitists in the 1970's. The test of the vitality and responsiveness of the city school systems will come in the next decade. There will be those (as there were on the integration issue) who will claim that educational institutions should not be used to solve the ills of the society and that these institutions can only be a reflection of the larger system. Others will recognize the potential of school systems as a viable community force for change in the city. The future of city schools may well rest on the kind of response that is forthcoming.

This selection of articles was compiled to present a cross-section of current research and thinking on the problems of urban education as they are developing in the social sciences. The authors represent several different disciplines; each of them, however, is currently engaged in field research on some significant aspect of urban education. Although their specific research efforts differ in subject matter and methodological approach, there is a common interest in the changing character of school populations and the means of adjustment to these new demands. All of the authors have conducted their research with a consistent framework of concern for the broader implications of urban development and the policy-making processes. They are involved not only with the question of what is necessary, but also how it can be achieved.

The book is divided into three sections. The first part, *Demands on School Policy,* is concerned with the range of pressures that have developed on urban educational systems in recent years.

The Campbell-Meranto article provides a general empirical setting for a discussion of the relationship between demands and resources in urban education. The authors have carefully delineated the elements in urban growth that have influenced the performance of the education function in urban centers.

The Havighurst selection on Chicago could well be a description of the school system in any of the large cities in the country. Although the particular evidence concerns Chicago; the implications are general. Havighurst's intimate knowledge of the Chicago system makes his discussion of pressing needs more compelling.

The Sacks-Ranney piece analyzes suburban education with special emphasis on the determinants of school support in these communities. The general tone of the group of articles in Part I suggests the magnitude of the problems faced by our urban school systems. Integral to those problems is the seeking out of new resources to meet pressing demands. However, the ability to meet these demands will depend in large part on those who control policy and the policy process.

Moving from the more general demands on education policy which result from urban and suburban development, the remaining selections deal with the particular demands on education in the legal requirements of school desegregation (Buss), the issue of fiscal independence (Hollander) and the use of demographic data (Glatt-Roaden).

Part II presents a series of research findings in several areas of school policy-making.

The Crain-Street study of school desegration and school decision-making is a comparative analysis of eight northern big city districts which was carried out by the National Opinion Research Center. The implications of this study reach beyond the question of desegration, for the authors provide a discussion of the basic inadequacies of the large systems to adapt to a social change. The Rodgers case study of New York City desegregation provides a more detailed analysis of the role of the various participants. In some ways it substantiates the conclusions of the Crain-Street study but it adds several dimensions to the analysis of desegregation policy.

The Rosenthal article is a comparative analysis of the views of leaders of teachers' organizations in five large cities. It compares leadership perceptions of power and attitudes concerning power with regard to several areas of policy-making. Rosenthal's approach is significant because it provides insights into the attitudes of teachers toward power and provides a basis for comparison with actual findings in studies of the distribution of power in school systems.

The Gittell and Masotti selections analyze participation in school policy in their respective studies of New York City and Cleveland. The latter is concerned with the role of a particular segment of the community—the Negro—and its area of study is the school vote. The Gittell research is related to five areas of school policy pinpointing the roles of several groups as participants. The conclusions in the Gittell study suggest a very narrow or closed participating decision-making system in education.

The conclusions reached in these seemingly different types of political analyses are quite similar. Each identifies an inability of the urban education system to respond to the pressing demands made upon it. The circle of school decision-makers is apparently confined to the school professionals and the school board with restricted participation by others. The presentation or consideration of alternative policies is limited and preservation of the status quo is secured. The newer groups in the cities have not been able to achieve the influence necessary to promote change or convert their demands into policies. Since all of the selections affirm the context of the schools in the political system of which it is an integral part, it is clear that political realities will have to be faced by urban educators in the coming decades.

Part III is concerned with solutions, presenting the approaches of four types of social scientists (sociologist, political scientist, economist, and educator) to the means of adapting aspects on school systems to the major demands of urban education. The proposals range from overall planning of education outposts, a comprehensive device for long-range policy-making by Hirsch, to the specialized considerations of preparing school personnel by Klopf and Bowman. Pettigrew discusses the crucial problem of school desegregation and its implications for the urban Negro and for our society. Minar deals with the impact of school politics stressing the need for adjustment in "educational government." Implicit in these proposals is the urgency of a broader conceptual framework for resolving school problems as well as a broader base for school policy-making. More extensive discussion among social scientists on the growing complexity of urban education is a prerequisite to achieving solutions, in the context of a realistic appraisal of the social, economic and political resources. This volume is an effort to encourage that discussion.

MARILYN GITTELL

Revised for second printing,
New York, N.Y. 1969

PART I

DEMANDS ON SCHOOL POLICY

The Nature of the Problem

ALAN K. CAMPBELL and PHILIP MERANTO

Alan K. Campbell is Professor of Political Science and Director of the Metropolitan Studies Center, Maxwell Graduate School of Citizenship and Public Affairs, Syracuse University. Philip Meranto is Assistant Professor of Government and Research Associate in the Public Administration and Metropolitan Affairs Program, Southern Illinois University, Edwardsville.

THE

METROPOLITAN

EDUCATION

DILEMMA: Matching

Resources To Needs

THE METROPOLITANIZATION of American society has gained widespread attention in recent years from a notable variety of scholars, popular writers, and public officials. Some scholars have preoccupied themselves with tracing the historical roots of metropolitanism, while others have attempted to demonstrate empirical relationships between metropolitanism and the social, economic, and political dimensions of society. Popular writers have interpreted some of these findings for the general public, and they have usually stressed the so-called "decay" of large American cities and the multitude of problems plaguing these urban centers. While journalists and scholars have been describing and analyzing the metropolitan phenomenon, public officials have been struggling with its policy implications. For these officials, the fact of metropolitanism, however dimly perceived, complicates

AUTHOR'S NOTE: *This article is based, in part, on a Carnegie Corporation-supported larger study of* Policies and Policy-Making in Large City Education Systems *being done at the Metropolitan Studies Center, Maxwell Graduate School, Syracuse University. A description of the entire study is available.*

many of the problems with which they must deal and influences many of the decisions they make.

The extent of this concern with one of the major forces of change in postwar America has been beneficial but, on occasion, misleading. On the one hand, it has stimulated popular interest and knowledge of the changing character of American culture. Further, it has prompted a wide assortment of research efforts about the causes and consequences of metropolitanism. On the other hand, there has been a tendency to see nearly all of the changes and problems which characterize contemporary America as consequences of the metropolitan process. Too often the interrelationships between substantive problems and metropolitanism have been blurred rather than clarified by this kind of perception. Similarly, there has been a tendency to assume that the problems involved in the provision of any public service (education, welfare, health, transportation, and so forth) are all related to or result from metropolitanism. This is not the case. With every function there are problems that would exist even if the country had not become metropolitan. Further, the fact of metropolitanism is not a problem in itself, but the dynamics which underpin it and the patterns which accompany it may be perceived by individuals and groups within the society as creating problems, and in many instances the problems thus perceived can be solved only by public action.

The tendency to equate both social change and functional concerns with metropolitanism is evident in the field of education. Much of the literature which purports to discuss the implications of metropolitanism or urbanism for education is, instead, simply a catalog of the substantive issues which characterize the education function. The metropolitan component of the problems is often assumed to be self-evident, and no effort is made to demonstrate the relationship between metropolitanism and the substantive issues.

It is the primary purpose of this article to delineate those aspects of metropolitanism which produce important consequences for the performance of the education function in large urban centers. Such an analysis necessitates, first, an investigation of basic population trends and an examination of the distributional results of these trends on income, educational attainment, race, and the nature of school population. Second, the relationships between these population attributes and the provision of educational services are analyzed, as are the relationships between education needs and the quantity and quality of resources available in the various parts of the metropolis. And finally, the public policy alternatives are examined in terms of their ability to meet the demonstrated needs.

Characteristics of Metropolitan America

The most often cited statistic about metropolitanism is the growing proportion of the American population which lives in metropolitan areas.[1] By 1964 this proportion had reached 65 percent, and projections indicate that it will approach 70 percent by 1970. A simultaneous phenomenon, perhaps of even greater significance for the education function, is the redistribution of people between the central city and its suburbs. There has been a gradual but consistent decrease in the proportion of total metropolitan population which lives within central cities. In 1900 over 60 percent of the metropolitan population lived within central cities; by 1965 this share had declined to under 50 percent.

This decline in the proportion of the metropolitan population living in central cities represents for many cities, particularly those in the largest metropolitan areas, an absolute decline in the central city population. Table 1 illustrates this fact by presenting the percent of population change for both central city and outside central city between 1950 and 1960 for selected large cities. The

---

1. The Census Bureau definition of the metropolitan area and of its component parts is followed throughout this article. That definition is as follows: "Except in New England, a standard metropolitan statistical area (an SMSA) is a county or group of contiguous counties which contain at least one city of 50,000 inhabitants or more or 'twin cities' with a combined population of at least 50,000. In addition to the county, or counties, containing such a city or cities, contiguous counties are included in an SMSA if, according to certain criteria, they are essentially metropolitan in character and are socially and economically integrated with the central city." In New England, towns are used instead of counties.

few instances of an increase in central city population were caused, in most cases, by annexation rather than by population growth within the original boundaries of the central city. Clearly, the population within the largest metropolitan areas is decentralizing.

TABLE 1

Population Change in 15 Largest SMSAs
Central City and Outside Central City: 1950-1960

	CENTRAL CITY		OUTSIDE CENTRAL CITY	
SMSA	1960	Percent Change since 1950	1960	Percent Change since 1950
New York	7,781,984	— 1.4	2,912,649	75.0
Chicago	3,550,404	— 1.9	2,670,509	71.5
Los Angeles*	2,823,183	27.1	3,919,513	82.6
Philadelphia	2,002,512	— 3.3	2,340,385	46.3
Detroit	1,670,144	— 9.7	2,092,216	79.3
Baltimore	939,024	— 1.1	787,999	72.4
Houston	938,219	57.4	304,939	44.8
Cleveland	876,050	— 4.2	920,545	67.2
Washington	763,956	— 4.8	661,911	87.0
St. Louis	750,026	—12.5	1,310,077	51.9
Milwaukee	741,324	16.3	452,966	41.7
San Francisco†	1,159,932	— 4.5	1,075,495	55.0
Boston	697,197	—13.0	1,892,104	17.6
Dallas	679,684	56.4	403,997	30.7
New Orleans	627,525	10.0	240,955	109.6
United States (all SMSAs)	58,004,334	10.7	54,880,844	48.6

* Includes Long Beach.
† Includes Oakland.
SOURCE: U.S. Bureau of the Census, **U.S. Census of Population: 1960.** Vol. I, **Characteristics of the Population,** Part A. Number of Inhabitants, Table 33.

The significance of these shifts for the education function would be substantial even if the population redistribution between central city and suburbs was random relative to the socioeconomic characteristics of the people involved. But this is not the case. The shifting is not only a matter of numbers of people; it also involves a sorting-out process. In general, it is the poor, less educated, nonwhite Americans who are staying in the central city and the higher income, better educated, whites who are moving out, although this description must be qualified somewhat in terms of the size of the metropolitan area and region of the country in which it is located. The larger the metropolitan area, however, the more accurate is this description.[2]

This sorting-out process has resulted in a median family income for central city residents in 1959 which was 88.5 percent of outside central city income; $5,940 for central cities, compared to $6,707 for the suburbs. Although median family income for both central city and outside central city residents has grown since 1959, the gap is widening, with central city median family income in 1964 at $6,697, while for outside central city areas it was $7,772, a proportionate relationship of 86.2 percent.[3]

These nation-wide averages hide important differences between metropolitan areas which can be explained, in part, by differences in population size. Overall, the larger metropolitan areas have higher family incomes than the smaller ones. In metropolitan areas having populations of over 3 million—the largest size category—the percent of families earning over $10,000 a year is almost double the percent earning less than $3,000 a year. Further, it is only in this category that the central cities have a higher proportion of their population over $10,000 than under $3,000.

The large metropolitan areas have less poverty proportionately than the small ones. This finding, however, is not as significant for the performance of the education function as is the contrast between central cities and their suburbs. It is the large, relatively affluent areas which possess the greatest income disparity between central cities and their suburbs. In the size category of over 3 million, for every 100 families in central cities earning under $3,000, there are 127 earning over $10,000. In the suburbs, the comparable number of families with an income over $10,000 is 312 for every 100 families earning under $3,000. In other words, there are 185 more families with income over $10,000 in the suburbs for every 100 families under $3,000 than is true for the central

2. For a complete discussion of these differences relative to size and region, see Advisory Commission on Intergovernmental Relations, *Metropolitan Social and Economic Disparities: Implications for Intergovernmental Relations in Central Cities and Suburbs*, Washington, D.C.: U.S. Government Printing Office, 1965.

3. U.S. Bureau of the Census, *Consumer Income*, Series P-60, No. 48, April 25, 1966.

cities. The magnitude of this difference in income distribution between central city and outside central city declines as the size of the area decreases and, in fact, reverses itself for the two size-categories below 250,000 population.

The differences in income characteristics between central cities and their suburbs is reflected in the educational attainment of the respective populations. Again, the contrast between central city and suburbs is substantial: 40.9 percent of central city pupils have completed four years of high school or more, while outside the central cities the comparable percentage is 50.9. Once more the differences are greatest when one examines the data for individual large metropolitan areas.

TABLE 2

Educational Attainment of Persons 25 Years or Older in 15 Urbanized Areas By Residence, by Color: 1960

FOUR YEARS OF HIGH SCHOOL OR MORE (IN PERCENT)

Urbanized Area*	Central City	Urban Fringe*	Central City Nonwhites
New York	36.4	48.7	31.2
Chicago	35.3	53.9	27.3
Los Angeles	53.4	53.4	43.6
Philadelphia	30.7	48.0	23.6
Detroit	34.4	47.5	26.5
Baltimore	28.2	42.3	19.7
Houston	45.2	50.1	26.2
Cleveland	30.1	55.5	28.1
Washington	47.8	67.5	33.5
St. Louis	26.3	43.3	20.2
Milwaukee	39.7	54.4	26.0
San Francisco	49.4	57.9	39.1
Boston	44.6	55.8	36.2
Dallas	48.9	56.4	25.2
New Orleans	33.3	44.6	15.0
All Urbanized Areas	40.9	50.9	28.3

* This table utilizes urbanized area and urban fringe as units due to the availability of data. The Census Bureau defines an urbanized area as "the thickly settled portions of the SMSA." The urban fringe constitutes the urbanized area minus the central city.

SOURCE: Computed from U.S. Bureau of the Census, **U.S. Census of Population: 1960, General Social and Economic Characteristics**, Washington, D.C.: U.S. Government Printing Office, 1961; and **U.S. Census of Population and Housing: 1960, Census Tracts**, Washington, D.C.: U.S. Government Printing Office, 1961.

The explanation for the income and education differences between central city and suburb rests in part on differences in the distribution of nonwhite population within metropolitan areas.[4] Although the nonwhite component of the American population has now distributed itself between metropolitan and nonmetropolitan areas in approximately the same proportion as the white population, the distribution within metropolitan areas follows a quite different pattern. It is well known that the proportion of nonwhites in central cities has been increasing, while the proportion in the suburban areas has been declining. This larger proportion of Negro population in central cities helps to account in part for the differences in educational achievement and income between central cities and suburbs. Due to a history of discrimination in all aspects of life, the Negro has a lower income and less education than does his white neighbor. In central cities, for example, the 1964 median family income for Negroes was $4,463, while for whites it was $7,212. In 1964 the percentage of all Negroes twenty-five years old and over having completed four years of high school was 17.1; the comparable percentage for whites was 31.3.

The impact of the growing proportion of nonwhite population in central cities is intensified for the schools by the even higher proportion of public school enrollment which is nonwhite. This difference in population and enrollment proportions is a result of age distribution, family composition, and the greater tendency of white parents to send their children to private and parochial schools. Table 3 shows, for 1960, the proportion of the total population of the largest cities which was nonwhite and the proportion of public school enrollment which was nonwhite. The ratio of nonwhites to whites is considerably higher in the school population than in the total population, and indications are that this is becoming increasingly the case.

---

4. The terms nonwhite and Negro are used interchangeably in this article since Negroes constitute 92 percent of the nonwhite classification as defined by the Census Bureau.

TABLE 3

Nonwhite Population Contrasted With Nonwhite School Enrollment for 15 Largest Cities: 1960

City	Percent Nonwhite of Total Population	Percent Nonwhite of School Population	Difference in Proportions of Nonwhite School Enrollment and Nonwhite Population
New York	14.0	22.0	8.0
Chicago	22.9	39.8	16.9
Los Angeles	12.2	20.5	8.3
Philadelphia	26.4	46.7	20.3
Detroit	28.9	42.9	14.0
Baltimore	34.7	50.1	15.4
Houston	22.9	30.2	8.7
Cleveland	28.6	46.1	17.5
Washington	53.9	77.5	23.6
St. Louis	28.6	48.8	20.2
Milwaukee	8.4	16.2	7.8
San Francisco	14.3	30.5	16.2
Boston	9.1	16.4	7.3
Dallas	19.0	26.0	7.0
New Orleans	37.2	55.4	18.2

SOURCE: U.S. Bureau of the Census, U.S. Census of Population: 1960, Selected Area Reports, Standard Metropolitan Statistical Areas and General Social and Economic Characteristics, 1960.

The sorting-out process which produces significant differences in socioeconomic characteristics between central city and suburban populations is the chief background factor against which the educational implications of metropolitanism must be examined. To the extent that these differences in characteristics produce different kinds of educational problems, the fact of metropolitanism is important to the provision of educational services.

Population Composition and Educational Problems

The redistribution process described in the preceding section has left the central city school system with a disproportionate segment of pupils who are referred to as "disadvantaged," and this appears to be a trend that is continually increasing. These students are disadvantaged in terms of the income level and educational background of their parents, their family composition, and their general home environment. To the extent that education of the disadvantaged is a more complex phenomenon than the education of middle-income pupils, the central city school systems face a different and more serious set of problems than do suburban education systems.[5]

In the immediate postwar period, the most striking phenomenon in education related to the metropolitanization of the country was the impact on suburban areas of a rapidly increasing population. The suburbs, however, responded well to the challenge and rapidly met the new requirements in building the necessary physical facilities and the provision of a teaching staff. The significance of the suburban expansion for the central city schools, however, was only dimly, if at all, perceived. It is now clear that the suburbanization of the country, by draining the higher income families and much economic activity from the central cities, produced greater problems for education in central cities than it did for the suburbs.

As the proportion of disadvantaged students in the central cities has increased, there has been a simultaneous increase in what are known in the community as "undesirable" schools, schools to which parents would prefer not to send their children. Many of these schools are so characterized because of the large proportion (in many cases, nearly 100 percent) of the students who are Negro. Because of population trends and the residential pattern of most of our cities, it is increasingly difficult to rearrange district lines to achieve what is referred to as "racial balance" among schools. As a result, more and more central city schools are being designated as "undesirable."

The underlying cause for the undesirable label in educational terms, however, is low income, not race. Several studies have now substantiated that the single most important determinant of edu-

---

5. For a sampling of the literature which deals with this topic see Frank Riessman, *The Culturally Deprived Child*, New York: Harper and Row Publishers, Incorporated, 1962; Judith R. Kramer and Seymour Leventman, *Children of the Gilded Ghetto*, New Haven: Yale University Press, 1961; A. Harry Passow (Ed.), *Education in Depressed Areas*, New York: Teachers College, Columbia University, 1963; and C. W. Hunnicutt (Ed.), *Urban Education and Cultural Deprivation*, Syracuse, N.Y.: Syracuse University Press, 1964.

cational achievement is family income.[6] In the high correlation between income and test scores, income undoubtedly is a proxy, and a fairly accurate one, for a combination of factors—family characteristics, educational attainment of parents, home environment. When white parents resist sending their children to undesirable schools, this is not necessarily a racial issue, although it is often difficult to separate the racial and educational questions which currently surround controversies over central city schools.

The undesirable schools are unattractive not only to parents but also to first-rate teachers. Teachers seek to be assigned to the "better" schools within the city system, and many abandon central city districts entirely for more attractive suburban districts. Furthermore, central city systems find it increasingly difficult to attract choice graduates of the universities as new teachers.

The resource needs for central cities relate not only to teachers but to other educational needs as well. Cities have much older school plants than do suburbs, and the site costs for building new schools within central cities are substantially higher than those for the suburbs. In addition, there is greater competition within the cities for resources for such noneducation functions as police protection, street maintenance, and welfare than is true in the suburban areas. These noneducation needs compete for the same resources which the central city schools need to meet their pressing educational problems.

This set of central city education problems exists in a society which is in need of a continuous improvement in its educational output. The very fact of metropolitanization implies extended specialization in a society which is increasingly complex. The need, therefore, is for a better and better educated work force. To some extent, the suburban areas have responded to this need through the gradual improvement and sophistication of its curricula and

6. Patricia Sexton, *Education and Income: Inequalities in Our Public Schools,* New York: The Viking Press, 1962; H. Thomas James, J. Alan Thomas, and Harold J. Dyck, *Wealth, Expenditures and Decision-Making for Education,* Stanford, Calif.: Stanford University Press, 1963; Fels Institute of Local and State Government, University of Pennsylvania, *Special Education and Fiscal Requirements of Urban School Districts in Pennsylvania,* 1964; and Jesse Burkhead, *Cost and Performance in Large City School Systems,* forthcoming publication of Metropolitan Studies Center, Syracuse University, as part of the Carnegie supported study of Large City Education Systems, 1967.

teaching. Curriculum improvement in central cities, however, is much less discernible and is particularly lacking in the education of the disadvantaged.[7]

The answer to this problem does not rest with providing education with a different purpose for disadvantaged pupils. A suggestion by James Conant that disadvantaged pupils should be concentrated in vocational education hardly seems appropriate.[8] Improvement in the quality of vocational education is needed, but it should not be made especially for the disadvantaged. Among the disadvantaged, there are those who are capable of achieving high educational accomplishment in a great variety of fields and options, and in terms of equity the opportunities should be the same for them as for other pupils. Further, it is apparent that the greatest employment growth of the future will be in the white-collar occupations, not in vocational fields offered by most of today's vocational schools.

One of the central issues confronting large city schools, therefore, becomes the allocation of sufficiently massive resources to the field of education for the disadvantaged to help them overcome their present handicaps. To what extent are large central cities capable of providing the resources needed to meet these problems and where are these resources to come from if the central cities cannot provide them from local assets?

The Availability of Resources

The educational problems confronting large cities would not be nearly as critical if cities had at their disposal an ample supply of resources to deal with these difficulties. But this is not the case. The metropolitan process has not only redistributed the population in a way that presents the central cities with a population having special educational difficulties; the process has simultaneously op-

---

7. William W. Wayson, *Curriculum Development in Large City Schools*, forthcoming publication of Metropolitan Studies Center, Syracuse University, as part of the Carnegie supported study of Large City Education Systems, 1967.

8. James B. Conant, *Slums and Suburbs*, New York: The New American Library, 1964, pp. 33-49.

erated to weaken the local resource base which must be used to meet their needs.

It has already been noted that the central city component of the metropolitan area population has lower income levels than the population outside the central city. This pattern is particularly significant because it has become increasingly apparent that income is the single most important variable in explaining the expenditure levels of a community for both educational and noneducational services.[9] To a large extent, it is the income available which influences the ability of a governmental unit to meet the service requirements of its population. Central cities are simply losing ground in this respect, while their functional needs are simultaneously increasing.

Metropolitanism is characterized by the decentralization of economic activities from the core city to the surrounding areas, as well as by decentralization of population. Evidence of this trend can be found by examining the distribution of economic activity within specific metropolitan areas over time. For example, an investigation of the proportion of manufacturing carried on in the central city portion of twelve large metropolitan areas demonstrates that the central city percentage has clearly declined over the past three decades, particularly in the post-World War II period. Whereas the twelve cities accounted, on the average, for 66.1 percent of manufacturing employment in 1929, this proportion decreased to 60.8 percent by 1947 and then declined to less than half (48.9 percent) by 1958.[10]

A similar decentralizing trend for retail activity can be demonstrated by examining the growth of retail store sales in the metropolitan area as a whole, in the central city, and in the central business district of the core city for the period 1948 to

9. Alan K. Campbell and Seymour Sacks, *Metropolitan America: Fiscal Patterns and Governmental Systems*, forthcoming publication, Metropolitan Studies Center, Syracuse University, 1966.

10. See Raymond Vernon, *The Changing Economic Function of the Central City*, New York: Committee for Economic Development, 1960; and U.S. Bureau of the Census, *Census of Manufacturing, 1958*. The cities include: Baltimore, Boston, Chicago, Cincinnati, Cleveland, Detroit, Los Angeles-Long Beach, New York, Philadelphia, Pittsburgh, St. Louis, and San Francisco-Oakland.

1958. Such a comparison was made for a sample of twenty-two large cities. It was found that with the exception of one (Birmingham, Alabama), the entire metropolitan area had increased its retail sales more than had the central city and far more than the central business district. This evidence illustrates that the historical dominance of the central city and its business district over regional retail activity is on the decline.[11] The patterns for manufacturing employment and retail sales reflect the fact that economic activity, like population, has migrated from the central city outward. This push for dispersal is related to a number of factors, including the need for physical space, the introduction of new industrial processes, the ascendance of the automobile and truck as means of transportation and shipping, the building of vast highway systems, and the spreading of the population throughout the metropolis.[12]

The consequences of this economic migration for the tax base of the central city have been widely discussed. As industries continue to move outward, taxable assessed valuation, the source of local property taxes, has barely held its own in many cities and has actually declined in several large cities. For example, in a recent five-year period, the percent changes in taxable assessed valuation for seven cities were as follows: Baltimore, − 10.5 percent; Boston, − 1.2 percent; Buffalo, − 1.0 percent; Detroit, − 2.0 percent; St. Louis, + 1.1 percent; Philadelphia, + 2.8 percent; and Cleveland − 3.4 percent.[13] These changes in taxable valuation do not yield the necessary resources to deal with the problems facing these urban centers.

Translated into educational terms, the recent performance of the tax base in large cities has not kept pace with the growth or nature of the school population in these cities. Indeed, an examination of the per pupil taxable valuation over a five-year period shows that ten large cities out of fourteen experienced a decrease

11. See U.S. Bureau of the Census, *Census of Business, 1958* for the twenty-two cities which reported all three figures.

12. Edgar M. Hoover and Raymond Vernon, *Anatomy of a Metropolis*, Garden City, N.Y.: Doubleday and Company, Inc., 1962.

13. The Research Council of the Great Cities Program for School Improvement, *The Challenge of Financing Public Schools in Great Cities*, Chicago, 1964.

in this source of revenue. Since local property taxes are the most important source of local educational revenues, large city schools can barely meet ordinary education needs let alone resolve the problems resulting from the shifting population distribution.

TABLE 4

Five-year Changes in Per Pupil Taxable Assessed Valuation

	Percent of Change over a Five-year Period*	
	City	State (minus cities listed)
Baltimore	—19.3	10.2
Boston	— 5.3	not available
Buffalo	— 8.6	26.1
Chicago	— 6.0	— 0.2
Cleveland	— 9.9	4.2
Detroit	— 5.7	3.4
Houston	— 2.8	18.9
Los Angeles	5.1	5.6
Milwaukee	— 9.6	— 1.1
New York City	32.4	26.1
Philadelphia	— 0.6	13.6
Pittsburgh	2.2	13.6
St. Louis	—10.6	3.1
San Francisco	5.9	5.6

* Change is for the most recent five-year period for which data are available.
SOURCE: Research Council of the Great Cities Program for School Improvement, **The Challenge of Financing Public Schools in Great Cities**, Chicago, 1964.

There is an additional factor which weighs against the capacity of central cities to meet their pressing educational needs. The postwar intensification of urbanization and metropolitanization has resulted in a demand for a wider range and higher quality of public services than at any other time in the nation's history. These demands are particularly great in the largest cities, where the necessity for providing a wide variety of welfare, public safety, sanitation, traffic control, and street maintenance services has been most pressing. The fact that central cities have responded to these demands is reflected in the data included in Table 5. An investigation of the fiscal patterns in thirty-six Standard Metropolitan Statistical Areas revealed that for the year 1957, the central cities in these areas were spending $25.66 more per capita in total expenditures than the communities in the outlying areas. Unfortunately for education systems, this difference was not due to higher educational expenditures in the central cities. In fact, their education expenditures were $27.82 per capita less than what was spent on education in the corresponding suburban areas. It was in the noneducational category that the central city exceeded the outside central city area in expenditures. In this sample, central cities spent about $53.00 more per capita on noneducation services than their surrounding communities. Further, this difference is largely due to the "all other" classification, which includes the

TABLE 5

Fiscal Characteristics
Central City and Outside Central City Areas,
36 Sample SMSAs: 1957

Per Capita	Central City	Outside Central City	Differences Central City —Outside Central City
Total General Expenditure	$185.49	$159.83	25.66*
Education expenditure	58.02	85.84	—27.82†
Current	49.16	61.72	—12.56†
Capital	8.86	24.12	—15.26†
Noneducation expenditure	127.48	73.95	53.53†
Total highways	16.55	14.41	2.14
Health and hospitals (current)	14.84	7.09	7.55†
Public welfare	10.22	8.34	1.88†
All other	85.70	43.80	41.90†
Taxes	109.07	85.78	23.29†
Property tax	92.06	78.58	13.48
Nonproperty tax	17.01	7.20	9.81†
Proxy Variables			
Nonaided education expenditure (education taxes)	42.24	56.43	—14.19†
Nonaided noneducation expenditure (noneducation taxes)	108.33	60.39	47.94†
Total Aid	34.65	39.72	— 5.07
Education Aid	16.12	28.43	—12.31†
Noneducation aid	18.60	11.83	6.77*
Exhibit:			
Per capita income	1,998.86	2,280.50	—281.64*

* Significant at .05 level of confidence.
† Significant at .01 level of confidence.
NOTE: Totals do not add because of unallocated aid.
    All figures in per capita terms unless otherwise indicated.
SOURCE: Alan K. Campbell and Seymour Sacks, **op. cit.**

traditional municipal services that cities, unlike suburban communities, must provide. The cost and number of noneducational governmental services tend to increase with the size and density of a district and to consume a larger proportion of the budget in major cities where many services are provided for nonresidents as well as for residents. It is reasonable to suggest that this "municipal overburden" is supported at the expense of the education function.[14]

The figures in Table 5 also show that the central cities were supporting these expenditure levels by taxes that were $23.29 per capita higher than in areas outside the cities. In contrast, the cities received about $5.00 per capita less in total intergovernmental aid and, most importantly, $12.31 less per capita in education aid than did suburban areas, where income was higher. In other words, not only are central cities pressed to support a large array of services by a relatively shrinking tax base, but they tax themselves more heavily to do so and they receive less intergovernmental aid than the more wealthy communities in their metropolitan area. This fiscal pattern borders on the ironic when it is realized that central city education systems must compete for educational resources with suburban school districts which have higher income levels and receive a greater amount of state aid. In fact, the state aid system actually works to intensify rather than to resolve the educational crises facing large city school systems.

The multitude of fiscal difficulties faced by the central cities results in a lower per student expenditure in the cities than in surrounding suburbs. Specifically, an examination of the thirty-seven largest metropolitan areas in the country indicated that the central city school districts in 1962 were spending an average of $144.96 less per pupil than their suburban counterparts.[15] This considerable difference in expenditures per student between central city and suburb would be serious even if the educational problems

---

14. David C. Ranney, *School Government and the Determinants of the Fiscal Support for Large City Education Systems*, unpublished doctoral dissertation, Syracuse University, 1966.

15. For a breakdown by individual city, see the Sacks-Ranney article in this issue.

were the same for the two type areas; but, as has already been demonstrated, such is not the case.

It is not known what amount of additional resources per student would be necessary to provide an adequate education for the culturally disadvantaged. On the basis of studies yet to be published, it is clear that the present small amounts of additional resources being used in some cities for what is generally referred to as "compensatory education" are accomplishing very little.[16] The additional resources currently being allocated to these programs are simply not sufficient.

In this respect it is interesting to note the amount per student which is being expended in the urban Job Corps Centers which have been established by the Federal Anti-Poverty Program to provide a meaningful education for disadvantaged pupils. Present costs for establishing and organizing the centers amount to $10,500 per student per year.[17] It is estimated that once the camps are in full operation and their costs level off, the expenditures per student will be reduced to $7,350 per year. Even if the subsistence cost (which in the regular public school system is absorbed by parents) is subtracted from this $7,350 figure, there remains a vast gap between the resulting figure and what is currently being spent in central city public schools. Assuming that the subsistence costs are $3,000 per year, this leaves a per pupil education expenditure of approximately $4,350. This figure presents a vivid contrast to education expenditures in many cities. New York City, for example, with the highest large central city expenditures per pupil in the country, expended $603.95 per pupil in 1961-1962, while Chicago spent $409.78 per student.

Obviously the quantity of resources being put into Job Corps education exceeds what is available or likely to become available for general central city education. Nevertheless, it does point the direction which must be followed if the disadvantaged schools in our central cities are to come near accomplishing their educational purposes. Such educational services as extensive counseling of individual students, small, specialized classes, and effective job

16. Jesse Burkhead, *op. cit.*
17. "The Job Corps," *The New Yorker*, May 21, 1966, p. 112f.

training, all of which are furnished by the Job Corps, are not provided cheaply. The Job Corps Center at Camp Kilmer, New Jersey, has a student enrollment of approximately 2,000 and a teaching and administrative staff of about 450, a student-professional ratio of about 4.5 students to 1 professional. The present ratio in larger city school systems is between 25-30 students to 1 professional.

It may be argued that comparing general public schools to the Job Corps schools is not realistic, since the Job Corps concentrates on those whom the regular schools failed. The point, however, is that the regular school systems failed these students, in part because they did not have the resources to provide the kind and quality of education needed. The obvious need is for more resources and an allocation system which recognizes the areas and students with special needs.

This analysis of the resources available for central city education demonstrates the disparity between needs and resources. There is little indication that present trends will substantially alter these circumstances; in fact, there is good reason to believe that the situation is becoming more serious. If these trends are to be modified, imaginative public policy decisions must be identified and pursued. What public policy alternatives exist and to what extent are they politically feasible?

Public Policy Implications

A variety of means exists for attacking the lack of fit between educational needs and resources. Some of these are politically more feasible than others.

Perhaps the most obvious solution would be to redistribute the population so as to reduce the concentration of disadvantaged pupils in cities. The demand for racial integration within public education points in this direction. There are, however, both physical and political obstacles to this course of action which, at the moment, appear to be insurmountable. First, the disadvantaged are concentrated in wide geographic areas within many cities. To redistribute these pupils throughout the city and throughout the metropolitan area, which would be necessary to achieve integration in the future, would require a transportation network so extensive and costly that it is both physically and politically impractical.

Obviously, there are neighborhood school districts where the redrawing of attendance areas within cities and perhaps the redrawing of district lines between cities and suburbs would substantially alter the present student balance in the schools. Where this is the case, however, political resistance is likely to be stiff. The recently discovered attachment of many people to the neighborhood school has produced powerful political support for present district lines and attendance areas. To assume that such changes could be accomplished on a metropolitan-wide basis is unrealistic.

There is, in fact, an inverse relationship between the intensity of political opposition to accomplishing some redistribution of pupils and the size of the area and proportion of the population involved. In cities where the proportion of disadvantaged students, particularly the proportion of Negro students, is relatively low (thereby making the redrawing of attendance area lines a meaningful alternative), the political resistance seems capable of preventing any substantial changes. Boston is a good example of this situation: On the other hand, where the political strength of the disadvantaged is great enough to initiate some change, the high proportion of students and large areas involved present a practical limitation on how much can be accomplished in this manner.

An alternative to the decentralization of disadvantaged students is the much-discussed creation of education parks or campuses which would contain many more pupils than the present single-building schools. By drawing on a larger enrollment area, school campuses would be able to concentrate services and would contain a more heterogeneous population, thereby, presumably, providing a higher quality of education for all students.

The concentration of disadvantaged students also would be lessened by the return of middle-income families to cities from the suburbs. It had been anticipated by some students of urban affairs that urban renewal would contribute to such a return. This reversal of the outward flow of people would have been beneficial in two ways: The mix of students in the schools would be improved and the tax base for supporting education would be strengthened. However, the contribution of urban renewal to revitalizing the central city has not been great. Much of the current disappointment over urban renewal has resulted from the lack of recognition of the importance of low-quality education as one of the primary factors motivating the move out of the city. It seems apparent that physical redevelopment, unless it is accompanied and closely interrelated with a variety of social improvements, particularly improvements in public education, will not attract the suburbanite back to the city.

Whatever the possibility of pupil redistribution, the central need is and will remain additional resources for the education of the disadvantaged. Whether educated where they are presently located or elsewhere, the disadvantaged have special education needs. To meet these needs, which is the only way of guaranteeing equality of educational opportunity, additional resources are required.

The present allocation pattern of state aid does little to accomplish this. In fact, the aid pattern runs exactly counter to the need pattern. It is possible that as reapportionment is accomplished and as the nature of the problem becomes more evident, state aid formulas will be revised to correspond more closely with needs. It is important to note, however, that reapportionment will result in a much greater gain in representation for the suburbs than it will for central cities.[18] It may be that the suburban representatives will recognize their stake in an improved central city education system; but if they do not, the present pattern of higher aid to the suburbs may well be accentuated rather than reversed by reapportionment.

Perhaps the single most significant policy response to the set of problems described here has been the response of the Federal government as reflected in the Elementary and Secondary Edu-

---

18. Robert S. Friedman, "The Reapportionment Myth," *National Civic Review*, April, 1960, pp. 184-188.

cation Act of 1965.[19] This program, combined with the antipoverty program, has given recognition for the first time to the problem of allocating more resources to education for the disadvantaged. However, although the concept underpinning the legislation is sound, the amount of aid provided for large cities is relatively small in relation to the need. In the case of New York City, for instance, the new Federal aid amounts to only 6.2 percent of total 1962 education expenditures. For Chicago, the figure is 2.9 percent, for Los Angeles 2.6 percent, with the highest figure among the fifteen largest cities being for New Orleans, where the new aid will amount to 17.5 percent of 1962 school expenditures. This program is clearly moving in the right direction; the task is to fortify it with enough money so that it can have a substantial impact.

Whatever means are used to provide the resources for the provision of adequate education services, they will have to come, in large part, from the middle- and higher-income suburbanites. If, therefore, the suburbanites resist a redistribution of population or a redrawing of school district lines to create a more equitable balance in the present pupil ability distribution, the alternative— if the problem is to be met—is greater Federal and state taxes paid by persons of middle and high income.

The fundamental issue, therefore, really revolves around the ability and willingness of Federal and state governments to raise revenue and redistribute the resources according to need. If this is not done, no major improvement in the situation confronting central city school systems can be expected.

---

19. Title I of this law, which accounts for about $1.06 billion of the approximately $1.3 billion authorized, provides for grants to be made to local school districts on the basis of 50 percent of the average per pupil expenditures made in their state for the school year 1963-1964 multiplied by the number of five- to seventeen-year-old children in the local school district from families with an annual income below $2,000, or with a higher income resulting from aid to dependent children relief payments. Local districts receive their proportion of the funds under this formula only after plans they have submitted indicating how they will meet the special educational needs of disadvantaged students are approved by their state education department. The politics surrounding the enactment of this legislation are analyzed in Philip Meranto, *The Politics of Federal Aid to Education in 1965: A Study in Political Innovation*, unpublished doctoral dissertation, Syracuse University, 1966.

There remains, of course, the issue of the ability of school systems to make good use of additional resources. This question, which is discussed elsewhere in this issue, relates to the kinds of changes needed in both curriculum and teaching techniques if the educational disadvantages of many young people are to be overcome.

However that question is answered, the fact remains that quality education for all will not be accomplished until the resources are found to do the job.

ROBERT J. HAVIGHURST

Robert Havighurst is Professor of Education and Human Development at the University of Chicago. He is the author of The Public Schools of Chicago: A Survey Report.

CHICAGO'S EDUCATIONAL NEEDS – 1966

M OST OF THE BIG Northern industrial cities have very similar educational problems which have grown out of their postwar experience. They are more alike than different if we look at a broad band of cities commencing with Boston and continuing with New Haven, New York, Syracuse, Buffalo, Baltimore, Philadelphia, Pittsburgh, Cleveland, Cincinnati, Columbus, Toledo, Detroit, Chicago, Milwaukee, St. Louis, and Kansas City. These cities all have Negro populations greater than 10 percent and this population has approximately doubled between 1950 and 1960. These cities all have seen massive migrations of middle-income people moving out from the central city to the suburbs. The average educational level of the adults in these cities has gone down since 1950 in the face of a rising educational trend in the country as a whole. These cities all have experienced a rapid increase of school enrollment since 1952, which is continuing through the 1960s at a somewhat reduced rate.

To write of Chicago, then, is to write of all the Northern industrial cities mentioned above.

The common educational problems of these cities are:

1. A relatively low educational background of the majority of parents that is reflected in their children's school achievement

2. A high degree of *de facto* racial segregation in the public schools, amounting to some 70 percent or more of Negro elementary

school pupils attending schools which have a 90 percent or higher Negro enrollment

3. A high degree of socioeconomic segregation in the public schools, with children of low-income families concentrated in certain areas of the city—usually the inner shells of the city

4. A tendency for teachers with experience and seniority to move to the higher status schools where discipline is not much of a problem

5. A need for flexible and varied curriculum development suited to the varying achievement levels of the various schools and of the pupils within the schools

6. A need for new high schools located where school population is increasing and also located so as to contribute to social integration of the school population

7. A need for innovation coupled with responsible experimentation and evaluation of the results of experimentation

8. A great deal of dissension and controversy within the public concerning the policies and practices of the school system

The Crisis of the Big City

The educational problems of the big city arise partly from changes in composition of the population since the close of World War II. There has been a vast redistribution of jobs and of people, which has produced the contemporary complex metropolitan area in place of the prewar central city partially surrounded by dormitory suburbs.

The postwar economic boom brought hundreds of thousands of people to Chicago, mainly people of relatively low education and low occupational level and mainly from the rural South. At the same time, hundreds of thousands of people moved out from the central city to the suburbs. These were people of relatively high income and high level of education.

These facts come out most clearly if we compare the city of Chicago with the suburbs on occupational level. This has been done by means of the socioeconomic ratio (SER). This is a ratio of white-collar to blue-collar workers, that is, of business and professional workers to factory and manual workers. The ratio goes up with increasing proportions of white-collar workers.

Looking at the SER for the United States, we see that this ratio has been increasing since 1940, and especially since 1950. This expresses the fact that the proportion of white-collar jobs in the American economy is increasing while the proportion of blue-collar jobs is decreasing. The SER for the Chicago metropolitan area shows a similar increase and is higher at all three dates than the SER for the United States as a whole.

In 1940, the city of Chicago was slightly below the average of the metropolitan area. In 1950, the Chicago city SER had increased from .69 to .72, while the total metropolitan area increased from .71 to .77. Clearly, the suburbs were carrying up the metropolitan area total, for they increased from .77 to .86. The city was lagging. The flight of middle-class people to the suburbs was in full course.

But the decade after 1950 saw even greater changes. The city of Chicago decreased in SER from .73 to .69, while the total SMSA increased from .77 to .92, and the suburbs jumped from .86 to 1.28. The central city was decreasing in average socioeconomic level in the face of a countrywide increase as well as a sharp increase in the Chicago area suburbs.

TABLE 1

Socioeconomic Ratios of the Chicago Area
(Based on male labor force, aged 14+)

YEAR	USA	CHICAGO SMSA	CHICAGO CITY	CHICAGO SUBURBS	CHICAGO CITY White	Nonwhite
1940	.66	.71	.69	.77	.75	.17
1950	.71	.77	.73	.86	.84	.18
1960	.82	.92	.69	1.28	.82	.25

The racial aspect of this phenomenon for the city of Chicago is shown in Table 1. While the SER of white male workers was going up from .75 to .84 and down to .82 between 1940 and 1960, the SER for nonwhites (almost all Negroes) was increasing rapidly —but from a low base, from .17 to .25. Since the proportions of nonwhites in Chicago increased from 8.2 percent in 1940 to 22.9 percent in 1960, it was the in-migration of nonwhites with relatively low occupational level that caused a substantial part of the change in Chicago.

The past twenty years have seen an increase of economic and racial segregation in Chicago as well as in the other large metropolitan areas of the country.

Changes in Birthrate and in School Enrollment. In addition to changes in the type of child and of family living in Chicago, there have been birthrate changes which have thrown and are throwing an increasing load on the schools. These changes are seen in Tables 2, 3, and 4.

TABLE 2

Births in the City of Chicago

1941:	57,300
1947:	82,700
1950:	78,600
1951:	82,100
1954:	88,800
1957:	98,100
1959:	98,200
1961:	92,800
1962:	86,800
1963:	83,700
1964:	81,600

SOURCE: **Facts and Figures.** Chicago Public Schools, September, 1965.

Table 3 shows how the enrollments have risen since the close of World War II. Enrollments reflect the births of a decade earlier, which are shown in Table 2.

The first big increase of school enrollment since about 1930 came after 1953, when the postwar upsurge of the birthrate was registered in the schools. First the elementary schools and then the high schools responded to the increased numbers of births.

The big Northern industrial cities differ from the rest of the country in their second increase in numbers of births which came

TABLE 3

Public School Enrollment in Chicago: 1950-1965

YEAR	AVERAGE DAILY MEMBERSHIP	
	Elementary School	High School
1946-1947	243,000	102,000
1949-1950	253,000	91,000
1951-1952	279,000	88,000
1955-1956	312,000	87,000
1959-1960	341,000	97,000
1960-1961	368,000	97,000
1961-1962	377,000	104,000
1962-1963	390,000	112,000
1963-1964	397,000	124,000
1964-1965	408,000	127,000
1965-1966	418,000	128,000

SOURCE: Facts and Figures. Chicago Public Schools, September, 1965.

Table 4

School Enrollments in the City of Chicago (Age Five Through Eighteen)

	1930	1940	1950	1960	1963
Public Schools	470,000	420,000	350,000	476,000	536,000
White and other	440,000*	374,000*	276,000*	290,000*	286,000
Negro	30,000*	46,000*	74,000*	186,000*	250,000
Catholic Schools	157,000	143,000	184,000	232,000	234,000

* Estimated by the author.
SOURCE: Havighurst, The Public Schools of Chicago. p. 54.

after 1950, as shown in Table 2. The numbers of births in Chicago increased from 78,600 in 1950 to 98,100 in 1957, a gain of 25 percent. This number dropped back to the 1950 level by 1965, which heralds a decrease of school enrollment in the 1970s.

This second wave of increased births was due to the arrival in Chicago in the early 1950s of large numbers of vigorous young men and women looking for work and ready to start their families. Most of these young people were Negroes. Therefore, their children, born mainly in the period from 1951 to 1964, have changed the racial composition of the Chicago schools.

The figures of Table 3 show that the elementary school enrollments have increased up to 1966. It appears from Table 2 that the elementary schools will soon reach a plateau of enrollment, while the high schools will continue to increase until about 1975.

Urban Renewal. In Chicago, as in several other large Northern cities, a continuation of present population trends might result in a growing, segregated Negro population in the city, together with a decrease in the white population, which in turn will grow rapidly in the suburbs. Furthermore, racial segregation may be accompanied by economic segregation, as high-income people continue to move to the suburbs and low-income people cluster in larger groups in the central city.

Both of these forms of segregation would be undesirable from the point of view of one who believes in democracy. They would also be undesirable from the point of view of one who is interested in the public services of the city—the schools, streets, police, fire department, and parks. With a population of reduced income, the city would find it more difficult to support the public services adequately.

Chicago's chief problem is this: how to keep and attract middle-income people to the central city and how to maintain a substantal white majority in the central city. Present trends lead to a decrease of middle-income people and a decrease of whites in the central city. The task is to change these trends.

The cure for the ills of the central city was thought to lie in urban renewal. But after fifteen years of urban renewal, people have come to believe that the process needs to be revised and reformed if it is to do the job. Some aspects of urban renewal have succeeded, while others have failed. Success has come in certain middle-class areas where the homes were obsolescent and there was danger that these areas would become slums. These areas have been cleared of the poorest housing and large apartment houses or large blocks of single-family dwellings have been built by private enterprise and sold or rented to middle-income residents.

The low-rent public housing has been far less successful. Even though it has improved the sheer physical housing of thousands of low-income families, it has tended to increase economic and racial segregation. The public housing has been so administered that most of the projects are segregated racially. Also, most of the housing projects are either high-rise apartment buildings or blocks of two- or three-storied row houses. The average housing project has over a thousand residents with three or four hundred school-age children. Some housing projects are so large that the children fill up an elementary school. One especially large public housing project in Chicago has a small high school and three elementary schools serving it alone. In this project, in 1965, were 2,070 children (not all of school age) who received Aid for Dependent Children; 661 families with annual income of less than $2,000; 612 school pupils severely retarded in reading, and 53 percent of the children in the first grade who tested on a test of reading readiness as not ready to learn to read.

Another subsidized housing project in Chicago, the Robert Taylor Homes, is a series of high-rise apartment buildings stretching for almost two miles along South State Street in Chicago. Not only do the children living in these homes make up most of the enrollment of several elementary schools; at the close of 1964 there were fifty-six elementary school classes meeting in apartments in the housing project due to lack of space in the neighborhood schools. The Robert Taylor Homes has practically all Negro occupancy. When it was proposed to build these high-rise homes, there was objection from some people on the grounds that it would tend to segregate low-income Negroes, but the City Council voted to approve the project. Professor Roald Campbell[1] later commented on this situation as follows:

> In many cases, housing patterns do more to determine the nature of the school than any action of the board of education. One might cite the decision to erect the Robert Taylor Homes, twenty-eight high-rise public housing apartments, down State Street in Chicago as one of the most dramatic examples. Apparently city council members were pleased not to have public housing dispersed over

---

1. Roald F. Campbell, "School-Community Collaboration in Our Cities," *White House Conference on Education: Consultants Papers*, 1965, pp. 144-151. Washington: Superintendent of Documents.

the entire city as had been advocated by Elizabeth Wood, then Director of the Chicago Housing Authority. In any case the two-mile strip of public housing on State Street did more to perpetuate *de facto* segregation in schools than any policy decision by the school board or any other body. But why was there not more collaboration between the board of education, the housing authority, and the city council? This lack of collaboration among agencies at both program and policy levels is a notable problem in our cities. . . .

What has happened in urban renewal in Chicago has happened in practically all of the big cities. From the point of view of those who are interested in social integration, the same mistakes have been made. Yet, it was not necessary to make most mistakes. Subsidized housing in other countries is not generally built so as to entrench economic stratification. It is possible to build small public housing units spread widely over the city, so that families living in public housing have neighbors with average incomes and send their children to schools of mixed socioeconomic status. In fact, the Chicago Committee on Urban Progress,[2] reporting in 1965, went on record as opposed to the kind of public housing policy which had built these segregated projects. It said:

> High density projects should be discontinued as a policy, but subsidized public housing, of appropriate scale and pleasing design, should be blended into normal residential neighborhoods in all parts of the city. . . . Experimentation should be initiated in designing public housing projects for resale to their occupants over a period of time, on a cooperative or condominium basis.

The need is for a concept of urban renewal which may be called *social* urban renewal. This consists in taking advantage of physical urban renewal in a local community area under the leadership of local community organizations to create communities which are attractive to all kinds of people—rich and poor, Negro and white. One sees this concept in action in several areas of Chicago—in the near North Side, in the Hyde Park–Kenwood area, in the area

---

2. Chicago Committee on Urban Progress, *A Pattern for Greater Chicago* and *Sub-Committee Reports*, 1965, pp. 30-31.

between Congress Circle (the new University of Illinois site) and the Michael Reese–Prairie Shores–Lake Meadows–Illinois Institute of Technology area. These are areas of hope for the future of the central city.

The City and the School System. The program of the schools is the greatest single factor in the decision of middle-income people to live in the central city or to live in the suburbs, and to live in one section of the city or another.

There are two opposite schools of thought among educators concerning the conduct of public schools in the big city. One may be called the "four-walls" school. The basic principle is to do the best possible job of educating every boy or girl who comes into the school, whoever he is, whatever his color, nationality, IQ, or handicap. This means building good school buildings, equipping them well, and staffing them with well-trained teachers. At its best, it means being courteous and friendly to parents and to citizens who are interested in the schools, but making it quite clear to them that the schools are run by professionals who know their business and do not need advice from other people. It means making use of the cultural resources of the city—museums, theaters, orchestras, TV programs—under a system which guarantees the safety of the children and meets the convenience of the teachers.

It means keeping the schools "out of local politics." Staff appointments are to be made on the basis of performance. It means a limited cooperation with other social institutions, public and private. The welfare and public aid and public health agencies are asked for help when the schools need it, but they cannot initiate school programs. Youth welfare and delinquency-control agencies have their jobs to do, which meet and overlap the work of the schools. On this common ground, the schools' administration must have full control of the use of school personnel and school facilities. In the area of training youth for employment, the school system will use the facilities of local business and industry for on-the-job training according to agreements worked out. Overall policy for vocational education is the responsibility of the school administration under the board of education, and local business and industry are not closely related to policy determination in this area.

The four-walls type of school system works for efficiency and economy and attempts to free the creative teacher to do the best possible job of teaching under good conditions. The community outside of the school is regarded as a source of complexity and of tension-arousal if the boundary between community and school is not clearly defined and respected.

The other school of thought may be called the "urban community" school. The educators who advocate this believe that the big city is in a crisis which has been in force for some years and will last for at least ten years and requires the active participation of schools in the making and practicing of policy for social urban renewal. This big city crisis is reflected in feelings of uncertainty and anxiety on the part of parents and citizens. There is danger of a collective failure of nerve which saps the vitality and flexibility of the city's efforts at urban renewal. Parents and citizens of middle income are tempted in this situation to escape to the suburbs, where life seems simpler and safer, especially for children.

The urban community school attempts to act constructively in this crisis by involving the parents and citizens in the decisions about school policy and practice. The educator accepts the frustration of working with people who themselves are confused and uncertain about the schools, believing that the only way to solve the problems of the city is to work on a give-and-take basis with citizens and community organizations.

The urban community school includes the intraschool program of the four-walls school, but differs at important points on the relation of the school to the community.

Those who take the urban community school point of view believe there is no viable alternative. They believe that the four-walls school actually causes some of the problems of the community through its rigid rules about attendance districts and about keeping the public away from the classroom. They believe that the schools by their policies and practices either attract or repel people in the local community. Under present conditions, the typical school system repels people whom the central city cannot afford to lose as citizens. They believe that the present trend toward economic and racial segregation in the metropolitan area will continue, and the central city will lose quality unless the schools take a more active part in social urban renewal.

Civil Rights

The other aspect of Chicago's crisis which especially involves the schools is the civil rights controversy. The public schools are heavily segregated as is shown in Table 5. This has come about through the working of the forces that produce residential segregation. In 1963 and 1964, 87 percent and 89 percent respectively of elementary school Negro children were in schools with 90 percent or more Negro enrollment.

TABLE 5

Extent of Integration of Teachers and Students in Chicago Public Schools

STUDENTS

Percent of Student Body Negro	Elementary Schools				High Schools			
	Negro 1964	White 1964	Negro 1963	White 1963	Negro 1964	White 1964	Negro 1963	White 1963
99 +	66	.09	64	.16	39	0	36	0
90-99	23	.9	23	.8	23	.8	24	0.8
50-89	7	3	10	4	17	4	26	4
10-49	3	9	3	8	18	19	12	18
1-9	0.5	14	0.5	12	2	29	2	24
0-1	0.05	73	0.06	75	0.7	47	0	54
Total No. of Students	189,000	175,000	193,000	183,000	48,000	81,000	43,000	82,000

TEACHERS

Percent of Negro Teachers in School	Elementary Schools		High Schools	
	Negro 1966	White 1966	Negro 1966	White 1966
99 +	6	0	0	0
90-99	23	1	0	0
50-89	54	11	58	6
10-49	16	22	37	27
1-9	1	10	5	37
0-1	0	56	0	30
Total No. of Teachers	5,276	9,068	1,403	4,807

47

In the judgment of the writer, there was no deliberate attempt by school authorities to segregate Negro pupils. Also, there was not until recently any deliberate attempt by school authorities to promote integration. The school administration officially took the position that it was "color-blind," and would not take color into consideration in its treatment of students or teachers.

The civil rights organizations were not content with this policy and acted through lawsuits and boycotts in 1963 to 1965 to induce the school board to establish a more positive policy toward integration. As a means of settling a lawsuit, the board of education agreed to appoint an Advisory Panel on Integration of the Public Schools, under the chairmanship of Professor Philip Hauser, sociologist at the University of Chicago. In the spring of 1964, this panel reported to the board, recommending a number of practices that it believed would increase the amount of integration in the schools. Chief among these recommendations was a plan for the "clustering" of two or more neighboring schools into a single attendance district, allowing children and their parents to choose which school of the cluster they would attend. It was expected that, by clustering Negro and white schools together, some Negro pupils could attend the predominantly white schools, even though it would mean a longer journey to school. Another recommendation was for a "permissive transfer" policy to allow pupils from crowded schools to transfer to schools that were not crowded. Since most of the Negro schools were crowded, this would presumably have the consequence of placing some Negro students in schools with white majorities.

Although the board of education officially adopted these and other recommendations, not much integration resulted. Opponents of the school administration argued that the superintendent and his staff did not work hard or intelligently to apply the recommendations.

With a new superintendent taking office in October, 1966, some action on the integration front is expected.

Next Steps for Chicago Schools

The most pressing needs for Chicago schools may be described under the following headings: These were all recommended, along with other recommendations, in the 1964 Survey.[3]

1. *New High Schools.* Enrollment projections indicate clearly that there will be further substantial increases in high school enrollment, while the elementary school enrollment will soon stabilize. Already, in 1965, thirty of the forty general high schools were operated at more than 125 percent of capacity, which means that they were open for twelve or more class periods a day instead of the "regular" nine-period day. The survey recommended the immediate construction of ten new high schools and plans for enough new buildings to serve 30,000 more students as well as to relieve existing overcrowding. By 1966 there were five new schools or additions with a capacity of 5,280 pupils that could be open within the calendar year. Any large new building program depends upon approval of a bond issue, which will be voted on in November, 1966.

2. *Compensatory Education.* With Federal government funds under the Elementary and Secondary Education Act, the Chicago schools have ample money for a significant program of compensatory education for socially disadvantaged children. A total of $32 million was allocated to Chicago for the school year 1965–1966. This was to serve approximately one in five Chicago pupils, whose families are below the poverty level.

The money has been used during the first year largely to provide afterschool instruction and summer school instruction, to purchase mobile classrooms, to reduce class size, to provide cultural experiences such as field trips, and to give in-service training to teachers.

When linked to a program of preschool classes for disadvantaged children financed under the Economic Opportunity Act, this vast effort may substantially increase the educational achievement of pupils in the innercity schools.

---

3. Robert J. Havighurst, *The Public Schools of Chicago: A Survey Report*, Chicago: Board of Education, 1964.

It is important that the elements of this program be fully and objectively evaluated. Unless there is evidence that such programs are effective, the extra funds are not likely to be provided indefinitely.

3. *Curriculum Improvement for All Schools.* For elementary and high schools in all sections of the city there is need of improved curriculum work; that is, better adaptation of textbooks and other instructional materials to the particular children in the schools.

It is a reasonable goal to raise the quality of the work done by pupils to the point where it compares favorably with at least the average suburban schools. This will require improved work by classroom teachers, which in turn will require better assistance and stimulation from principals and curriculum specialists.

The expert educators who surveyed classroom teaching found that the *average* classroom was not being taught as well as it should be. They recommended more in-service training for teachers, more time for the department chairman (in the high school) to work with his teachers, more assistance from curriculum specialists, and more attention by school principals to the supervision of their teachers.

4. *Improvement of Teacher-Recruitment and Assignment.* In Chicago, as in all the great cities, there is a strong tendency for teachers with greatest seniority to move toward the schools which serve middle- and high-income areas of the city. Table 6 shows this tendency in the elementary schools.

The "high status" and "conventional" types of schools serve areas of predominantly upper-middle and lower-middle residents. The "common man" schools are in districts of stable working-class population, while the "inner city" schools serve the lower half of the population in terms of income and education. This table shows that 94 percent of teachers in high-status schools are "regularly assigned," having passed the Chicago examination for a regularly assigned teacher. These teachers in the high-status schools have a median of nineteen years experience. On the other hand, 64 percent of the innercity teachers are regularly assigned and 36 percent are full-time substitutes; that is, teachers with a teacher's certificate

TABLE 6

Type of School and Type of Teacher

TYPE OF ELEMENTARY SCHOOL

	High Status	Conventional	Common Man	Inner City	Totals
Number of Elementary School Pupils	26,500	60,400	68,800	176,000	331,500
Percent of Total Enrollment	8	18	21	53	100
Percent of Regularly Assigned Teachers	94	91	86	64	
Percent of Full-time Substitutes	6	9	14	36	
Percent Distribution of Regularly Assigned Teachers	11	23	22	44	100
Percent Distribution of Full-time Substitute Teachers	1	6	11	82	100
Median Years Experience of Regularly Assigned Teachers	19	15	9	4	

SOURCE: R. J. Havighurst, **The Public Schools of Chicago:** A Survey Report, Chicago; Board of Education, p. 170.

who have not passed the Chicago examination. Those who are regularly assigned have a median of four years experience.

Some way should be worked out to interest the more experienced teachers in teaching innercity children.

5. *Decentralization of Administration.* It is generally agreed by specialists in school administration that it would be well in the great cities to decentralize some of the administrative authority and responsibility. Such a recommendation has been made for Chicago by Superintendent Willis and also by Professors Morris Janowitz and David Street after their study of the administrative structure of the system. In their report, Janowitz and Street conclude:

. . . the organizational structure of the public school system can be seen as constituting a significant barrier to continuous and effective innovation. We are dealing with generic characteristics of the school system. While it is essential to increase the amount of decentralization of effective authority, the problem is more complex in that it

51

is necessary simultaneously to increase the articulation and communication among the various elements, both teaching and supervisory, in the school system and the central staff.

They called for strengthening the role of the principal and for creation of four or five regional districts, each with a high degree of autonomy. They said:

> Our central recommendation is that a new level of administration is needed between the central staff and the existing school districts in order to achieve significant decentralization. It is proposed that four or five "super districts" or sector districts be set up in the city of Chicago. These sectors would be geographically defined, each serving a large portion of the city. The school board, the general superintendent and the central staff would be responsible for broad policy, long-range planning, recruitment, fiscal control and relations with state and federal government agencies. The sector districts, operated by sector school superintendents having strong supporting staffs, would be highly autonomous units with power to adapt and develop educational programs for their regions and to develop the types of regional school-community relations which appear necessary. Each district would have an advisory board. The appointment of these boards would go a long way to overcoming the lack of communication that currently exists, especially with the Negro communities. The sector district superintendent, acting on general directives, would have the responsibility for achieving and maintaining racial integration and some of the general principles set forth below. It would be the purpose of the staff of the sector school district to assist teachers and principals in curriculum construction.

Such decentralization would place more authority and responsibility in the hands of regional superintendents, district superintendents, and principals. The survey report paid special attention to the principals. It said:

> Again and again the staff and consultants of the Survey reported that the principal is the key person in the educational system. Sometimes they reported the principal as the source of success in a school, and sometimes as a source of failure. In order to increase

the amount of success which comes from the work of principals, certain facts can be pointed out and certain recommendations made.

There are almost 500 principals in the Chicago schools. They range in age from the early 30's to the mid 60's. Their salaries range from $9,500 to $14,500. Some salary increases are automatic, depending on years of service, but others depend on being promoted by the central administration. Most offices in the central administration (assistant and associate superintendents, bureau directors, etc.) are filled from the ranks of principals within the system. Therefore the principalship is a complex hierarchy of positions, not a single position one holds for 10 or 20 years, as is the case in a small city. . . .

The principal in the Chicago schools leads a far different life. Starting at the lowest of the principals' levels, he has eight salary lanes above him to which he can be promoted by action of the administration (not automatically). Above that are four ranks, from district superintendent to assistant, associate, and general superintendent, if he aspires that high. If his job as principal starts at the young age of 35, he has a 30 year career, and is likely to be promoted between five and 10 times, which means he will average three years to six years at a particular school. Thus the Chicago principal is likely to be a mobile person.

6. *Evaluation and Research.* Chicago and all big city systems need innovation and they need changes. But they also need careful evaluation of their programs. Yet it is difficult to find any school system with an adequate program of research and evaluation. The Chicago projects for the socially disadvantaged illustrate the difficulties that big city systems face in the conduct of research and development. Several such projects have been carried on with funds from the Ford Foundation, the Wieboldt Foundation, and the U.S. Department of Health, Education and Welfare.

Although the projects were set up with enthusiasm and with creative originality, they were seldom accompanied by a careful design for collecting data on what actually happened to children and teachers before, during, and after the experiments.

If the public is going to be asked to contribute more millions of dollars to the school budget for new educational practices, it would be wise for the board of education to arrange for a thorough reporting and evaluation of these innovations so as to keep the new practices that work and to discard those that are not successful.

For this function there should be a Division of Educational Research and Development with responsibility for evaluating the on-going program of the school system and for supplying research assistance to people who are experimenting and innovating in the schools. The cost of such a division might be about 1 percent of the operating budget of the schools.

7. *Integration.* In Chicago and other large cities, the Negroes are so fully segregated by residence that it is impossible to place the majority of Negro children in integrated schools without a program of mass transportation that would take them to schools far distant from their homes. Few Negro parents and few of the proponents of integration would support this kind of policy, unless it was tried out experimentally for small numbers for several years.

In this situation, the tendency for school administrators is to do nothing about integration beyond the policy of permissive transfer that depends upon the initiative of the parents and their ability to provide transportation for their children. The "neighborhood school" tradition is strong in this country, and it is convenient for nearly everybody—parents, children, and administrators.

Yet the conviction is growing that integrated schooling is necessary for good education of Negro children. The strength of this conviction is illustrated by the following quotation from John H. Fischer, formerly Superintendent of Schools in Baltimore and now Professor of Education at Columbia University. Professor Fischer at one time believed that a good education could be provided for Negro children in segregated schools. But he has become a strong proponent of integration in New York City. Writing on the problem he underlines two basic facts—the first is that any school enrolling largely Negro students is almost universally considered of lower status and less desirable than one attended wholly or mainly by white students;[4] and, in his words:

---

4. John H. Fischer, "Race and Reconciliation: The Role of the School," *Daedalus*, Vol. 95, No. 1 (Winter, 1966), pp. 29-44.

A second impressive fact, closely related to the first, is the unfortunate psychological effect upon a child of membership in a school where every pupil knows that, regardless of his personal attainments, the group with which he is identified is viewed as less able, less successful, and less acceptable than the majority of the community. The impact upon the self-image and motivation of children of this most tragic outcome of segregated education emphasizes the dual need for immediate steps to achieve a more favorable balance of races in the schools and for every possible effort to upgrade to full respectability and status every school in which enrollment cannot soon be balanced.

The purpose of school integration is not merely, or even primarily, to raise the quantitative indices of scholastic achievement among Negro children, although such gains are obviously to be valued and sought. The main objective is rather to alter the character and quality of their opportunities, to provide the incentive to succeed, and to foster a sense of intergroup acceptance in ways that are impossible where schools or students are racially, socially, and culturally isolated. The simplest statement of the situation to which school policy must respond is that few if any American Negro children can now grow up under conditions comparable to those of white children and that of all the means of improvement subject to public control the most powerful is the school. The Negro child must have a chance to be educated in a school where it is clear to him and to everybody else that he is not segregated and where his undisputed right to membership is acknowledged, publicly and privately, by his peers and his elders of both races. Although his acceptance and his progress may at first be delayed, not even a decent beginning toward comparable circumstances can be made until an integrated setting is actually established.

The strategy of integration should have two principal elements. The first is to stabilize integration in areas where the present population is mixed. This can be done where there is a substantial local community organization which favors integration and where the school administration works effectively with the local community.

Three such areas have been identified in Chicago. Each of these areas has a population of 200,000 to 400,000. Active programs for community redevelopment and social urban renewal are under way. Commencing with the high schools, integration can be promoted through procedures worked out by school administrators in close collaboration with community representatives.

A common objection to this proposal is that the area is already "changing" and nothing can stop it from becoming a segregated Negro area. This belief is based on experience of the past decade, where the pressure of Negro in-migrants cooped up in a ghetto often resulted in rapid segregation of areas on the margins of Negro residence.

The situation in the mid-1960s is quite different from that of the mid-1950s. Rapid changes of large residential areas are not now in prospect for two reasons. First, the rate of Negro in-migration is much less than it was in the 1950s. The demand for unskilled and semiskilled workers in industry has slackened off, due to the effects of automation in industry. Second, the area of Negro residence is so great, as compared with that area in 1950, that a given number of new Negro residents can be accommodated at many points on the perimeter of existing Negro residential areas without any large increase of segregated residential area. For example, the addition of 50,000 Negroes to the 500,000 who lived in Chicago in 1950 would cause much more apparent increase of segregated housing area than would the addition of 50,000 Negroes to the 1,000,000 who live in Chicago in 1966.

It is now possible, in Chicago, to maintain large stable areas which are integrated to the extent of having Negroes and whites living in adjacent blocks, if not in the same block.

With respect to the racial composition of the schools, there is also some publicly expressed concern over the fact that the public elementary schools of Chicago have more Negro than white pupils, although Negroes make up only about 27 percent of the total population. It is feared that Negro pupils will swamp the public schools.

In this connection, the projections of the Negro school population are useful. They indicate that the recent rapid increase of Negro pupils in the schools will soon come to an end. As Table 2 on birthrates indicates, there was a wave of high birthrates between 1951 and 1964 caused largely by in-migration of young Negro men and women in the early 1950s. This wave is now receding,

56

and the elementary school population will soon reach a plateau and then decrease somewhat, reflecting the reduction of births since 1960. Table 7 shows census data which lie behind this phenomenon. The numbers of nonwhite females of childbearing age were relatively higher in 1950 than in 1960 in Chicago. The analogous figures for Kansas City show that this phenomenon is likely to be common to Northern industrial cites.

Thus, there is no real basis for the idea that the proportion of Negro pupils in the public schools will continue to increase as rapidly as it has since 1950.

TABLE 7

Age Characteristics of Nonwhite Females: 1950, 1960

AGE	CHICAGO (Percent of total)		KANSAS CITY (Percent of total)	
	1950	1960	1950	1960
0-4	10.3	15.0	8.5	14.7
5-9	7.4	11.8	6.6	11.0
10-14	6.4	8.4	6.0	8.0
15-19	6.2	6.2	6.0	6.1
20-24	9.7	7.6	8.6	6.5
25-29	11.3	8.0	9.7	6.8
30-34	9.7	8.4	9.0	7.7
35-39	9.2	7.6	9.1	7.3
40-44	7.6	6.2	7.8	6.2
45-64	17.6	16.0	21.8	18.0
65 +	4.6	5.0	7.0	7.8
20-44	47.5	37.8	44.2	34.5
Median age	29.4	25.6	32.0	27.7
Total Number	265,000	436,000	29,166	43,935

SOURCE: U.S. Bureau of Census, Vol. I, 1950 and 1960.

The second element of integration strategy is to establish and maintain a *special group of integrated elementary schools,* located at places on the margins of Negro–white residence where a considerable group of white children are living. These schools should be operated in addition to the local neighborhood schools. They should be open to voluntary enrollment with the stipulation that they will have at least 60 percent white and Oriental pupils, and the further stipulation that they are open to every child who is not more than one year below his age-level in reading ability.

These schools should start at the fourth or fifth grade. Statements of intent by the Board of Education should be made, somewhat as follows:

1. The Board will maintain elementary and secondary schools with at least 60 percent white pupils in sites which are well located for Negro pupils to reach them. However, in many areas these schools will be farther from home than other schools with greater proportions of Negro pupils.

2. In the location of integrated schools (60 percent or more of white pupils) the Board of Education will cooperate with local community organizations to find or choose schools which are approved by the local groups. If there are areas where the consensus is opposed to the location of an integrated school, the board will respect this consensus, though it will also endeavor to help the people of the community meet their responsibilities in a pluralistic society.

3. The Board of Education will provide special remedial teaching (after school, summer school, tutoring, etc.) available to pupils who are more than one year below their age-level in reading ability.

4. Every pupil will have the right to attend the school of his home district or attendance area, regardless of his reading level, unless he is transferred to another school for a special class of some kind that he especially needs.

This program could be started immediately on an experimental basis in one or more areas of the city. Its success would depend on two things: (1) the willingness of large numbers of white parents to send their children to *good* integrated schools; and (2) the willingness of the Board of Education to spend a little extra money to maintain really superior schools.

Integration of faculty is another desirable goal for Chicago. Table 5 shows that 56 percent of white elementary school teachers were teaching in schools without Negro teachers, and 30 percent of white high school teachers were members of all-white faculties in 1966. There were 6 percent of Negro elementary school teachers who taught in all-Negro faculties.

Probably the normal course of securing seniority and exercising choice will increase the extent of integration of faculties, but this will happen slowly. Some cities are working directly on the matter by promoting a "balanced staff" policy. The aim is to attain within each school a balanced staff based on age, training, race, sex, and experience.

With such a policy stated and worked out with the aid of teachers' organizations, the balanced staff would be attained by assignment of new teachers, transfer of young teachers after about three years of experience, and basing promotion partly on the possession of teaching experience in different neighborhoods. The Detroit school system has such a plan in operation.

Conclusions

These recommendations for Chicago schools illustrate the close and essential connection between the narrow educational procedures within the classroom and the broad procedures of social renewal in the great cities.

It is not possible for the public schools to do their task well on the basis of the four-walls philosophy. They must become active and cooperative participants in the remaking of the urban community. When they build new schools, they must locate these schools and determine their size through cooperation with city planning personnel. When they develop new curricula, they must use the new teaching materials differentially among types of schools and among types of local communities within the city. When they reorganize their administration, they must do so with an eye on the social geography of the city. When they work toward racial and social integration, they must do so as part of a broad program of social urban renewal in which they cooperate with the business men, the church leaders, the labor union officers, and the civil rights workers of the city. They must be attuned to the varied sentiments and aspirations of the common people in the many local communities of which the great city is made.

SEYMOUR SACKS and DAVID C. RANNEY

Seymour Sacks is Professor of Economics, Maxwell Graduate School of
Citizenship and Public Affairs, Syracuse University. David C. Ranney
is Assistant Professor of Government
and Metropolitan Affairs, Southern
Illinois University, Edwardsville.

SUBURBAN

EDUCATION: A

Fiscal Analysis

THE AIM OF THIS paper is to contribute to a better understanding of the nature of suburban public education. Resources in suburbia, as measured by educational expenditures per
pupil or per capita, have increased enormously in recent years. This
increase has occurred not only in absolute terms but also in terms
relative to central cities. On the basis of the sample data for that
portion of the past decade for which the information is available
(1957–1962), current educational expenditures per enrolled pupil in
suburbia grew from $303 to $439. During the same period, expenditures per pupil in central cities grew from $310 to $376. Thus, in
1957 central cities were spending about the same per pupil as their
suburbs, but by 1962 the suburbs forged considerably ahead. This
relative growth in suburban school expenditures per student is even
more remarkable when one considers that suburban school system
enrollments grew between 1957 and 1962 at almost twice the rate of
their central city counterparts. Indeed, if account is taken of differentials in the proportions of the total population going to public

AUTHOR'S NOTE: *This article is based, in part, on a Carnegie Corporation-
supported larger study of* Policies and Policy-Making in Large City Education Systems *being done at the Metropolitan Studies Center, Maxwell Graduate School, Syracuse University. A description of the entire study may be
obtained by writing to the Metropolitan Studies Program, 607 University
Avenue, Syracuse, New York 13210.*

elementary and secondary schools by measuring expenditure growth differentials in per capita terms, the growth in the suburbs relative to the central cities is even greater.

Thus, in a five-year period, a similarity in the amount of resources spent per pupil in the suburbs and their central cities clearly disappeared. In part, the change reflects the substitution of current expenditures for the funds previously devoted to the construction of school facilities in suburbia. In part, it reflects the internal and external dynamics of suburbia itself, which in combination have so dramatically changed the balance in per pupil expenditures and increased an existing imbalance in the per capita expenditures on education. The social, political, and economic implications of the present pattern of educational finance in suburbs relative to their central cities have not been lost on the American people, whether they be those living in the suburbs, inside central cities, or the considerable but shrinking proportion of the population living outside of "metropolitan America."

Given these facts, the necessity of a better understanding of the fiscal patterns in suburban school systems is clearly evident. In the first place, it is important to understand the conditions that made possible the enormous differential between suburb and central city in the resources devoted to public elementary and secondary education. It is also necessary to look at the nature of suburbia itself by focusing on the patterns of educational finance within the area herein designated as suburban. To achieve these aims, suburban school systems will be examined from several perspectives. First, these systems will be analyzed in their *metropolitan context* by comparing the outside central city portions of thirty-five metropolitan areas to their central cities. (Since two metropolitan areas have more than one central city, there are thirty-seven observations in the sample.) From this perspective, a picture of the nature of the suburban schools will be sought. Further, the common notion that the suburban school system is generally better off than its central city counterpart will be tested.[1]

1. James B. Conant, *Slums and Suburbs*, New York: Signet Books, 1964.

A second perspective involves the *comparison of suburbs to one another.* In this section of the paper, the thirty-seven outside central city portions of the metropolitan areas are analyzed to see how the differences among these portions compare with the differences that were found relative to the central cities. Having noted the nature of the variations among suburban areas, an attempt is made to explain these differences.

Finally, a third level of analysis examines suburban variation in a somewhat more refined manner. The suburban school systems are *analyzed by county* in a single region. For this purpose, the school systems surrounding New York City, but outside of other central cities in the region, are compared. This area has the advantage of encompassing portions of three states so that the effect of the state policy itself can be assessed.

This paper is essentially a fiscal analysis in which particular fiscal variables are used to indicate different suburban school issues. That is, the resources used for public education are taken as an index of the level of service being provided and the effort which this level requires. The measures used reflect two aspects of the nature of suburban education. One is the educational aspect which involves the provision of a certain level or quality of education. In spite of its limitations, the best single measure of the level of education is current educational expenditures per student. While this is not a perfect measure, it does provide a reasonable means of quantifying the level of education being provided. Aside from the educational aspect, there is the fiscal problem of providing resources to finance the level of education desired. Two measures are employed to quantify the fiscal problem: (1) *total educational expenditures per capita,* which reflects the total fiscal effort from all sources being made for local schools; and (2) *local educational taxes,* which measures the local tax burden assumed by the community for its schools. Where no direct measure of local educational taxes is available, a proxy variable —total educational expenditures less intergovernmental aid—is used instead. This latter measure is in some ways better than the tax measure because it includes the entire "local contribution." Nevertheless, where checks have been possible the two measures have been found to be very closely related. To get a full picture of suburban education, it is necessary to use all three measures.

The basic hypothesis of the present analysis is that three major factors explain the level of education and the fiscal effort, or burden, which this level imposes on the suburban community. First is the fact that suburban school systems operate in a metropolitan context. The metropolitan area has the ingredients of a healthy, competitive environment which is advantageous to the school system within it. Where public school systems operate side by side, the respective levels of education in the two systems can be easily compared. Such comparisons can provide an impetus to the poorer school systems to raise their educational standards. Further, the metropolis provides a geographical labor market area within which the schools must compete to retain their senior staff and to recruit new teachers and other personnel.

A second important factor is a combination of the attitudes, tastes, and aspirations of the community as reflected by the social and economic characteristics of the population served by a given school system. Thus, the socioeconomic variables representing this factor are expected to be influential in determining the extent to which a community is willing to support its public school system.

A final factor is intergovernmental aid. Such aid at the present time comes primarily from the state, although with the passage of legislation for broader-based Federal aid in 1965, the Federal government is apt to be increasingly important in this respect. Aid can be an extremely important element in the educational and fiscal aspects of suburban education. There is sufficient evidence to believe that aid is used only to a very limited extent as a substitute for local effort and, in fact, is additive to that effort.[2]

---

2. Alan K. Campbell and Seymour Sacks, "Metropolitan America: Fiscal Patterns and Governmental Systems," forthcoming publication, Syracuse, N.Y. Metropolitan Studies Center, Syracuse University, 1966.

Fiscal and Socioeconomic Patterns

The contribution of the above factors, individually and in combination, to the educational and fiscal aspects of suburban education can partially be assessed by examining the patterns of the variables that represent these factors and aspects. Using these variables to compare suburbs to their central city school systems, greater insight into the nature of suburbia in general can be gained. Then, by comparing the outlying school systems of a number of metropolitan areas with respect to these variables, the differences among suburban school systems can be demonstrated.

The Nature of Suburbia. Table 1 compares suburban areas (or more accurately, outside central city areas) to their respective central cities. A number of socioeconomic characteristics are used for

TABLE 1

Means of Socioeconomic and Fiscal Characteristics of Suburban and Central City School Systems in 35 Standard Metropolitan Statistical Areas*

	Outside Central City Areas ("suburbs")†	Central Cities	Difference
Socioeconomic Independent Variables			
Per Capita Personal Income	$2,182	$2,068	$ +114
Public School Enrollment as a Percent of Population	22.6%	17.2%	+5.2%**
Fiscal Independent Variables			
Per Capita Education State Aid	$ 37.66	$ 20.73	$ +16.87**
Per Student Education State Aid	$ 165.54	$ 124.92	$ +40.62**
Per Capita Noneducation Expenditures	$ 126.44	$ 161.70	$ —34.76**
Current Educational Expenditures as a Percent of All Local Current Expenditures	55.0%	32.4%	+22.6%**
Dependent Variables			
Per Student Current Educational Expenditures	$ 439.11	$ 376.33	$ +62.78**
Per Capita Total Educational Expenditures	$ 127.24	$ 67.96	$ +59.28**
Local School Tax Proxy	$ 83.80	$ 47.23	$ +36.57**
Exhibit: U.S. Totals			
Median Family Income††	$7,114	$5,943	$+1,141
Median Family Income	$6,707	$5,943	$ +764

* Since two areas have two central cities there are actually thirty-seven observations.
† Includes all communities outside the central city but within the metropolitan area.
** The difference of means is significant at the .01 level of confidence.
†† Urban fringe is used here in place of outside central city.

SOURCE: Computed from U.S. Bureau of Census, **Census of Population,** 1960 and U.S. Bureau of Census, **Census of Governments,** 1962.

the comparison.[3] Income, which plays such an important role in explaining educational patterns, has also been used to define suburbia. In fact, income is the one variable which has clearly been associated with school expenditures and local support for schools.[4] The communities outside of the central city have, on the average, higher income levels than does the city itself. Table 1 shows this relationship in the sample of the largest metropolitan areas. Two kinds of comparisons are made. On the basis of census definitions, personal income per capita is, on the average, slightly higher outside the central city than within, although the difference of means is not significant.[5] The actual disparity in the case of "true suburbs" is really greater than this comparison indicates, because in many places the outside central city area includes rural territory which lowers the average income level. By comparing the median family income between the central city and the urban fringe, the extent of the difference is demonstrated. The difference between central city and the urban fringe in median family income is $1,141. This compares to a difference of $764 between the central city and the entire outside central city area. Even though suburbs tend to have higher incomes than the central city, however, the difference is not statistically significant.

A second variable that is representative of the demand that is made for public education (in terms of numbers of pupils) is the proportion of the population attending public schools. This variable, which is referred to here as the "enrollment ratio," varies considerably between outside central city areas and their central cities. The mean enrollment ratio in the thirty-seven large central cities is 17.2 percent, while the mean enrollment ratio in the outlying school sys-

---

3. These areas were chosen by David Ranney and are analyzed in his unpublished doctoral dissertation, "School Government and the Determinants of the Fiscal Support for Large City Education Systems," Syracuse University, 1966.

4. See, for example, Patricia Cayo Sexton, *Education and Income*, New York: Viking Press, 1961; H. Thomas James, J. Alan Thomas, and Harold J. Dyck, *Wealth, Expenditures and Decision Making for Education*, Stanford, Calif.: Stanford University Press, 1963.

5. The term "significance" as used in this section of the paper refers to the statistical significance of the difference of means. For this purpose, a conventional t test is used. Given 70 degrees of freedom, a difference is considered significant at the .01 level where $t > \pm 2.576$.

tems is 22.6 percent. This difference is both large and statistically significant.

A third variable that is an important element in school support is state aid. The difference of means between suburbs and central cities is again significant. It is clear that suburban school systems benefit much more from the present system of state aid to education than do central cities, both because they have a higher enrollment ratio and a greater average grant per pupil. On a per student basis, the cities average $124.92 in aid from their state while the suburbs get $165.54, or a difference of $40.62 for every student. The relative difference is larger on a per capita basis than it is on a per pupil basis. The mean per capita aid for education is $20.73 while the comparable figure for outside central city areas is $37.66, a difference of $16.93 per capita.

There is one further important difference between central cities and their outlying areas. This difference involves the extent to which a given municipality or unincorporated area and its overlying governments (e.g., counties, special districts, etc.) undertake local public expenditures other than education. Central cities clearly tend to have a far greater need for such services than their suburbs. This means that there are weaker competitive claims on local resources in the suburbs than in the city. This point is demonstrated by the fact that noneducational expenditures are higher in the central cities than in the suburbs.[6] The mean expenditure in the city is $161.70 while outside it is only $126.94, a significant difference of $34.76. The fact that suburban communities have relatively less demand for noneducational services is also reflected by the relative allocation of resources between education and other local functions. Such allocation is measured in Table 1 by the proportion which current educational expenditures are of all local expenditures. Using this measure, it is clear that suburban communities allocate a far greater proportion of their resources to education (even when capital outlays are excluded) than is the case with central cities. The average propor-

---

6. The difference is even greater than Table 1 suggests. The per capita amounts are computed by dividing through by 1960 population. Yet recent population figures indicate that the central city has lost people, while the suburbs have gained. Thus, the per capita differences in noneducation would, if 1962 population figures were available, be greater.

tion of funds used for current education in the city is only 32.4 percent, while in suburbia it is 55.0 percent. This difference is again statistically significant.

The above comparisons demonstrate that suburbs tend to have higher incomes, higher enrollment ratios, receive more state aid for their schools, and have a lower level of competing noneducational service requirements than the central city. The result of these characteristics is that suburban communities tend to devote more fiscal resources to their schools. Table 2 demonstrates this point in detail for the sample. The levels are significantly different in each case. Current educational expenditures per student, which are a rough index of the level of education being provided, is on the average $376.33 in central cities and $439.11 in the suburbs. The mean of total educational expenditures per capita in the central city is $67.96, while outside the city it is $127.24. With respect to the nonaided educational expenditures (the school tax proxy variable), central cities have an average per capita tax of $47.23 and the suburbs pay $83.80 in school taxes.

Differences among Suburbs. Although the above analysis clearly demonstrates that there is a generalization that can be made about suburbia and the kind of education that is provided there, it is also true that the suburban communities outside the central city vary extensively among themselves in their socioeconomic characteristics as well as in the level of education provided and the burden and effort which this level requires. These differences can be seen by looking at the variation among suburban areas with respect to the variables discussed above. This variation is shown in Table 3 in terms of the range, the standard deviation, and the coefficient of variation.[7] That there is a lack of homogeneity among suburban areas with respect to the variables discussed earlier is vividly demonstrated by the table. As measured by the coefficients of variation, educational expenditures and taxes vary from 24 to 30 percent, which is a considerably greater variation than their central city counterparts. One of the variables which is presumed to be partially responsible for the variation in educational fiscal support in the suburbs is state aid. Educa-

---

7. The coefficient of variation is the standard deviation divided by the mean.

TABLE 2

Current Educational Expenditures per Student, Total Educational Expenditures per Capita, and Total Nonaided Educational Expenditures per Capita (tax proxy) for Central City and Outside Central City Areas: 1962

CITY	Current Education Expenditures per Student 1962		Total Education Expenditures per Capita 1962		Total Non-Aided Education Expenditures per Capita 1962	
	CC	OCC	CC	OCC	CC	OCC
New York	536.88	684.34	77.29	194.05	47.10	127.88
Chicago	408.51	473.69	66.09	112.60	50.78	92.15
Los Angeles	437.14	555.54	101.01	174.83	64.82	72.53
Philadelphia	397.75	492.96	54.69	105.59	37.24	81.42
Detroit	461.67	434.10	93.78	128.08	70.16	88.59
Baltimore	366.07	421.61	80.50	112.82	60.67	81.21
Houston	290.09	450.35	63.75	143.85	32.42	91.87
Cleveland	370.59	459.50	65.01	113.74	58.25	100.98
St. Louis	386.58	423.73	55.31	100.70	37.11	75.87
Milwaukee	377.90	469.38	65.20	124.75	51.77	112.84
San Francisco	466.77	546.29	69.19	172.17	45.47	73.83
Boston	385.46	465.36	50.32	100.87	43.78	93.09
Dallas	301.96	325.40	74.42	100.37	47.29	61.63
New Orleans	271.87	233.05	41.74	66.63	12.68	27.62
Pittsburgh	368.00	450.98	51.19	96.05	39.76	61.52
San Diego	414.63	538.95	105.13	156.29	67.70	92.42
Seattle	409.89	415.72	89.39	138.86	46.93	58.83
Buffalo	447.03	561.20	59.27	137.32	33.82	77.52
Cincinnati	373.11	577.74	62.80	118.29	55.07	95.24
Memphis	227.58	245.71	48.74	96.59	26.54	64.25
Denver	418.30	380.74	81.19	151.07	67.13	116.37
Atlanta	272.52	287.80	57.42	90.49	36.17	51.47
Minneapolis	414.31	441.45	61.42	157.05	41.91	63.32
Indianapolis	352.87	467.92	69.83	144.17	51.30	116.28
Kansas City	409.19	350.67	75.09	156.54	54.40	126.33
Columbus	327.40	332.06	61.25	98.08	51.97	69.77
Newark	496.21	522.23	93.80	112.08	78.32	100.04
Louisville	301.44	477.73	42.81	134.33	25.28	106.31
Portland (Oregon)	421.59	480.14	79.37	149.10	58.32	95.58
Long Beach	426.33	555.54	85.99	174.83	51.08	84.77
Birmingham	194.43	223.89	49.93	61.49	18.23	23.64
Oklahoma	269.23	291.67	67.16	83.76	43.97	70.37
Rochester	580.05	573.07	79.35	158.58	54.79	91.53
Toledo	377.71	511.85	80.08	160.51	71.54	113.00
St. Paul	415.51	441.45	58.10	157.05	40.37	55.02
Norfolk	265.43	288.65	47.42	87.51	29.53	59.23
Omaha	282.58	394.90	49.48	136.83	43.88	126.37
Mean	376.33	439.11	67.96	127.24	47.23	83.80

SOURCE: U.S. Bureau of Census, Census of Governments, 1962.

tional state aid per capita ranges from $7.88 to $80.03; in per student terms, the range is from $42.57 to $307.57. The coefficients of variation (49.1 percent and 46.5 percent respectively) are very high. Per

TABLE 3

Range, Standard Deviation, and Coefficient of Variation with Respect to
Selected Socioeconomic and Fiscal Characteristics of
37 Outside Central City Areas

	Range	Standard Deviation	Coefficient of Variation
Income per Capita	$1347 - $2748	$336.62	15.4%
Enrollment Ratio	15.9% - 28.4%	3.0%	13.3%
Educational State Aid per Capita	$7.88 - $80.03	$18.48	49.1%
Educational State Aid per Student	$42.57 - $307.59	$76.93	46.5%
Total Non-Educational Expenditures (per Capita)	$65.50 - $199.41	$37.95	29.9%
Educational Expenditures as Percent of Total	33.8% - 75.9%	8.7%	15.8%
Current Educational Expenditures per Student	$239.89 - $684.34	$107.43	24.5%
Total Educational Expenditures per Capita	$61.49 - $194.05	$32.34	25.4%
Educational Tax Proxy per Capita	$23.64 - $127.88	$25.54	30.5%

capita incomes in outside central city areas range from $1,347 to $2,748 with a coefficient of variation of 15.4 percent. The enrollment ratio runs from 15.9 percent to 28.4 percent. The coefficient of variation is about the same as that for income. The extent to which suburban communities provide noneducational services also differs from suburb to suburb. Per capita noneducational expenditures in outside central city areas range from $65.50 to $199.41. The coefficient of variation is 29.9 percent. Finally, it should be noted that for all but one of the variables analyzed in Table 3, the average deviation from the mean among suburbs is as great or even greater than the average differences between central city and outside central city.

Thus, one thing is very clear from Table 3: The generalizations often made about the nature of suburban education are not as useful as is often supposed. When analyzed in detail, communities which are called suburbs because of their physical location, actually differ among themselves with respect to both their socioeconomic and fiscal characteristics. Of particular interest in the present context is the fact that the fiscal resources devoted to suburban schools vary from area to area considerably. For this reason, the determinants of this variation in suburban school support become of great interest.

The Determinants of the Variation
in Suburban School Support

At the beginning of this paper it was hypothesized that three factors have a major effect on the level of school support: the metropolitan context, attitudes or tastes, and intergovernmental aid. The metropolitan context is considered through the choice of the sample. The other two factors are put into three multiple regression models to assess the extent to which they can "explain" the variations among suburban areas. Each equation relates the independent variables to one of the educational and fiscal variables enumerated earlier. Metropolitanism is not measured directly in this context. Two variables used in the regression analysis reflect attitudes. These are income per capita and the enrollment ratio. The variables representing intergovernmental aid are state aid for education per capita and per student. These variables are related to each of the three educational fiscal variables in the regression equations below.

Equation (1)°
Current educational expenditures per student (1962) = $135.49 + .179^a

(.034)

per capita income − 8.393^b enrollment ratio + .617^a per pupil state aid
(3.847)   (.141) $R^2 = .672$

Equation (2)°
Total educational expenditures per capita (1962) = −$81.38 + .051^a per

(.012)

capita income + 2.867^b enrollment ratio + .837^a per capital state aid
(1.402)   (.214) $R^2 = .581$

Equation (3)°
Educational tax proxy per capita (1962) = −$44.39 + .043^a per capita in-

(.012)

come + 2.229 enrollment ratio − .402^c per capita state aid
(1.427)   (.218) $R^2 = .302$

° Unbiased errors are shown in parentheses below the net regression coefficients. Statistical significance using Student's t is indicated as follows: ^{a}.01; ^{b}.05 and ^{c}.10. Significance levels have been adjusted for degrees of freedom.

⁻) income, the enrollment ratio, and state aid "ex-
ι of the variation in suburban school expenditures

per pupil. Income and aid are positively associated with these expenditures, while the enrollment ratio has a negative relationship. The same variables "explain" 58 percent of the variation in the total effort suburban communities and their states are making in behalf of education as measured by total educational expenditures per capita. In equation (2), higher enrollment ratios lead to higher expenditure efforts—a contrary result to that found with respect to per student expenditures. This same model does not explain as much of the variation in local nonaided expenditures. Income, the enrollment ratio, and state aid explain only 30 percent of the variance. The most interesting relationship in equation (3) is the negative association between the tax proxy and state aid, which is considerably less than —1. This means that aid replaces only part of local effort.

The relative power of the three independent variables in explaining each of the dependent variables in the multivariate analysis can be better demonstrated by using the standardized regression coefficient, a transformation which makes net regressions comparable when all variables are expressed in units of their respective standard deviations. In all three models, the relative importance of the inde-

TABLE 4

Standardized Regression Coefficients

	Per Capita Income	Enrollment Ratio	Per Capita State Aid	Per Student State Aid
Current Educational Expenditures per Student	.561	— .237	not computed	.442
Total Educational Expenditures per Capita	.536	.269	.479	not computed
Educational Tax Proxy per Capita	.562	.265	— .290	not computed

pendent variables is: income, aid, and the enrollment ratio in that order. Income and aid are both far more important than the enrollment ratio.

The same variables can be also analyzed in a different context. It is possible by use of the elasticity coefficient to show the relative response of the educational and fiscal variables to a given change in each of the independent variables with the effects of the other two held constant. This coefficient indicates the percentage change in

71

the dependent variable that is associated with a one percent change in the independent variable at the point of their means. These coefficients are shown below. It is clear from Table 5 that expenditures and taxes for public education are most responsive to changes in income. This is especially true of education taxes for which it has been hypothesized elsewhere that there would be higher elasticity than in the case of education expenditures. A 1 percent increase in in-

TABLE 5

Elasticity Coefficients

	Per Capita Income	Enrollment Ratio	Per Capita State Aid	Per Student State Aid
Current Educational Expenditures per Student	.889	— .428	not computed	.233
Total Educational Expenditures per Capita	.875	.507	.248	not computed
Educational Tax Proxy per Capita	1.120	.600	— .180	not computed

come is associated with a 1.12 percent increase in the educational tax proxy. The educational fiscal measures are next most responsive to the enrollment ratio followed by state aid. The negative elasticity of —.180 between aid and school taxes indicates that only 18 percent of aid is used to replace local effort. These results highlight the true importance of aid in suburbia. Only a very small part of aid is used to replace local taxes. Further, aid is additive to total effort as measured by per student or per capita expenditures.

Suburban Differences in the New York Region

Current expenditures per pupil in suburbia clearly appear to be a function of the levels of income and state aid, offset to a limited extent by the enrollment ratio. The sample in the above analysis used suburban areas taken as a whole. The question arises, however, whether or not the same forces are operative among suburbs within a particular metropolitan area. Further, how do the forces compare to each other within a single large area? The area chosen for this last section has often been considered as the prototype "metropolitan region," with its multiple central cities and suburban rings. The region is the New–Northeast New Jersey Standard Consolidated Area plus Fairfield County, Connecticut, which except for a state boundary would ordinarily be considered as part of this region. The data are presented in county aggregate form. Central cities are subtracted from the county, leaving the suburban portions of counties as the unit of analysis. The only deviation from census definitions was to consider Yonkers, New York, as a central city. The fourteen-county area contains nine municipalities in addition to Yonkers which are classified as central cities. These cities are shown in Table 6 in parentheses to demonstrate that the suburban central city differences discussed earlier in this paper hold in the several state portions within the region. The only exception is Stamford, Connecticut, which is a central city by definition only, having exceptionally high per capita income, school expenditure, and tax levels. It should be noted that the detailed school district data, where available, follows the same pattern in all particulars as do the county aggregates presented below.

In Table 6, the expenditures per pupil, school taxes per capita, state aid per pupil, and income per capita are shown for the region. Unlike the earlier analysis where data was not available, school taxes are measured directly here. The region is an interesting one because it covers three separate states which differ in the extensiveness of their respective educational state aid programs and whose suburban communities have quite similar levels of income. Since it is clear that income and aid explain much of the variation in suburban school expenditures per student, it follows that their relative impact on per student expenditures can be highlighted through a comparison of the expenditures in a specific multistate environment.

The striking characteristic of the suburban portions of the fourteen-county area is that incomes are roughly uniform throughout the region while state aid, local school taxes, and expenditures per pupil are quite different. The difference in the latter variables are most pronounced among states, with New York counties having far higher levels of educational state aid, expenditures, and—most surprising—local school taxes than the counties in New Jersey and Fairfield County in Connecticut.

73

TABLE 6

School Systems in the Metropolitan New York Area*, 1964

	Current Educational Expenditures per Student	School Taxes per Capita	Educational State Aid per Student	Income per Capita
NEW YORK STATE				
New York SMSA				
New York City	(759.31)	(67.87)	(250.23)	(2306)
Nassau County	826.74	133.30	364.74	2874
Rockland County	719.44	128.47	333.33	2109
Suffolk County	696.07	119.04	406.86	1964
Westchester County	805.36	116.81	261.74	3252
Yonkers	(517.98)	(58.64)	(233.81)	(2685)
Westchester less Yonkers	871.28	134.78	264.46	3427
New York SMSA less New York				
City and Yonkers	790.35	129.90	358.59	2738
NEW JERSEY				
Newark SMSA				
Essex County	547.34	94.91	68.41	2452
Newark	(516.03)	(85.43)	(71.52)	(1792)
Essex less Newark	572.24	102.31	65.79	2967
Morris County	557.20	141.98	84.88	2527
Union County	521.44	107.54	69.13	2631
Newark SMSA less Newark	548.33	112.45	72.13	2746
Patterson-Clifton-Passaic SMSA				
Bergen County	553.64	113.85	68.85	2721
Passaic County	500.66	84.27	71.03	2088
Clifton	(436.50)	(73.17)	(58.35)	(2378)
Patterson	(451.88)	(63.89)	(83.24)	(1840)
Passaic	(512.20)	(72.22)	(71.03)	(2093)
Passaic less Clifton, Patterson,				
Passaic	562.09	119.68	78.82	2181
Patterson-Clifton-Passaic SMSA less				
Patterson, Clifton, and Passaic	555.02	114.66	70.48	2646
Jersey City SMSA				
Hudson County	501.89	60.06	65.32	2039
Jersey City	(473.68)	(53.27)	(56.47)	(1964)
Hudson County less Jersey City	523.28	66.26	72.03	2101
Other Metropolitan Counties				
Middlesex County	445.08	107.14	84.26	2073
Somerset County	506.60	133.33	82.10	2381

TABLE 6 (continued)

School Systems in the Metropolitan New York Area*, 1964

	Current Educational Expenditures per Student	School Taxes per Capita	Educational State Aid per Student	Income per Capita
CONNECTICUT				
Fairfield County	517.10	81.96	112.88	2792
Stamford	(578.64)	(82.80)	(113.65)	(2860)
Bridgeport	(388.54)	(42.04)	(112.08)	(1955)
Norwalk	(520.60)	(88.23)	(111.33)	(2523)
Fairfield less Stamford, Bridgeport, Norwalk	549.21	99.11	114.71	3208

* Fourteen counties; parentheses indicate central cities.
SOURCE: **Financial Data for School Districts, Year Ending June 30, 1964**, Albany, N.Y.: Department of Audit and Control, 1965; New Jersey Taxpayers Association, **Financial Statistics of New Jersey Local Government**, 1964 ed., Trenton, N.J., September, 1964; Connecticut Public Expenditure Council, **Local Public School Expenses and State Aid in Connecticut, School Years 1960-61 through 1964-65**, Hartford, Conn., January, 1966.

On the basis of the multiple-regression analysis, it was evident that income and aid were the major determinants of both school expenditures and taxes. Since suburban incomes are sufficiently uniform throughout the area, the differences in expenditures and local taxes appear to be due largely to the differences in the state aid and related policies of the three respective states.

It should be emphasized that New York State's exceptionally high state aid is accompanied by both higher expenditures and local school taxes relative to New Jersey and Connecticut. In any case, it is clear that the states have a significant impact on suburban school finances in the New York region. In the case of this region, aid appears to be stimulative to local taxes as well as to expenditures.

Conclusions

It is evident from the results of this analysis that one can generalize about suburban school systems by comparing them to central cities. But it is just as clear that such a generalization does not get at the nature of suburban education. For it has been demonstrated here that differences among suburban areas with respect to income, the enrollment ratio, state aid, noneducational expenditures, and the fiscal variables are of the same order of magnitude as the differences between central city and suburb. Variations in school expenditures per student and school expenditures and taxes per capita among suburban areas indicate that it is not appropriate to describe a "typical" suburban school system. Suburban communities are not all of similar character.

The variations in the measures of the educational and fiscal aspects of suburban public school systems have been largely explained by a few variables that indicate what kinds of suburban differences have an impact on education. These variables are per capita income, state aid, and the enrollment ratio. By looking at a single region where incomes are fairly uniform, it was discovered that state aid and related policies play a very important role in providing the fiscal resources for education.

The most significant set of implications of this analysis concerns the role of the state in suburban education. The educational levels in suburbia are far more than a passive reflection of income differences. State policies with regard to elementary and secondary education as reflected by intergovernmental fiscal flows play a powerful role in influencing the level of suburban education. In addition, a great portion of the educational disparities between suburbs and cities can be explained by state aid. Indeed, where incomes are homogeneous, the state becomes the major force in the determination of the nature of education in a given suburban area. That the potential role of the state in suburban education is great is attested to by the fact that aid, in its most dramatic statement, has even stimulated greater tax effort at the local level.

WILLIAM G. BUSS, JR.

The author, a lawyer, is presently a lecturer on education and Assistant to the Dean of the Harvard Graduate School of Education—giving particular attention to the problems of de facto segregation in public schools. He is the author of "The Mass Conflict-of-Interest Statute: An Analysis" in the Boston University Law Review *and "Racial Imbalance and Equal Educational Opportunity in New Haven, Connecticut" in a forthcoming issue of* Law and Society Review.

THE LAW AND THE EDUCATION OF THE URBAN NEGRO

T HERE IS SOMETHING arresting and even discouraging about the persistent identification of the law and the education of the Negro. In fact, it is a matter of some embarrassment that the education of the Negro merits special treatment at all.

In many ways the problems of urban education which the Negro shares with all other city children are more important than the problems which are unique to the urban Negro. Under the generally prevailing legal structure education is provided primarily through local school districts, and the financing, and hence the quality, of education is primarily dependent upon local resources. Throughout the United States, suburban areas tend to have high family income levels and to be free of the financial overburden which results from aging buildings, density of population, and concentration of commercial, industrial and government facilities. Consequently, the per pupil expenditures on education in the suburbs are often twice as great as those in the core city. Federal aid to education and more equitable state aid formulas have begun to qualify the educational impact of this structure. But it has long

77

been true, and it is true today, that the city school child — black or white — is at a marked disadvantage by comparison to his suburban counterpart.

Still, it remains a fact that long history and not-so-accidental circumstances have put the Negro at a special disadvantage. Because equality of opportunity is the promise of America, and particularly of education in America, the education of the Negro poses special problems. In 1954, in its decision in the case of *Brown v. The Board of Education,* the Supreme Court of the United States dealt with the most obvious of these problems when it held that a legally supported system of school segregation was unconstitutional. But that decision marked only the beginning of the painful and painfully slow attempt to provide equality through the elimination of racial segregation in the public schools.

This article will consider the legal implications of the Supreme Court's segregation decision on the type of segregation which is spawned by the conditions of the city — commonly called "de facto segregation." Before doing so, however, it is important to recognize that the law is sometimes included among these conditions. There are certain aspects of our legal structure — certain legal rules — which, usually unintentionally, tend to make desegregation of schools more difficult.

Segregation in the city's schools is indirectly encouraged, for example, by the law which governs landlord and tenant. With common-law origins in medieval relationships between lord and vassal, this law does not apply the principles which ordinarily determine the interdependent obligations of contracting parties. As a result, it is generally impossible for a tenant to obtain adequate remedies against his landlord for intolerable living conditions in a rented apartment. So long as the tenant wants (or is forced by circumstances) to occupy the apartment, he must pay the rent and the landlord accordingly has little incentive to make improvements.[1]

At the same time, the housing market and the laws which establish the city's tax structure discourage the tenant from making im-

---

1. In the form of legislative solutions, a beginning has been made toward the correction of this legal inequality, but these new approaches are only a beginning, and they have appeared very recently.

provements. As there is nowhere else for the economic bottom of the population to go, prices can be kept high; if improvements are made, taxes would be raised also. Together, these legal ingredients contribute to slum conditions and ghettoization within the city and hasten the so-called "white flight" to the suburbs. The result, with school assignments made largely by geographic districting, is segregation both within and between school systems.

School districts are traditionally organized on a local, largely autonomous basis. This legal framework for providing education further impedes desegregation, because it tends to limit solutions to small geographical areas and to permit segregation between districts to go without remedy. Of course, each state is ultimately responsible for the organization of its schools, and the allocation of the educational function among particular school districts is not permanently immune to change through adjudication. For example, the division of a single school district into separate Negro and white districts for the express purpose of preserving segregated schools would not withstand attack in court. Moreover, it is possible that, in time, inequality between districts will be prohibited, whether it is inequality based on racial segregation or inequality based on the uneven allocation of financial resources. And the time for such changes through state or federal law, may be sooner than we realize. But in the immediate future at least, it appears that desegregation between school districts will depend heavily upon the consent of the local populations and their elected representatives. School district consolidations usually encounter heavy opposition prompted by the proprietary impulses of local control. When race becomes a factor in consolidation, this opposition can become fanatical.

The law has also introduced desegregation obstacles which are not in any sense the product of time-worn or deeply ingrained legal principles. In quite recent legislative ventures the law has often been framed in such a way as to foster segregation rather than integration. For example, under urban renewal legislation very considerable economic advantages are available to local communities if schools are constructed in the renewal areas to serve children residing there. While new schools and new housing are better than decadent schools and decadent housing, the renewed areas are very often built in the old ghetto. And very often a new ghetto and a new ghetto school is produced. In a like fashion, Title I of the Elementary and Secondary Education Act of 1965 tends to increase the investment of public funds into ghetto schools rather than to bring about integration. Title I is the antipoverty provision of this act. Money is available under it to deal with the educational problems associated with the poor. The legislation itself does not absolutely preclude fighting poverty with integration but it tends in this direction, and it appears that the administration of the provision on both the Federal and state level has tended to complete the process. Even in those communities where a voluntary transfer plan would permit a particular child to attend an integrated school, this antipoverty provision sometimes forces a quite unfair choice between special services and facilities, on the one hand, and integration on the other.

To be sure, some affirmative legislative steps have been taken to deal explicitly with the problems of school segregation. But even here, the effort has been partly abortive. For example, the Commonwealth of Massachusetts enacted a racial imbalance statute, but it did not at the same time appropriate any funds to aid in the effective implementation of the statute. In Title IV of the Civil Rights Act of 1964, Congress included certain provisions under which various kinds of technical and financial assistance was made available to school systems engaged in the process of desegregation. But "desegregation" was defined in Title IV to exclude efforts to overcome racial imbalance. As actions which would overcome racial imbalance can ordinarily be taken as actions to eliminate segregation, this exclusion is probably of very little effect. Nevertheless, it does distort the picture by purporting to pass over the increasing segregation in the schools of the city where the segregation is not necessarily the product of conscious discrimination.

The remainder of this article will focus on the legal questions which are raised by school segregation — without regard to its cause. These are the questions which have held the attention of the courts and dominated public discussion. But it is unlikely that satisfactory or enduring solutions will be created so long as the conditions which produce segregation in the schools of the nation's cities go unchecked. Thus, changes in the law, where the law contributes to these conditions, are of perhaps even more fundamental importance than the response of the law once segregation exists.

Two Conflicting Legal Claims

Of course, school segregation is not uniquely a problem of the city. Rural areas are generally even more resistant to compliance with the Supreme Court's segregation decision than are urban areas. But once this hard core of resistance is broken, the sophisticated and circumstantial segregation of the cities will remain. And, in North and South alike, this urban school segregation may well prove to be a far more intractable problem in the long-run.

Segregation is a persistent condition in nearly every large city school system in the United States. It is caused by a variety of interrelated factors, including school assignment policies; residential patterns within the city; real estate practices; socioeconomic position; high Negro population density in the cities; "white flight" to the suburbs (which may or may not include flight from Negro schools and Negro housing but certainly includes flight from inferior housing, inferior schools, inferior municipal services, and inferior play areas); and outright bigotry. Whatever combination of circumstances may have produced segregated schools in a particular instance, the courts have been involved frequently in attempts to bring about desegregation. Two conflicting legal claims have been made repeatedly, one for the purpose of preventing desegregation and the other for the purpose of requiring it.

The first of these claims is based on the argument that racial neutrality is the legal norm and no action purposefully taken with a view to affecting the racial composition of a school is legally permitted. In its constitutional form, this claim is often premised on the so-called "color-blind" constitution. Insofar as desegregation relies upon such racially conscious action, it is barred according to those who make this claim. In their view, segregation which was not deliberately and officially planned calls for no legal response.

The second claim is based upon an opposite assumption. Because segregated schools are inferior, no matter how the segregation was caused, action must be taken to bring about desegregation by all feasible means. It is assumed by those who make this claim that such action will ordinarily entail conscious consideration of racial criteria.

In some cases, the explicit disposition of the legal issue raised by one of these claims will, of necessity, dispose of the issue raised by the other also. For example, if giving any consideration to race is prohibited, segregation cannot be eliminated except in those cases, and to the extent, that it was caused by a racially conscious policy, as was the dual school system ruled unconstitutional by the Supreme Court's decision in *Brown v. The Board of Education.* On the other hand, if the law positively requires action toward the elimination of segregation, effective action will nearly always depend upon considering racial criteria in the development of a desegregation plan. It should be noted, though, that both claims could be rejected. It could be decided that the law neither prohibits utilization of racial considerations nor requires the elimination of segregation which did not result directly from overt official discrimination.

For both positions, it is often argued that the claims are derived from the equal protection clause (or sometimes the due process clause) of the Fourteenth Amendment of the United States Constitution.[2] In many states, comparable claims are also made on the strength of provisions of the state constitution or a state statute. It is not uncommon for these parallel state and Federal questions to become intertwined and even confused. In some cases, the adjudication of one or both of these claims has not clearly indicated whether state or Federal law was relied upon. Where Federal and state legal standards are inconsistent, the Federal standard must

---

2. "No State shall . . . deprive any person of life, liberty, or property, without due process of law; nor deny to any person within its jurisdiction the equal protection of the laws." Amendment XIV, Par. I.

be followed because of the supremacy clause of the United States Constitution.[3]

So far as Federal law is concerned, there is no authoritative decision of the legal issues raised by these claims. Only the Supreme Court of the United States can make such a decision, and the Supreme Court has not yet considered either claim. Contrary to much popular thinking, the legal questions which they raise were not decided by the Court's opinion in the *Brown* case.

It is probably true that the *Brown* opinion is *consistent* with both claims. In dictum statements in subsequent cases individual members of the Court have suggested that *Brown* should be construed to require absolute disregard of race as a legislative criteria. And in *Bolling v. Sharp*, the companion case to *Brown* from the District of Columbia, the Court observed that racial classifications were inherently suspect. On the other hand, much has been made of the Court's statement in the *Brown* case that separate schools for Negroes are inherently unequal, and the statement in *Brown* (which was really a quotation from the trial judge's opinion) that the detrimental effect of segregated schools has a greater impact when the segregation has the sanction of law. From these latter statements, it has been inferred, from *Brown*, that schools segregated even without the sanction of law have a detrimental effect, are inherently unequal, and constitutionally forbidden.

While all of these points are relevant in beginning analysis, they fall far short of completing the process. The legal issues growing out of adventitious segregation in public schools were not argued in 1954, and they were not considered by the Court. Courts do not decide controversies which are not before them. The Supreme Court did not have these issues in mind in passing upon legally required school segregation in its opinion in *Brown v. The Board of Education*.

Nor has the Supreme Court's subsequent action answered these questions. The Court has declined to exercise its discretionary authority to review cases in which both claims have been rejected

---

3. "This Constitution, and the Laws of the United States . . . shall be the supreme Law of the Land; and the Judges in every State shall be bound thereby, any Thing in the Constitution or Laws of any State to the Contrary notwithstanding." Article VI, Par. II.

by the lower court. Such a refusal to review does not indicate approval or disapproval of the disposition of the case by lower court. It indicates only that fewer than four justices believe it would be desirable for the Supreme Court to consider the issues raised by the case. Because the Court has refused to review decisions rejecting both the color-blind and duty-to-act arguments, there has been speculation that the Court has decided to leave the matter of appropriate action to the discretion of local school districts. In a broad sense this is no doubt true. Granting either claim would have limited local discretion; therefore, refusing to reconsider the denial of the claims necessarily means that local officials have retained maximum freedom. But it is probably misleading to suggest that this outcome represents a deliberate judgment of the Court or that it can be counted upon as the Court's permanent solution.

The Englewood Litigation

Although these legal issues remain unsettled, they have been considered and decided by a number of state and Federal courts and by state education officials who perform an adjudicatory function concerning educational questions brought before them in an administrative proceeding. Nearly every aspect of these issues has been dealt with in an unusual variety of litigation that has arisen in the relatively simple factual situation of Englewood, New Jersey. By tracing the Englewood litigation chronologically, one can see in concrete terms the central legal issues growing out of the *de facto* segregation which is characteristic of city school systems. A comparison of the treatment of these issues in the several cases involving Englewood with their treatment in certain other cases will provide a general outline of the present state of the law.

In some respects Englewood is not representative of the problems of segregation in city schools. It is more suburb than city. And, because it is quite small, the segregation problem there was much more confined and manageable than is often the case. But school segregation has been a problem in many such smaller cities, and it does no harm to observe that problems of urban education will increasingly become the problems of the outer ring of communities in the urban metropolis. Moreover, it seems desirable to remember that the problem of segregated education is not so uniformly insoluble as undue attention on Harlem and Chicago's South Side would suggest. In any event, the legal issues are well illustrated by the several Englewood legal actions.

Englewood is a city of approximately 30,000 people. It is nearly a square in shape, 2 miles on a side. In 1955, Englewood had five elementary schools (grades 1-6), two junior high schools (grades 7-9), and one senior high school (grades 10-12). The precise racial percentages at the several schools at that time are not known. But, in general, the enrollments of Lincoln Elementary School and Lincoln Junior High School included a very high proportion of Negroes, and the other schools had predominantly white enrollments. The two Lincoln schools were located in the southwestern quadrant of the city, which was a heavily Negro residential area and in which nearly all of the city's Negroes lived.

A legal proceeding was initiated before the New Jersey Commissioner of Education on behalf of two Negro children who were students in the Englewood schools. It was alleged that the Englewood Board of Education had discriminated in the assignment of these two children and other Negro children similarly situated. The plaintiffs contended that Negro children were assigned to Lincoln although white children living in the same area were assigned to Liberty School, located a very short distance to the north of Lincoln. The board of education admitted impropriety in the one case, but claimed it had not known of the assignment. The child was reassigned to Liberty School prior to the commissioner's decision.

The other plaintiff's case proved to be more complicated for the commissioner. First of all, he noted that standards of shortest distance and equal treatment should have governed assignment practices. And he observed that Englewood, through its attendance districts for Liberty and Lincoln, had plainly violated these standards. Moreover, at the kindergarten level, at which the plaintiff was a student, the districting placed 100 Negro and two white students in Lincoln and fifty-four white and no Negro students in

Liberty. The commissioner ordered a revision of the attendance district lines.

But the commissioner's decision was equivocal with respect to the charge that the unequal districts had been racially motivated. He seemed to say that it looked suspiciously like racial discrimination was involved. But he refrained from saying so explicitly. He said, "Without impugning the motives of the Board of Education in fixing boundary lines, . . . the result is discrimination, regardless of intent or motivation."

In private statements by persons in Englewood privy to information concerning school decisions, less caution was used. These persons had no doubt that district lines were intentionally drawn to keep white children out of the "Negro school." But such testimony is rarely available to the deciding tribunal.

The commissioner did come a small step closer to a finding of intentional discrimination in relation to a matter not found by him to be directly relevant to the case of either plaintiff. The commissioner observed that Lincoln Junior High School had an enrollment of less than 200 pupils, practically all Negro, while the Engle Street Junior High located only three blocks away and serving all elementary school districts except Lincoln, had an enrollment of between 500 and 600 pupils, most of whom were white.

The commissioner's reason for ordering the termination of the separate Lincoln Junior High was clearly a response to the resulting racial separation. Echoing the Supreme Court's *Brown* opinion of just the year before, he said, "The pupils of the Lincoln Junior High School are entitled to attend classes and to participate in school activities with other pupils of the city of their age. The commissioner is convinced that these pupils, denied such a right, are being discriminated against." But here, too, the commissioner stopped short of stating that this striking division along racial lines was intentionally created by a board policy of racial discrimination.

This ruling of the commissioner was explicitly based on the education law of the State of New Jersey. A similar standard of equality might have been derived from the equal protection clause of the Fourteenth Amendment of the United States Constitution. Several years after the commissioner's decision, a Federal court judge did reach a similar result on similar reasoning in reliance upon the Fourteenth Amendment. This case arose in Manhasset, New York, in 1964. Manhasset had three elementary schools. Two of these had enrollments of 600 and 574 and were both all white; the third had an enrollment of only 166 and was over 98 percent Negro. The judge expressly disclaimed any intention of dealing with "racial imbalance" but refused to ignore the virtually complete segregation which existed under suspicious circumstances.

> The defendants are, and for several years have been, fully aware of the total separation of the entire Negro elementary school population from over 99% of their white contemporaries. With knowledge of this fact, were they to prescribe today the attendance area lines which now exist could such action be justified by the normal criteria supporting the neighborhood school policy? Were the Board to create out of the total District one disproportionately small attendance area, provide a school for a disproportionately small student body composed almost entirely of Negro children and representing 100% of the Negro student population of the District, and couple such action with a rigid no-transfer policy — were the Board to take such action today would it not be reasonable to regard it as a rather ingenuous device to separate the races, protestations to the contrary notwithstanding? Could such attendance lines, if drawn today, be insulated from the Fourteenth Amendment merely because the bylaw or rule of the Board did not mention the word Negro, but, rather, was cast in terms of residence?

The Case of the Lincoln School

There was a lull of several years before the second, larger wave of litigation came to Englewood. The first new legal ripple came with an action commenced in the United States District Court for the District of New Jersey in 1962. Parents of certain Negro students assigned to Lincoln Elementary School sued on behalf of their children. The Lincoln Elementary School was about 98 percent Negro at the time of suit. The situation was otherwise similar to that in 1955 except that Lincoln Junior High School had been eliminated. These Lincoln parents argued that the segregation at

Lincoln was caused by the board of education's conscious acts, but they also argued that, without regard to the cause of the segregation, the board was obliged to take steps to desegregate Lincoln School.

The Federal court did not consider the case on its merits. The judge, taking note of certain seemingly relevant administrative procedures under the state's education law, held that the plaintiffs had to exhaust the remedies available under these procedures before a Federal court could address itself to the constitutional questions under Federal law.

A new action relying upon these administrative remedies was not started immediately because it appeared, for a time, that Englewood was going to solve the Lincoln school segregation on its own initiative. When this hope disappeared, a lawsuit was initiated before the commissioner — this time by different Negro parents, again claiming that the board of education had both a duty to compensate for discrimination and an affirmative duty to act against segregation. In his 1963 decision, the commissioner found no discrimination but nevertheless concluded that the Englewood board was required to take action to alleviate the inequality brought about by the segregated condition of the Lincoln school.

Before considering the commissioner's positive holding and the order and plan which followed, the negative holding should be noted. The commissioner found no evidence of discrimination. Necessarily, this meant either that the possible relevance of the 1955 case did not occur to him or that he saw no causal connection between the circumstances of the 1955 case and the segregation at Lincoln School in 1963. The commissioner's 1963 opinion did not mention his earlier decision.

Yet, in a case decided by a Federal court two years earlier, discriminatory acts which occurred no later than 1949 were held to have contributed significantly to the segregation of a school (also named "Lincoln" by unhappy coincidence) in 1961. In that case, the Federal judge had held that gerrymandering of school attendance districts in the early 1930s by the Board of Education of New Rochelle, New York, and the board's subsequent discrimination in applying a transfer policy had, and was intended to have, the effect of creating a segregated school. The judge concluded that, in purposely creating a segregated school, the law of the board of education was not constitutionally different from the statutory law which required the maintainance of separate Negro and white schools throughout the South before 1954. He therefore held that the Negro plaintiffs before him had been denied the equal protection of the law.

There was at least a rough parallel between these circumstances and those which might have been found in Englewood. In addition, the commissioner might well have concluded, as the court did in the New Rochelle case, that the failure of responsible officials to take ameliorative action clearly contributed to the continued existence of the segregated school and therefore brought the good faith of these officials into question. In both instances, the segregated school had been the focus of considerable attention, and a positive plan of action had been suggested. But no action had been taken in either case by the time the litigation was being decided.[4]

An analysis of the New Rochelle litigation has pointed out that the success of the plaintiffs in proving the gerrymander was practically a legal miracle, depending as it did upon the failure of the board's attorney to object to hearsay evidence.[5] It might not have been possible in the Englewood case to prove that any such deliberate official acts had contributed to Lincoln's segregation. The 1955 case had skirted around a finding of racial motivation at the elementary level and the commissioner may not have been prepared to make such a finding eight years later. But an alternative explanation is possible also. Once the commissioner held that there was a positive duty to do something about the segregated school, there remained only an incidental interest in whether the board had previously been engaged in wrongdoing. No doubt, the Negro plaintiffs would have preferred such a ruling, but they were concerned mainly with obtaining relief. The commissioner granted

---

4. In Englewood, the board of education had attempted to achieve desegregation at Lincoln school through the establishment of city-wide fifth and sixth grade school. But the Englewood Board of Estimate had refused to appropriate the necessary funds.

5. John Kaplan, "Segregation Litigation and the Schools — Part I: The New Rochelle Experience" *Northwestern University Law Review*, 1, 16 (1963).

this relief without any finding of discrimination. Moreover, the commissioner may have had a practical incentive for avoiding such a finding. After his decision, he would have to continue to work with the local school board and the local school administrator. He might just as well not jeopardize his relationship with them. And, with respect to the particular case before him, he may have felt that the odds in favor of board action in compliance with his order would not be improved if he labeled the board members as racists.

Developing Affirmative Policies for Correcting Racial Imbalance

In granting plaintiffs their request that affirmative action be taken to deal with the segregation at Lincoln, the commissioner held that compulsory attendance at a virtually all-Negro school constituted a denial of educational opportunity which the board of education was required to correct.

> In the minds of Negro pupils and parents a stigma is attached to attending a school whose enrollment is completely or almost exclusively Negro, and that this sense of stigma and resulting feeling of inferiority have an undesirable effect upon attitudes related to successful living. Reasoning from this premise and recognizing the right of every child to equal educational opportunity, the Commissioner is convinced that in developing its pupil assignment policies and in planning for new school buildings, a board of education must take into account the continued existence or potential creation of a school populated entirely, or nearly so, by Negro pupils.

This legal ruling, like the earlier 1955 decision, was determined under New Jersey's education law. Comparable conclusions have been reached in other states. In New York, this position was based on a policy statement of the board of regents. In Massachusetts, a state statute establishes a policy of "promotion of racial balance and correction of existing racial imbalance." The California Supreme Court has held that there is an affirmative duty to reduce racial imbalance, although it is not clear whether its decision is based on state or Federal law. In some instances, affirmative action to eliminate racial concentrations has been taken by a local board of education without any state legal requirement to do so.

It has been argued, also, that an affirmative duty to desegregate is required, as a matter of Federal law, by the equal protection clause. Although some Federal courts have so held, this argument has not generally succeeded in the Federal courts. In cases originating in Gary, Indiana; Kansas City, Kansas; and Cincinnati, Ohio, the courts found no board of education responsibility for the existence of segregation in the schools and, therefore, held that the board of education had no constitutional obligation to desegregate. On the other hand, as noted earlier, a Federal district court ordered affirmative action to be taken to reduce segregation in Manhasset, Long Island. While that order was strongly influenced by the rather special circumstances that were present in the Manhasset schools, it did not rely upon any finding that the Manhasset school board had purposely caused the segregation. In another New York case, a Federal court used rather sweeping language in denying a motion for a summary judgment in 1962. The motion had alleged absence of official responsibility and argued that the action for relief therefore necessarily failed. The court said segregation, however caused, required corrective action:

> Segregated education is inadequate and when that inadequacy is attributable to state action it is a deprivation of constitutional right. Education is compulsory in New York. The educational system that is thus compulsory and publicly afforded must deal with the inadequacy arising from adventitious segregation; it cannot accept and indurate segregation on the ground that it is not coerced or planned but accepted.

Similar language was used by a Federal judge in Massachusetts in ordering the Springfield, Massachusetts School Committee to act to end segregation.

> It is neither just nor sensible to proscribe segregation having its basis in affirmative state action while at the same time failing to pro-

91

vide a remedy for segregation which grows out of discrimination in housing, or other economic or social factors.[6]

Compliance Plans and Reaction

On the basis of his legal conclusion, the New Jersey Commissioner of Education ordered the Englewood Board of Education to submit a plan to eliminate the aggravated racial imbalance at the Englewood Lincoln School. Under the plan submitted by the board, this was accomplished by discontinuing Lincoln as a regular elementary school. Children in grades 1 through 5 who were formerly assigned to Lincoln were reassigned to the other elementary schools in the city, with the exception of Liberty, where the enrollment was already over 60 percent Negro. All Englewood sixth graders were assigned to a school located in the center of the city and used at that time for school administration offices. Kindergartners continued to attend Lincoln, and the administration headquarters were moved to the Lincoln building.

The board's plan met resistance from a group of white parents and taxpayers. At least three suits including an appeal from the commissioner's decision, were initiated in various New Jersey state courts by this group, some of whom had intervened on the board's side in defending the suit of the Negro parents before the commissioner. In addition, these parents and taxpayers brought a suit in the United States District Court for the District of New Jersey, where the Negro parents had begun this second round of litigation before being remanded to the state administrative procedures. At this juncture, the board became the defendant in a case in which it was defending action rather than inaction. The board's former adversaries in the suit before the commissioner appeared as inter-

---

6. The Springfield case was subsequently dismissed by order of the Federal appellate court on procedural grounds. The Springfield School Committee had voluntarily adopted a resolution to "take whatever action is necessary to eliminate to the fullest extent possible, racial concentration in the schools within the framework of effective educational procedures." The appellate judge reasoned that, because of this initiative, the school committee should not be directed to do what it had undertaken to do by a court order using identical language.

vening defendants on the side of the board. The state suits were either withdrawn or permitted to become inactive prior to any final decision.[7] The Federal claim was actively pursued.

This Federal suit asked that the Englewood Board of Education be enjoined from carrying out its compliance plan and from spending funds pursuant to the implementation of the plan. The plaintiffs argued, in essence, that any segregation which existed in Englewood's schools was fortuitous and not the result of official action and that the Constitution of the United States prohibited resort to racial criteria in the formulation of school assignment policies.

Of course, the board of education did not argue that it had been responsible for the segregation.[8] But, rather surprisingly, the board also argued that its plan did not entail any use of racial criteria. By this, the board meant that the actual assignments were made on the basis of a child's place of residence, not skin color. In that sense, of course, racial criteria were not involved. But there was absolutely no doubt that the board's action, taken to comply with the commissioner's order,[9] had as its primary objective the elimination of segregation at the Lincoln school. This necessarily meant taking race into account because the assignment pattern adopted by the board was required to be one which did not leave an overwhelming Negro majority at the Lincoln school.

The Federal court rejected the plaintiffs claim that the board's action was prohibited by a "color-blind" constitution. The court expressly conceded that race had been at the foundation of the board's action and that racial considerations were involved. The court nonetheless concluded that use of racial criteria in this fashion

---

7. Possibly these cases were not diligently prosecuted because the New Jersey Supreme Court had ruled, in a case which originated in Montclair, New Jersey that a local board of education was permitted to utilize racial criteria in its school assignment policies.

8. Nor did the Negro parents who participated as intervening defendants in the suit so contend. As noted earlier in this article, none of the participants in the suit had any substantial interest in insisting that the board had actively discriminated, once a decision was made that the board had to alleviate the segregated conditions.

9. The plan being challenged was entitled, "Proposal of a plan to comply with the decision of the State Commissioner of Education of New Jersey directing the Englewood Board of Education to reduce the extreme concentration of Negro pupils in the Lincoln School."

for the purpose of accomplishing more integrated schools was constitutionally permissible.

This conclusion has also been reached, where the same constitutional claim has been made, in Federal or state courts in Massachusetts, Connecticut, New York, and New Jersey; and such a conclusion was a prerequisite of the California Supreme Court's decision that action must be taken to reduce racial imbalance whenever possible. There have been lower court decisions upholding the contention that a state statute or the Federal constitution imposes a requirement of absolute racial neutrality and prevents any consideration of race in furtherance of desegregation. But every such case has been reversed on appeal. There is not a single decision, not subsequently reversed, which has prevented a board of education from acting to accomplish integration through the utilization of racial criteria.

Appeals

An appeal was taken from the Federal trial court's decision upholding the Englewood Board of Education's desegregation plan. The Federal appellate court remanded the case to the Federal district court on procedural grounds without making any decision on the merits of the case. It also directed the trial court to consider the effect of a recently decided New Jersey case upon the Englewood desegregation plan. In this case, which originated in Plainfield, New Jersey, the state Supreme Court held that a desegregation plan which eliminated a 98 percent Negro school but left several schools at between 50 percent and 98 percent Negro, was insufficient.[10] The Liberty school in Englewood was over 60 percent Negro. As the Englewood desegregation plan had not affected Liberty, the Plainfield case raised obvious doubts concerning its adequacy.

The Englewood case has become inactive since its remand to the Federal trial court in New Jersey. A new suit before the commis-

---

10. This Plainfield decision was based on the standards initially established by the New Jersey commissioner of education, even though the commissioner had found the more limited Plainfield plan to be satisfactory.

sioner has been started by Negro parents, however, and this most recent action asks for the desegregation of the Liberty school. While this action remains pending, the Englewood superintendent of schools has drawn up a plan to deal with the Liberty segregation. This plan would create a city-wide fifth and sixth grade and would reassign Liberty children in grades 2 through 4 to the other three elementary schools in Englewood. Children in kindergarten and grade 1 would remain at Liberty.

These several phases of the Englewood litigation, and the other cases referred to, present an accurate picture of the legal questions posed by urban segregation and the judicial and administrative answers to these questions. As observed earlier, none of these cases authoritatively answers the Federal questions considered. Any question of Federal law remains open until it is decided by the Supreme Court of the United States. Thus, it can be expected that persons who believe that they are affected by school segregation (or desegregation) will continue to claim that a color-blind constitution proscribes desegregation based upon considerations of race and to claim that desegregation is affirmatively required by the Constitution without regard to evidence of previous wrongdoing.

Future Judicial Decisions: Problems and Prospects

In the remaining pages, this article will provide a framework for analysis to suggest how the Supreme Court might deal with these claims, if and when it considers them. This, of course, is speculation about what the Court will do in the future, but it is also a recommendation for what state and Federal courts should do in the meantime.

The concept of the color-blind constitution had its origin in the late Mr. Justice Harlan's dissent from the majority's acceptance of the "separate but equal" doctrine in *Plessy v. Ferguson.* The main thrust of his dissenting opinion was that the majority on the Court ignored what was obvious to all: The exclusion of a Negro from the railroad car reserved for whites by reason of his race, as required by the Louisiana statute involved in the case, was discriminatory and harmful to the man excluded; the parallel "exclusion" of whites from the car reserved for Negroes did not bring about equality in anything other than a form of words. In other words, he argued that equality must be defined within the context of the real world.

We have already seen that the state and Federal courts have uniformly rejected arguments which would have foreclosed considering race as a means toward integration. As some of these courts have observed, there can be no neutrality in the matter. If a law is interpreted to bar consideration of race as a basis of desegregation, that law would affirmatively foster or preserve segregation.

The Supreme Court has never adopted the concept of a color-blind constitution as a legal standard. The Court has repeatedly shown its distaste for color and race classifications, but it has not stated that such criteria are automatically barred. In some cases, notably the Japanese exclusion cases, it has actually permitted racial classifications when very special circumstances were thought to be present. In others, particularly those involving segregation, a racial classification has been rejected because it was not related to any permissable legislative purpose.[11] It is exceedingly unlikely that the Supreme Court would hold that integregation is not a permissable legislative purpose.[12]

As acutely put in an Opinion of the Attorney General of California:

> Rejection of *Plessy* did not convert Justice Harlan's metaphor into a constitutional dogma which compels the striking down of affirmative steps to accomplish the purpose of the Fourteenth Amendment. Only invidious discrimination is forbidden. "Our Constitution is color-blind" was Justice Harlan's admonition against

---

11. It is actually somewhat misleading to speak of racial "classifications." The desegregation plans involved in the cases considered in this article did not assign individual students on the basis of skin color. They utilized the race of the students for purposes of making decisions, such as the selection of assignment areas, which were implemented without regard to race.

12. The validity of any classification depends upon the use to which it is put. For example, it would ordinarily be a denial of equal protection for a state to establish separate requirements for criminal defendants on the basis of their economic position. Yet the constitution has been construed to require states to furnish transcripts for defendants who cannot afford to pay for them.

the "separate but equal" doctrine. To decide that the combined thinking and efforts of persons of all races may not recognize a present inequality as the starting point in a program designed to help achieve that equality which Justice Harlan sought would be to conclude not merely that the Constitution is color-blind, but that it is totally blind.

Color-blindness is no doubt one of the high aims of American democracy, but we all know it does not exist today. A small child can see that the emperor is wearing no clothes; the Constitution does not charge us with the folly of praising his garment.

It is more difficult to predict the Supreme Court's likely resolution of the duty-to-act argument. But some of the briars which have overgrown the path to a consideration of the essential constitutional question can be rooted out and eliminated. The best place to begin this gardening is the Federal appellate court's decision in the Gary, Indiana case. As noted earlier, the court held that the Gary Board of Education had no duty to eliminate segregation. In reaching this conclusion, the court pointed out that the board had not been responsible for creating the many segregated schools in Gary.[13] The court found that the board had no intention of segregating the races; school attendance areas were not created for the purpose of including or excluding children of certain races. The court concluded, therefore, that there was no affirmative duty to change innocently arrived at attendance districts. It quoted with approval the oft-repeated statement of a South Carolina Federal court: "The Constitution does not require integration. It merely forbids discrimination." The implicit conclusion that there is an alternative other than segregation or integration would seem to

---

13. Out of forty schools in Gary, twelve had enrollments which were from 99 percent to 100 percent Negro, and five additional schools had enrollments which were between 77 and 95 percent Negro. There were no Gary schools in which Negro enrollments amounted to between 37 percent and 77 percent Negro, although the school system as a whole was 53 percent Negro. It had been argued in the trial court, although not in the appeals, that the segregation had been deliberately caused in at least some instances. In an analysis of the Gary litigation, Professor Kaplan developed certain arguments which might have been more effective for the plaintiffs in refuting the conclusion that the board of education had not been responsible for the segregation. John Kaplan "Segregation Litigation and the Schools — Part III: The Gary Litigation" *Northwestern University Law Review*, 1, 21 (1964).

require more thorough examination than the court provided. ,

The Fourteenth Amendment prohibits any state from denying any person the equal protection of its laws. For purposes of applying the Fourteenth Amendment, a local board of education is an agent of the state. Its actions are the actions of the state. There can be no doubt, then, that in assigning children to schools, which they are forced to attend by the state's compulsory education law, local boards must meet the Fourteenth Amendment's strictures against inequality.

But the Gary case suggests that the board satisfies its constitutional obligation when it refrains from overt racial discrimination. There may be state action, it seems to say, but there is no violation of any constitutional standard. Any inequality which may have resulted is fortuitous; it may be the product of the state's inaction, but not the state's action. This exegesis would seem reasonable if the assignment of a particular child to a particular school were inevitable and irrevocable. Otherwise it would appear unreasonable. Surely, a school board is obligated, so far as it is able, to provide educational conditions conducive to learning and to provide these on terms which are substantially equal for all students. If a board of education has the power to remove inequality through its choice of assignments or the size or location of a school, it seems inexcusable not to exercise this power in a fashion which will tend to provide equality to all of its students. Thus, if segregation impedes education and if segregated schools put the children assigned to them at a disadvantage, the board must act to eliminate the segregation insofar as it is able to do so by reasonable measures. In short, the fact that segregation results from the board's inaction does not suggest that the board had no choice or no responsibility.

The apportionment cases shed light on the concept of Fourteenth Amendment responsibility through state inaction. Suppose that the legislature of a given state was initially responsible for a particular apportionment of representation through voting districts. When the districting pattern was established, it provided equal representation for the state's voters. In fact, the districts were set up long ago by a legislature with a substantially different membership. Because of population shifts over which the legislature had no control, the districts now are extremely malapportioned. It is plain that these circumstances would not excuse the present legislature from its constitutional obligation to reapportion in order to provide the state's existing voters with substantially equal representation.

It would seem that the state, through its legislature or local school board, is similarly obliged to take steps toward the elimination of segregated schools, even though innocently created. At least this is so if segregation of the *de facto* variety does produce harm in the same sense as did the segregation considered in the *Brown* decision. In many cases in which relief from segregation has been allowed, it has been assumed or concluded that injury did result to the segregated student, even though the segregation was not the product of a legally imposed dual school system. This was true in those cases where relief was based on the Fourteenth Amendment either on grounds of school board discrimination as in New Rochelle, or merely by reason of circumstances, as in Manhasset. It was true also in those cases, as in Englewood, where relief was based on state law on grounds of aggravated Negro concentrations. In all of these cases, it was concluded evidently that the Negro student is put at a disadvantage when racial isolation in school results from assignment policies and related circumstances as well as when it results from more formal legal requirements. It seems particularly relevant that in those cases in which relief has been denied, as in Gary, Indiana, the denial was not based upon the absence of harm to the plaintiffs, but evidently on the premise that, if harm does result, it is not the fault of the school board.

There is no reason to assume harm would not result in the North as well as in the South. While there may be no overt policy of segregation, it is nonetheless true that segregated schools in the cities of the North and South alike do not result from fortuitous circumstances or mutually free choices. On the contrary, they grow out of a long history of racial discrimination and cumulative disadvantage. In the appeal of the Springfield, Massachusetts case in Federal court, the school committee's attorney was arguing that segregation in the *Brown* case was the product of legal requirements but the accidental segregation which existed in Springfield's schools was different. Listening to these arguments, Chief Judge Aldrich asked from the bench whether the children perceived the difference.

This analysis suggests that the Fourteenth Amendment might eventually be construed by the Supreme Court to require affirmative action toward desegregation of schools, without regard to the cause of the segregation. It is clear, though, that very complicated problems for judicial judgment would be presented by such a decision. There is the elusive problem of definition: What is "segregation"? There are also complicated problems in creating standards for enforcement: When has the board afforded proper weight to integration compared to distance, safety, cost, and other potentially competing considerations? No doubt the answer to such questions are interrelated. "Segregation" would not seem to require absolute separation of all Negro and white children, but it should involve the element of racial isolation and the resulting stigma attached to it. A local board of education would have performed its obligation satisfactorily when it had moved toward the elimination of isolation and stigma to the extent it could reasonably do so, in view of all the circumstances (probably including a comparison with alternative courses of action which were available). But these are, nevertheless, hard problems and they would impose substantial burdens on the judiciary so long as significant resistance to desegregation forced a case-by-case judicial determination of the adequacy of the action taken.

Whether the Court will choose to assume these burdens may depend very much upon what happens in the courts and in the society at large in the period immediately ahead. Separate facilities for Negro and white children are *not*, in all circumstances, unequal. In theory, it would be possible for two races, which had equal status and equal power in a society, to come to a mutual decision to maintain racially separate schools. The Supreme Court had the very different circumstances of twentieth-century American society in mind in its assertion that separate schools were "inherently unequal." For example, it seems very likely that the Court's decision was influenced by the notorious fact that separate schools were almost never equal. The isolation of the Negro child from the dominant white society and the related sense of inferiority were inextricably bound up with the low status and the low quality of the Negro schools.

It seems likely that circumstances will similarly effect the constitutional fate of *de facto* segregation in the long run. An affirmative duty to act may be found, if it becomes increasingly evident that "Negro schools," though not created by an official system of segregation, tend to be educationally inferior; that white families fight tooth and nail against sending their children to Negro schools or even receiving Negro children in "their" schools; that school boards continue to permit their schools to remain equally segregated or to become more segregated. Such a result would be made more likely also if, from the attempt of the courts to work out remedies in the segregation cases in the South makes it more and more clear that there is no middle ground between segregation and integration; that without an explicit requirement of integrated results the inherited tradition of segregated schools remains resistant to change. In these circumstances, the Constitution will appear to be a very impotent document for proscribing segregation unless it also requires steps toward integration. In this context, it will become increasingly more difficult for courts to avoid the conclusion that equality can be provided only if such affirmative steps are taken.

History has on more than one occasion revealed the unworkability of the Supreme Court's initial resolution of a constitutional question. It took many years before the linguistic equality of separate but equal foundered on the reality of actual conditions. A smaller gap separated the Court's initial decision upholding the white primary and its subsequent holding that the nominally private political party in the South was an integral part of the election process and an effective means of nullifying the Negro's right to vote.

In this perspective one might rejoice at the Supreme Court's failure thus far to review claims that affirmative action must be taken to desegregate the apparently unintended segregation which is characteristic of city schools. It may be an act of judicial wisdom for the Court to bide its time until circumstances fully develop and

101

a decision which is truly responsive to those circumstances becomes more likely.

Conclusion

School integration alone can not solve the racial problems of the entire society, although it may provide hope and opportunity in many individual cases where they would not otherwise exist. Nor can it solve alone the problems of urban education. It has been assumed in this article that school integration is just one indispensable part of equalizing educational opportunity, and that the law will continue to be involved in the process of providing it.

But perhaps even this is too optimistic a view. There is considerable evidence that the attempt to achieve school integration has been a failure. As United States Commissioner of Education Howe has recently pointed out, what little desegregation has taken place in the South has been offset by an increase in segregation in the cities of both the North and South. Moreover, there has been such a hard core of resistance to integration in all parts of the country that the desegregation process has been embittered by the knowledge of the deep racial hostility which exists. The appeal of "Black Power" is at least in part a symptom of disenchantment with the once high hopes for integrated schools in an integrated society.

In the end, the United States will have to choose between a society which is racially integrated and one which is rigidly divided along racial lines. And it seems clear that we are moving toward greater separation in many areas — including schools — even as the formal legal support of segregation is dissipated. It is not likely that this direction will be reversed unless the law moves beyond formal neutrality to a position of affirmative support of integration in the public schools and in other instruments of government.

T. Edward Hollander, Ph.D., C.P.A.,
is an Associate Professor at the Ber-
nard M. Baruch School of Business
and Public Administration, the City
College of the City University of New
York. He has also served as Studies
Director of the Education Task Force
of the (New York) Mayor's Tempo-
rary Commission on City Finances.

FISCAL INDEPENDENCE AND LARGE CITY SCHOOL SYSTEMS

M ANY OF THE PROBLEMS facing urban areas — integration, poverty, juvenile crime, large expenditures for public protection, extensive public assistance — focus on education. Perhaps we expect too much from our school systems, but they offer the only practical hope at the present time for long-range solutions to the most pressing social and economic problems facing urban society. If city school systems are to function effectively, if they are to play a meaningful role in helping arrest the social and economic deterioration in urban areas, they require extensive public support. They also must be made responsive to changing social needs and be sufficiently viable to adjust rapidly. To achieve these ends is a critical problem for our school systems today. Fiscal independence has often been advocated as one means of assuring greater school support and providing for better adaptability.

Interest in the question of fiscal independence was renewed in New York City when, in 1964, the Regents of the State of New

AUTHOR'S NOTE: *The author is indebted to Joseph D. McGoldrick, Queens College, Secretary of the Mayor's Temporary Commission, City Finances (New York City), who has given freely of his time to review this manuscript and suggest changes for its improvement.*

York included in their legislative proposal a recommendation that the legislature amend the constitution to permit the state's five largest cities (excluding New York City) to establish fiscally independent school districts.[1] They further recommended that a special study be undertaken to determine how fiscal independence can be fully achieved for the New York City school system. Subsequently, the mayor of New York City asked the Temporary Commission on City Finances to examine the whole question of city-school relations with special emphasis on the appropriateness of fiscal independence in the city.[2] This study was undertaken at the request of the Temporary Commission on City Finances to test the validity of fiscal independence for the New York City school system.[3] The study has implications for other large city school systems as well.

Fiscally Independent and Dependent School Systems: The Current Issues

Fiscal status is defined in terms of whether a school system is fiscally independent of, or fiscally dependent upon local government.

A fiscally independent school is one in which the state has delegated to the board of education complete authority in all matters pertaining to the financial management of public schools, the board having the power to determine the amount of the budget and to levy or cause to be levied a tax rate to raise the required funds.[4]

In such a case, the school board would possess full budgetary and debt-incurring powers. It would not be responsible to the

---

1. Board of Regents, State of New York, *The Regents Major Legislative Proposals for 1964*, Par. 6b. The five dependent city districts are Albany, Buffalo, Rochester, Syracuse, and Yonkers.

2. *Local Laws of the City of New York*, 1965, No. 181.

3. A pilot study of other large city school systems is being performed persuant to a contract with the U.S. Department of Health, Education, and Welfare, Office of Education, under the provisions of the Cooperative Research Program.

4. Carter V. Good (Ed.), *Dictionary of Education*, New York: McGraw-Hill Book Company, 1945.

local electorate nor would its budget be subject to review by a municipal government or an agency of local government. It would keep its own accounts and within the total amount of the budget adopted, it would spend funds without the outside approval of another unit of local government. If there are statutory or constitutional limitations on the amount of debt that can be incurred or the tax rate that may be established, fiscal independence would require that the school district have available an adequate tax base or at least have sufficient tax and debt leeway to permit it to raise amounts necessary to provide the trained staff and facilities needed to ensure an adequate education for every child. Few, if any, school districts enjoy this degree of independence.[5]

A variant of fiscal independence that does exist widely provides for dependence upon the electorate for budget approval and/or election of the school board. Or, alternatively, the board may have budgetary powers within a defined tax limit and it would have to secure voter approval of state legislation to raise the tax limit. Such school boards are considered to be fiscally independent because no agency of local government is interposed between the electorate and the school board. In practice, fiscal independence means dependence upon the electorate or some higher form of government.[6]

A school board is fiscally dependent upon the municipal government if it depends upon local funds either because it has no taxing power or its taxing power is limited to an amount which is insufficient to raise all of the local funds necessary to finance the school program, or if the law requires that the school budget be submitted regularly for approval by some local government agency. Dependent city school districts must periodically appeal to the municipal government for funds; in such cases, the municipal government determines the total amount of money spent for

---

5. The James study points out that fiscal independence, so defined, requires that the school government have no legal relationship with any agency of local government or electorate. The members of the school board would have to be appointed by county or state government. H. Thomas James, Thomas J. Alan, and Harold J. Dyke, "Fiscal Relationships in Budget Decisions," *NEA Research Memo 1963-22*, Washington, D.C.: National Education Association, 1963, p. 7.

6. James et al., *ibid.*

education and usually exercises some control over how the school district's moneys are spent.

The advocates of fiscal independence contend that a city school district functions most effectively when it is fiscally independent of municipal government.[7] They argue that public support for education is greatest where the public is able to determine directly the level of expenditures for education and where education need not compete with other municipal functions for the tax dollar. They insist that this is the only sure way to avoid the diversion of funds from education to other municipal functions. It allows greater economic efficiency by permitting long-range planning, greater stability in programming, and fixing responsibility for education in a single local governmental unit, the school board.

On the other hand, those who oppose fiscal independence have taken the position that fiscal independence, though appropriate for small districts, is not appropriate for large urban districts.[8] They reason that education is not unique, that it is important but no more so than health, housing, welfare, or other municipal services. A municipality functions best when a single unit of government directly responsible to the electorate, assumes responsibility for the allocation of public funds among all of the competing needs.

Whether or not fiscal capability is increased by independence from the municipal government, opponents claim, depends upon whether it is easier to secure additional funds from the municipal tax levy, state aid, or through direct appeal to the school district's voters. Economic efficiency may be achieved through long-range planning, but such planning depends upon the availability of funds when needed and where they can be most easily obtained.

Advocates also assert that fiscal independence is designed to

---

7. The arguments in favor of fiscal independence are summarized in a number of publications. Especially complete is the statement of arguments by Frederick C. McLaughlin in *Fiscal and Administrative Controls of City School Systems, New York State*, New York: Public Education Administration, 1949.

8. A good summary of this viewpoint was presented by Robert M. Haig and Carl S. Shoup in "Fiscal Independence for Public Education in the City of New York," *The Financial Problem of the City of New York*, New York: Mayor's Committee on Management Survey, 1952, Appendix to Chapter XIII.

free education from control by municipal authorities. If municipal authorities appropriate funds for education, they can influence educational policy by directing funds into specific programs and influence school board members and the professional staff with respect to technical and professional matters. Similarly, it is argued, freedom from municipal involvement frees education from partisan politics. This freedom, they contend, is essential if education is to be in the interest of all its citizens, that is, free from partisan positions on specific issues and educators are free to analyze honestly social and political issues of current relevance.

The opponents of fiscal independence point out that political involvement is always present when decisions are to be made. Freedom from municipal control does not assure freedom from politics; it only changes the participants and the rules of the game. The location, nature, and extent of political control exercised by the various "school politicians" may be defined by the mode of operation of the school district, but there is no a priori reason to assume that fiscal independence or municipal control is the best method of operation.

Finally, advocates of fiscal independence argue that elimination of any municipal agency between the electorate and the school board encourages greater community interest in education and encourages higher expectations, more support, and greater community involvement.

Although the opponents of fiscal independence concede that public interest in the operation of the school system and public expectation as to what it can achieve may be increased in fiscally independent small school systems, they argue that there is no reason to assume that the absence of municipal involvement would reduce public apathy toward education in large city school districts.

In view of these current issues, this study attempts to determine whether fiscal independence would contribute to the viability of the New York City school system. The financing of selected city school systems and decision-making in the New York City school system were studied. Specifically, the study attempts to answer these questions:

107

1. Do large city school districts that are fiscally independent receive greater fiscal support than dependent districts? We may call this issue "fiscal capability."

2. Does fiscal independence insulate school operations from local municipal control, thereby permitting the school administration to innovate with minimal municipal interference? This we may call the issue of "adaptability."

Fiscal Independence and Fiscal Capability

Few empirical studies of fiscal independence have been carried out. Those that have been undertaken attempt to measure whether fiscal independence does or does not make for greater fiscal support.

In his 1922 study, Frasier used an "efficiency index" to correlate fiscal independence with efficiency of operation. Based on a sample of 176 city school districts, he found a −.27 correlation between dependency and school efficiency; the more dependent the school board, the less efficient was its operation.[9] The 1924 McGaughy investigation used Frasier's index in comparing 377 cities divided into groups of fiscally dependent and fiscally independent districts. This investigation found fiscally independent cities received greater financial support than did dependent cities.[10]

The reverse was found to be true in Henry Woodward's study conducted twenty years later.[11] In 1948, Woodward statistically analyzed expenditures in eighty-five cities with populations between 100,000 and 1,000,000 for the fourteen-year period ending 1943-1944. During this period, the highest expenditure per pupil was found in dependent districts. He concluded that it makes no difference whether a school board is fiscally independent or fis-

9. George W. Frasier, *The Control of City School Finances*, Milwaukee: The Bruce Publishing Company, 1922, p. 82.

10. J. R. McGaughy, *The Fiscal Administration of City School Systems*, New York: The Macmillan Company, 1924.

11. Henry B. Woodward, *The Effect of Fiscal Control on Current School Expenditures*, New York: Teachers College, Columbia University, 1948.

cally dependent insofar as the amount of current expenditures is concerned. A more recent study by J. J. Naughton compared the levels of expenditure, taxation, and bonded indebtedness among sixty-six fiscally independent and dependent school districts that serve populations between 40,000 and 50,000 persons.[12] No significant differences were found in levels of expenditure, per pupil costs, and ratio of bonded indebtedness for schools to other bonded indebtedness. The study did find a higher proportion of state aid to total expenditures in states with fiscally independent districts. In the most recent study, H. T. James identified a number of variables that correlate highly with educational expenditures. Whether a district was fiscally independent of municipal government was found to be less significant than any of the other variables in explaining school expenditure patterns.[13]

That fiscal capability is not greatly influenced by fiscal status has been corroborated by a study of the eighteen largest school districts in the country.[14] In this study, data were collected for the years 1942-1943, 1952-1953, and 1962-1963, together with information to permit identification of the degree of fiscal independence enjoyed by the school boards in each of these districts. No significant relationships were found to exist between the level of expenditures and fiscal status, except for the tendency of dependent districts to receive more state aid, pay lower average salaries and maintain larger class size. Selected data for 1962-1963 are shown in Table 1.

The results of the study suggest that the fiscal advantages claimed for independent districts do not apply to large city school

---

12. James J. Naughton, *A Comparison of Selected Fiscally Dependent and Independent School Districts*, unpublished doctoral dissertation, Storrs, Conn.: University of Connecticut, 1959.

13. H. Thomas James, *Fiscal Independence and Other Factors Affecting Resources for Schools*, a paper presented before the National Conference on School Finance, St. Louis, Mo., April 7-9, 1963.

14. The data on eighteen large city school districts were collected by Dr. William S. Vincent and the staff of the Institute of Administrative Research, Teachers College, Columbia University, as part of a broader study of the relationship of fiscal status to various expenditure patterns and selected measures of school quality in city school districts. The study was supported, in part, by funds made available by the Mayor's Temporary Commission on City Finances (New York City).

TABLE 1

Comparison of Selected Data for Independent and Dependent City School Districts with 100,000 or More Pupils, 1962-1963*

Selected Data	Independent n = 8	Dependent n = 10
Net current expenditures per average daily attendance	$ 402 (n = 7)	$ 433
Amount raised locally per average daily attendance	$ 329	$ 321 (n = 9)
State aid per average daily attendance	$ 131	$ 191
Average teachers' salaries	$7,089	$6,581
Teachers per 1,000 average daily attendance	38.4	40.5

*The independent districts are Atlanta, Chicago, Cleveland, Detroit, Houston, Los Angeles, and St. Louis. The dependent districts are Baltimore, Baltimore County, Dade County, District of Columbia, Duval County, Indianapolis, Philadelphia, Memphis, New York, and Orleans Parish.

districts. Data were collected from about 1,200 school districts of varying size to determine if size was a critical factor in measuring the relationship of fiscal status to school spending. It was found that smaller independent districts spent more on schools than their dependent counterparts but that the differences diminished as the size category increased. Data relating to net current expenditures per pupil in average daily attendance are shown in Table 2.

TABLE 2

Comparison of Net Current Expenditures per Pupil in Average Daily Attendance for Independent and Dependent Districts Classified by Size of District, 1962-1963

Size Category	Number of Pupils Enrolled	Independent		Dependent	
		No.	Amount	No.	Amount
1	Over 100,000	7	$402	10	$433
2	50,000 to 99,999	26	366	21	372
3	25,000 to 49,999	22	395	29	375
4	12,000 to 24,999	115	410	72	377
5	6,000 to 11,999	207	453	110	371
6	3,000 to 5,999	402	442	156	361

The results were not so clear with respect to the amounts raised locally per pupil in average daily attendance. In size categories 1, 3, and 4 the dependent districts raised more locally in support of schools while in the other three categories, the reverse was found to be true.

At the very least, the data collected suggests that fiscal capability is generally related to factors other than fiscal status. With respect to the largest city school districts, fiscal independence has not resulted in any financial advantages over districts dependent on municipal (or state) government for financing.

The study did identify that among the eighteen big city and big county school districts, the widest practices obtain with regard to fiscal responsibility of school boards. They range from the highest degree of fiscal independence to the highest degree of fiscal dependence. Pure independence was found in only one of the large city school districts, Atlanta, where the school board may determine its budget, set the necessary tax rate and is not required to submit its budget for the approval of any other agency of the electorate. In five districts, Cleveland, Detroit, Houston, Los Angeles, and St. Louis, the school boards enjoyed independence up to an established tax limit and a public vote was required to raise the limit. In Chicago, the school board operates under a statutory tax limit with the state legislature having the power to change the tax limit.

Pure dependence was identified in five of the large city school districts: Baltimore, Baltimore County, District of Columbia, Philadelphia, and Memphis. The school boards in these districts obtain their funds from the taxing power of the local government and either submit their budgets to a local government agency for approval or else work out their budgets in concert with local government officials as the total estimated yield of public revenue is being allocated among the various public functions. New York City is technically independent up to a mandated tax limit which is far below a rate necessary to support current needs. Effectively, the school district looks to municipal government for its financial support. In several districts, Dade County, Duval County, Indianapolis, and Orleans Parish, the school boards require both local government and state agency approval of the school budget.

The experiences of several of the large independent districts suggest one of the major reasons why fiscally independent large districts do not spend more on education than do districts dependent on municipal government. The simple fact is that the public is not so open-handed with respect to educational expenditures as had been assumed.

In 1949, the Michigan legislature granted Detroit's school board independence from the mayor and common council. The board had the authority to impose a school tax of 8 mills, but had to obtain voter approval for any subsequent increase. Ten years later the voters approved an increase of 7.5 mills for a five-year period. In 1963, it sought an additional 5.3 mills, but the voters turned down the increase.[15]

In Los Angeles, voter approval was equally hard to obtain. School tax rate increases in 1959 and 1962 were voted down by decisive votes. A school bond issue was defeated in 1962 but did pass in 1963. The Los Angeles School Board considered but decided not to seek a school tax rate increase in 1964.[16]

In St. Louis, fiscal independence shifted dependence from the municipal government to the electorate. In 1959, St. Louis voters rejected a tax increase for the schools; it was finally passed in 1960. In a recent two-year period, the voters rejected a bond issue four times before it was finally approved.[17]

A second related reason that explains why fiscally independent large city school districts do not spend more on schools is that they are not permitted to enjoy any tax leeway. In six of the fiscally independent districts, the school boards enjoy independence up to an established tax limit, *and in each case, the board was operating at the maximum limit.* Further increases in the tax rate required either a change in the state law (Chicago) or voter approval (other five districts). Only in Atlanta does the school board have adequate tax leeway. If fiscal independence were established in New York City, it is likely that a constitutional tax limit would be imposed on the school board (especially if it was an appointed

---

15. *The Evening Bulletin*, Philadelphia, February 11, 1964, p. 11.

16. William H. Wilcox, *Memorandum of Summary of Visitation to School Districts of Los Angeles, St. Louis, Mo., and San Francisco, Cal.*, Philadelphia: Greater Philadelphia Movement, 1964, pp. 13-15.

17. Wilcox, *ibid.*, p. 15.

one) and the tax limit would be barely sufficient to cover current expenditures.[18]

The study suggests that fiscal independence in a large city school district is not likely to result in greater fiscal capability; in fact, in New York City fiscal independence might well result in fiscal restraints because periodic voter approval would be required to raise the tax limit as school needs increase faster than the real estate tax base available to support them.

Fiscal Independence and the Formulation of School Policy

The issue of fiscal independence is generally discussed in relation to financial needs and how they can best be met. Not so apparent but far more significant is the way in which fiscal status relates to the determination of school policy, the decision-making process, the role of municipal government in school affairs, in short, to the whole operation of the school system and its responsiveness to public needs. What attention the problem has received has taken the form of a series of "independent commission" studies that have dealt with the problem conceptually without attempting to collect data that might test the hypotheses presented.[19] Such studies either describe the political and administrative relationships between boards of education and other governmental agencies or review the salient points in support of or opposed to fiscal independence. If conducted by educators or under educational auspices, the studies stress the position that public education should be segregated from other public functions fiscally, politi-

---

18. Several bills were introduced at the 1964 meeting of the New York State Legislature to establish fiscal independence for the New York City school district (Bills prefiled at the 1964 New York State Legislature, Senate Intro. 2516, and Senate Intro. 2517). Each would have established real estate tax limits barely sufficient to cover current expenditures. The limits could be raised by small amounts through referendum up to a constitutional tax limit. An increase in the constituitional tax limit would require approval by two separate legislatures and then voter approval.

19. For example, *Administrative Management of the School System of New York City*, Strayer-Yavner Study, New York, Mayor's Committee on Management Survey, 1951 and *Report by Mark C. Shinnerer, Consultant on New York City School Reorganization*, New York State Education Department, 1961.

cally, and administratively. The studies follow a pattern: They begin with the assumption that municipal involvement in school affairs is undesirable; they identify cases of municipal involvement; they conclude that only through fiscal independence can this involvement be prevented.[20]

The author questions the assumption that municipal involvement in school affairs is per se bad and that educators, if left free to operate without municipal pressure, best secure the needs of public education.

Thus, in evaluating recent proposals for fiscal independence for the New York City school district, we asked Dr. Marilyn Gittell to explore intensively the character of policy formulation. Five diverse areas for decision-making were selected for study to determine the roles of city officials, the board of education, the school staff, and others in the formulation of school policy.[21]

The study found that the major decision-makers in school policy formulation are the supervisory staff and the superintendent, with the board of education and the United Federation of Teachers playing substantial roles. The municipal government plays a relatively limited role.[22]

From this study of New York City, it is clear that the professionals are the base of power, though the system is fiscally dependent. They shape the character of education in New York City. Municipal interference is minimal, even on issues such as integration, that involve public as well as educational policy. The role of the board of education is also relatively limited except in the selection of the school superintendent.

But although school policy is in the hands of professional educators, the New York City school system is unable to adapt to

---

20. The Strayer-Yavner and Shinnerer studies are examples of this approach. See also Rose N. Cohen, *Financial Control of Education in the Consolidated City of New York.*

21. This phase of the study was carried out for the Mayor's Temporary Commission on City Finances as part of its overall study of the appropriateness of fiscal independence for the city school system. The five areas were (1) the budget process, (2) integration policy, (3) selection of the superintendent, (4) salary increases, and (5) curriculum development.

22. The results of Dr. Gittell's study are reported in detail in separate article. See pp. 205-239.

changing social and educational needs. The system has become atrophied, partially because of size but largely because of rigid institutional arrangements which operate against change. Paramount among these are the constraints established by the power of the "professionals" and the United Federation of Teachers. These two groups, active participants in policy formation, generally represent the interests of their members. They form an effective barrier against any meaningful change within the system.

Fiscal Status for Large City School Systems: The Relevant Issues

The "conventional wisdom" that fiscal independence assures a school district adequate financing does not apply to large city school districts. On the contrary, fiscal independence has become a device to limit school expenditure increases. School expenditures can rise only to the extent of increases in the real property tax base to which they generally are tied through a rigidly prescribed tax limit.

Real property values tend to lag behind economic growth especially since the tax limit in most cities is based upon average (three to five years) rather than current valuation. Voter approval is necessary to increase the tax limit and voter approval has been difficult to achieve.

In contrast, school districts which are financially dependent upon city government are usually able to draw upon rapidly rising municipal revenues drawn from the city's broader taxing powers. Such taxing powers extend to revenue, excise, and income taxes which are much more responsive to economic growth than property values.

Even if fiscal independence had financial advantages, these would be more than offset by the inherent disadvantages in the separation of school from city government. Large city school systems, following the pattern of large administrative organizations, are overly bureaucratized, with extensive decision-making powers in the hands of a large central staff. Such systems are also atrophied because of the power of teachers' and supervisory associa-

115

tions within the professional staffs which tend to favor the *status quo*. As a result, the systems are highly resistive to change and are slow to adapt to changing social needs. These institutional factors suggest the reasons for Swanson's finding that "large systems appear to have an absolute rigidity that defies the forces which are so important in shaping the operation of small systems."[23]

Fiscal independence would not make large city school systems more adaptable because it would transfer further power to those institutions which now stand as major obstacles to change. What is needed is a countervailing power which can stimulate basic organizational and policy changes within a system. Only an elected mayor can wield such power and what may be most needed is a mayor personally involved and committed to education.

These findings are preliminary and tentative. They must be validated by more intensive study of large city school systems, preferably on a comparative basis. But clearly, they point to discarding the oversimplified "conventional wisdom" that fiscal independence offers the most appropriate fiscal status for large city school systems.

Further research is needed, for an optimum mode of operation for large city school systems has yet to be defined.

---

23. Austin O. Swanson, "Relations Between Community Size and School Quality," *IAR-Research Bulletin*, III (October, 1961), p. 3.

CHARLES A. GLATT AND ARLISS L. ROADEN

Dr. Glatt is Associate Professor of Education at the Ohio State University, and has served as a consultant to the National Teacher Corps and the National Education Association. Dr. Roaden is Associate Director of O.S.U.'s School of Education. He edited the 1965 monograph Problems of School Men in Depressed Urban Centers, *and with Dr. Glatt, recently co-authored a series of eight articles on educational problems in large cities published in* Baltimore Public School Teachers Association Newsletter.

DEMOGRAPHIC ANALYSIS AS A TOOL FOR EDUCATIONAL PLANNING

EDUCATION PLANNERS — boards of education, superintendents of school systems, and others charged with developing education — are in dire need of all the data available about the nature of the populations to be served by the schools. Every facet of school planning calls for population information including the numbers of persons in the system, age variations, stability of the populations, family income, occupational distribution, nativity and parentage, and other related facts. Most especially are those data needed in the large urban centers that are fraught with economic, racial, and ethnic imbalances. Educational sociologists are called upon to lend their skills in demographic analysis for the formulation of policies essential to the selection of meaningful educational programs.

Educational research has taken many forms in the past century. Even a cursory survey of professional literature reveals the tremendous variety of research interests that has motivated students of professional education. Beyond question the entire profession is indebted to scholars with psychological leanings for their trail-blazing efforts. Early mistakes and tangential interests that led educational psychologists astray have served the negative purpose of helping contemporary students from other disciplines to avoid similar, often fruitless, pursuits.

Educational sociology is rapidly approaching a stage of development where other students of learning problems are becoming aware of some of the contributions that can be made by this behavioral discipline. And yet, even as sociology is not one science but many, educational sociology similarly is composed of many areas and methods of investigation. A review of popular textbooks in the social foundations of education quickly reveals what the most common of these are.

Stanley, Smith, Benne, and Anderson, in their *Social Foundations of Education,* constructed their thinking around five basic categories: (1) the school as a social institution; (2) the school and the structure of the community; (3) American ideals and conflicts and the social function of the school; (4) social aspects of school organization and pedagogical method; and (5) social aspects of the teaching profession.

Havighurst and Neugarten, in their *School and Society,* include the following as basic areas of study: (1) a general introduction that focuses on social structure; (2) the child's social environment; (3) the school; and (4) the teacher. Gross, Hanson, and Wronski took a somewhat different approach in their collection of readings entitled *School and Society.* They include as major categories: (1) the role of the school in society; (2) the role of education in a democratic society; (3) the social context and purposes of education; and (4) the teacher and the profession of teaching.

The sixtieth yearbook of the National Society for the Study of Education, *Social Forces Influencing American Education,* began with analyses of the relationships between education, politics, and economic growth. These were followed by chapters dealing with

118

demography, social-class influences, values, the impact of students on schools, teacher organizations, mass media and educational policy, and stability and social change.

Within these broad categories, often followed by persons who compile textbooks in educational sociology, can be found a wide variety of sociological interests: race relations, religious differences, marriage and family structures, juvenile delinquency, social policy, social origins of teachers, peer group relations, schools as social systems, community institutions, social agencies, welfare levels, contrasting conceptions of the role of the school in society, and so forth.

A chapter, or part of a chapter, is commonly devoted in these textbooks to population changes. Almost without exception the chapter is descriptive. Birth and death rates are examined; migration patterns are indicated; racial differences are sometimes tied to a larger demographic picture; and some indications for effects of these factors on teaching and learning may be indicated.

Census data provide a wealth of information that can be used quite effectively to facilitate educational planning, but a survey of the research that currently is being done by educational sociologists reveals little interest in utilizing these data. The purposes of this paper are: (1) to call attention to the kinds of information that can be gained from basic demographic sources; and (2) to illustrate how these data can be converted to a useful form for educational planning. Students of comparative education can find census data from other nations invaluable to their work. Even where accurate enumeration and publication of population statistics are lacking, estimates can be useful.

For the remainder of this chapter the writers have chosen to focus only on reports from the United States Bureau of the Census. Information that is available from the 1960 Census of Population will be utilized mainly, although data from previous censuses and from special reports of the Bureau will be referred to at times.

Data relative to school enrollment were obtained for the 1960 Census from answers to these questions:

119

P16. Has he attended regular school or college at any time since February 1, 1960?

If he has attended only nursery school, business or trade school, or adult education classes, check "No"

Yes...[]   No...[]

P17. Is it a public school or a private school?

                    Public school...........[]

                    Private or
                    parochial school........[]

Answers to these questions were obtained for persons who, as of April 1, 1960, were from five to thirty-four years of age. "Regular" school was interpreted to mean schooling that could advance a person toward an elementary school certificate or a high school diploma, or a college, university, or professional degree. Four school levels were identified in the presentation of these data: (1) kindergarten; (2) elementary school (includes grades one to eight); (3) high school (includes grades nine to twelve); and (4) college.

Data on years of school completed were obtained from a different set of questions. For these answers only persons twenty-five years old and over were included.

P14. What is the highest grade (or year) of regular school this person has ever attended? (Check one box)

If now attending a regular school or college, check the grade (or year) he is in. If it is in junior high school, check the box that stands for that grade (or year).

Never attended school.....[]

Kindergarten..............[]

Elementary   1 2 3 4 5 6 7 8
school (Grade)...........[] [] [] [] [] [] [] []

```
                              1  2  3  4
    High school (Year)       [] [] [] []

                              1  2  3  4  5  6 or more
    College (Year)...........[] [] [] [] [] []
P15.Did he finish the highest grade (or year) he attended?


    Finished         Did not            Never
    this             finish             attended
    grade...[]       this grade...[]    school...[]
```

These data are available in the 1960 Census of Population Reports for a number of populations. They include the total number of inhabitants of the nation, populations of the various states, of counties, of cities and towns, of urbanized areas, of metropolitan areas, and rural areas. They also include the nonwhite inhabitants of most of these.

In addition to questions that relate directly to school enrollments and years of school completed, the Census Reports contain a wealth of other information that is pertinent to effective school planning. These data relate basically to the following categories: (1) birth and death rates; (2) migration and immigration; (3) family stability and disorganization; (4) employment status; (5) nativity and parentage; (6) occupational distribution; (7) income; (8) population increases and decreases; (9) urban-rural differences; (10) age and sex differences; (11) numbers and distribution of people; and (12) historical trends. How some of these data can be utilized by educational planners is exemplified in the following section.

Baltimore, Maryland, has been selected as an example of how demographic factors that affect school planning can be converted to useful form by educational sociologists. In June of 1966, the Public School Teachers Association of Baltimore invoked professional sanctions in the city because city officials had cut the education budget which was submitted by the Board of School Commissioners. Three days later, professional sanctions were endorsed by the Maryland State Teachers Association. An investigatory team appointed by the Professional Rights and Responsibilities Commission of the National Education Association conducted an inquiry in Baltimore in August of 1966. The authors have worked closely with that team and with the Public School Teacher's Association.

Although the Baltimore Standard Metropolitan Statistical Area gained over 320,000 inhabitants between 1950 and 1960, the city itself lost over 10,000 residents. Of more importance, the white population in the city of Baltimore decreased in number by over 113,000. In the same ten year period, the nonwhite[1] population increased numerically by over 100,000. These racial shifts and concomitant differences between the white and Negro populations have been chosen as the focal point of this analysis.

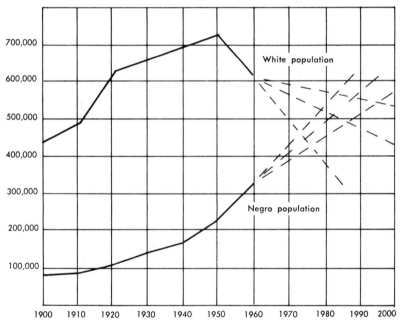

FIGURE A. TRENDS AND POSSIBLE GROWTH PATTERNS OF WHITE AND NEGRO POPULATIONS IN BALTIMORE, MARYLAND, 1900 TO 2000 A. D. (Source: United States Census Reports)

Many cities in the eastern part of the United States have been losing their white populations for as long as forty years. Baltimore did not experience such a loss until the 1950s. Patterns of change in the white and Negro populations of the city from 1900 to 1960

1. The term "nonwhite" includes Negroes, Orientals, and American Indians. Baltimore's nonwhite population was 99.14 percent Negro in 1960. Because of this high proportion of Negroes, the terms are used interchangeably here.

and possible patterns in the decades ahead are shown in Figure A. Baltimore, like Cleveland, Gary, East St. Louis, and other cities, may have more Negroes than whites in its population before 1980. Ratios of Negro to white in Baltimore's population for six decades are depicted in Figure B.

Three basic factors account for these changes: (1) natural increase; (2) migration; and (3) non-accessibility of housing for Negroes in suburban areas.

1. For each 1,000 *white* women in Baltimore (1960) who had ever been married, 2,029 children had been born. This ratio jumped to 2,539 children per 1,000 Negro women. Among younger women (ages fifteen to twenty-four years), the difference was even more pronounced — 1,113 children for each 1,000 white women, compared with 1,891 children for each 1,000 Negro women. The ratio of young children (under age five) to women who were or had been married was also much higher for Negroes than for whites. In 1960 there were 615 children under age five for each 1,000 *white* women who had ever been married, but 910 young children for each 1,000 *Negro* women ever married.

In the Baltimore metropolitan area, nonwhite families are likely to be larger in number than white families. Only 17.80 percent of all white families in the area had three or more children under age eighteen in 1960; but 26.83 percent of Negro families had three or more children in that age group. Or, whereas less than one-fifth of the total families were nonwhite, over one-fourth of the families that had three or more children were nonwhite. Again, only 2.78 percent of all white women had given birth to seven or more children; 7.14 percent of all nonwhite women had borne seven or more children.

The larger proportion of young Negroes is evidenced differently in terms of the ratio of persons of school age or below (zero to twenty years) to those in the working age group (twenty to sixty-five years). For each 100 white children in Baltimore in 1960, there were 168 white adults in the working age group. But for each 100 nonwhite children there were only 116 adults in the productive years of life. These differences are illustrated in Figure C.

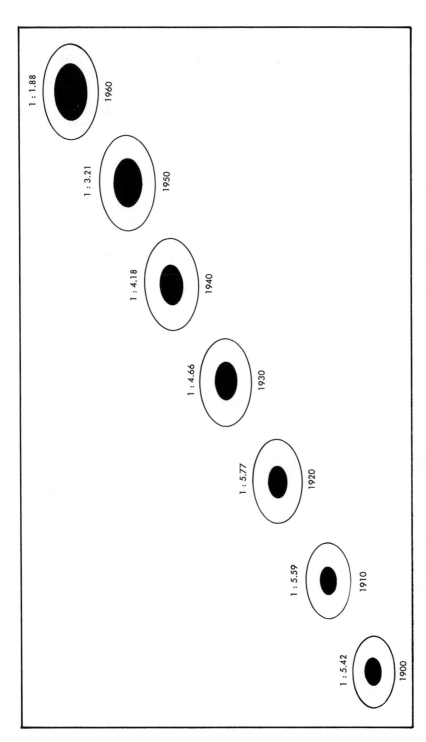

1 : 1.88   1960

1 : 3.21   1950

1 : 4.18   1940

1 : 4.66   1930

1 : 5.77   1920

1 : 5.59   1910

1 : 5.42   1900

FIGURE B. RATIOS OF NEGROES TO WHITES IN BALTIMORE, MARYLAND, 1900 to 1960.

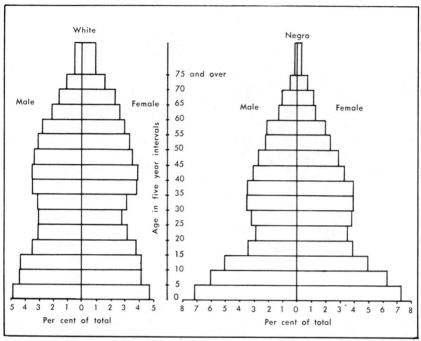

FIGURE C. AGE-SEX PYRAMIDS FOR THE WHITE AND NEGRO POPULATIONS OF BALTIMORE, MARYLAND, 1960.
(Source: United States Census Reports)

2. Approximately 75 percent of Baltimore's 1960 white population were born in Maryland, but less than 60 percent of the Negro residents were born in the state. Eight of each ten Negroes in the city who had moved across county lines between 1955 and 1960 had come to Baltimore from some other state. Sources of these migrants are indicated in Figure D. More than half of the Negro population over five years of age lived in a house in 1960 that was different from the one in which they lived in 1955.

3. A different kind of migration characterized the white population — movement to the suburbs. As indicated above, the white population in Baltimore decreased by over 113,000 between 1950 and 1960. During that interval the metropolitan area around the city experienced a numerical increase of 332,308 persons. Only 6,771, or 2 percent, of that increase were Negro. Figure E illustrates the ratios of Negro to total population in Baltimore and in the suburban area around the city.

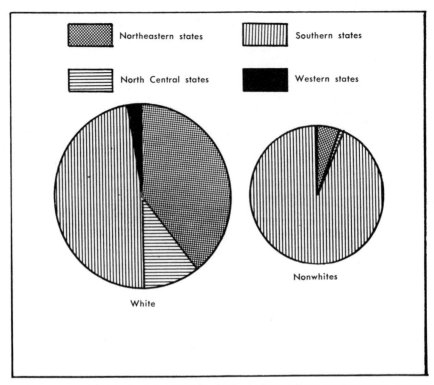

Northeastern states   Southern states

North Central states   Western states

White

Nonwhites

FIGURE D. SOURCES OF WHITE AND NONWHITE MIGRANTS WHO MOVED TO THE BALTIMORE METROPOLITAN AREA, 1955 TO 1960. (Source: United States Census Reports)

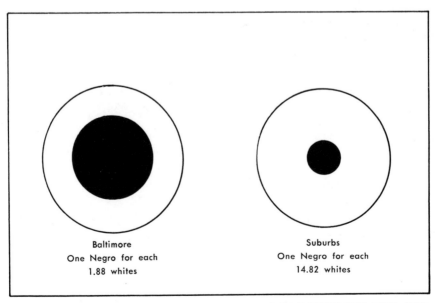

Baltimore
One Negro for each
1.88 whites

Suburbs
One Negro for each
14.82 whites

FIGURE E. RATIOS OF NEGROES TO WHITES IN BALTIMORE CITY AND IN THE SUBURBAN AREAS AROUND BALTIMORE, 1960.

School enrollment statistics are relatively unimportant census contributions to the school planner. By the time these figures can be collected, calculated, and published, they are dated. Local school districts, therefore, collect their own data each year in most instances. In 1960, however, a new dimension was added to the information collected and disseminated by the bureau — private school enrollments were made available for both white and nonwhite populations.

Because of the large numbers of white students who attend private schools, Negroes form a proportion of the public school population that is much greater than the proportion of Negroes in the total population of Baltimore. There were 100 Negroes in the city in 1960 for each 186 white persons. In the age group five to eighteen years, the ratio was 100 Negroes for each 142, which was approximately the ratio in the *total* school population. In the *public* schools, however, the ratio of Negro to white was 100 to 99. Or, although only 35.21 percent of Baltimore's population was Negro, over one-half of the students in the public schools were Negro (see Figure F).

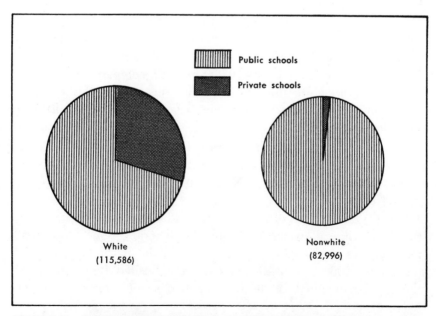

Public schools

Private schools

White
(115,586)

Nonwhite
(82,996)

FIGURE F. WHITE AND NONWHITE STUDENT ENROLLMENTS IN PUBLIC AND PRIVATE SCHOOLS IN BALTIMORE, MARYLAND, 1960. (Source: United States Census Reports)

In addition to the private school factor, Baltimore, during the 1950s, experienced a large increase in the total public school population. Prior to the *Brown, et al. v. Board of Education* decision, a great many Negroes dropped out of school after the ninth grade. When the schools were desegregated, more of these young people continued their education through the secondary grades. In the 1960 school year, 40,000 more young people were enrolled in Baltimore's public schools than in 1952, although the total population of the city had decreased in number by about 10,000.

Mere numbers of Negro children in the population and in the public schools form only a part of a broader demographic pattern. Social and psychological conflicts that have their roots in different economic settings, in varying family structures, and in transient living arrangements can be suggested from census data. That Negroes are "last to be hired and first to be fired" is too broad a generalization to be accurate, yet one that has some basis in fact. Differences in income and employment that characterize Baltimore's white and nonwhite populations can be illustrated by use of demographic figures. Income variations for the two racial groups are indicated in Figure G. The median annual family income for nonwhites in Baltimore is about $1,500 less than the median for the city as a whole, which means (since nonwhites are included in the total city population) that Negro families average about $2,500 less income than white families. Less than 6 percent of the city's Negro families earned over $10,000 in 1959, compared with almost 19 percent of white families who had incomes in this category. Approximately one-third of the Negro families in the city lived on less than $3,000 in 1959.

In 1960 the unemployment rate for Negroes was double that for whites (9.74 percent to 4.87 percent). Whereas the civilian labor force was one-third Negro, one-half of the unemployed were Negro.

Negro families are often described as having a matrilineal rather than a patrilineal structure. Again, the generalization is too broad. However, of the 76,928 Negro families in the Baltimore metropolitan area (1960), over 21 percent were headed by women. Although only one-fifth of the families in the metropolitan area were

Negro, almost one-half of the families with a female head and children under age eighteen were Negro. Of those Negro women who headed families, one in ten were over age sixty-five. These are the families that in America are most likely to be impoverished.

These statistics gain added meaning when the children themselves are considered. Over 86 percent of the white children in the city of Baltimore (under age eighteen) were living with both parents in 1960. Only 64 percent of the nonwhite children were in homes where their parents lived together. Or, whereas 43 of each 100 young people in the city were nonwhite, 67 of each 100 young people *not* living with both parents were nonwhite. Among single women who had three or more (illegitimate) children, over 98 percent were nonwhite, and 71 percent of women with children who were married, but separated from their husbands, were nonwhite.

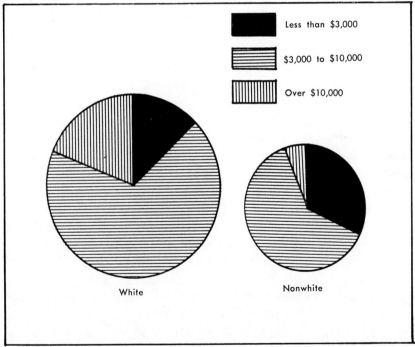

FIGURE G. ANNUAL FAMILY INCOMES OF WHITE AND NONWHITE FAMILIES IN BALTIMORE, 1959. (Source: United States Census Reports)

In some instances the above differences are even more accentuated for the *city* of Baltimore because, as indicated, certain of these statistics are presented in Census reports for the entire metropolitan area where the proportion of whites is much larger than only in the city. Conclusions that can be drawn from the data presented here are appropriate specifically to Baltimore; yet they are generally descriptive of many cities.

Educational planners in city school systems are faced with problems that challenge the best in ingenuity and intellect that American public leaders have to offer. It is easy for educational policy-makers and implementors to become immobilized and plead "victims of circumstance" caught in a web of inept political and social mal-planning. The overwhelming conclusion from demographic data is that racial, cultural, and economic segregation is rapidly becoming entrenched. This phenomenon is viewed with alarm by political leaders, by business and industrial leaders, and by educators. All agree that the tide must be reversed lest the cities crumble.

Yet, who will muster courage to exert leadership for reversing the tide? Why not educational planners? The superintendent's office, armed with demographic facts and knowledge of educational handicaps brought about by segregated classrooms, is the most obvious source of leadership. Educational planners are "victims of circumstance" only when they are ignorant of demographic resources or when they refuse to utilize these rich data.

With a high turnover of students and a disproportionate ratio of students with cultural and educational handicaps, how can a meaningful program of study be developed? Traditional curricular materials will guarantee continued and continuing frustration, failure, and force-outs. Standardized national curricular materials which were introduced in the sciences and in mathematics appear at first glance as means of insuring that third grade in Baltimore is the same as third grade in rural Alabama.

A knowledge of the student population in city classrooms, however, with vast ranges of educational abilities and achievements seems to call for more diversification of curricular materials than are currently available. Structurally, most schools are still graded;

the realities of grade-level ranges in the city classrooms render grade structures meaningless.

Demographic facts in Baltimore, i. e., growing school-age population and decreasing total population; growing unemployment and the growing unemployable and unskilled labor force; and disproportionate concentrations of low income families, large families, and matrilineal families; — these depict the folly of local support of education. The folly is especially significant with respect to income and property valuation. Aggressive leadership in gaining metropolitan, state, and Federal fiscal support is an obvious requirement of city educational planners. The metropolitan government of Davidson County and the city of Nashville, Tennessee may be a model for educational fiscal planning.

The best teachers want to teach where exciting educational programs are under way. Proper utilization of funds available through the Elementary and Secondary Education Act will guarantee that the most exciting educational innovations in American school systems will be in the inner-city schools. Job satisfaction comes from immediate feedback of educational achievement among the students. Nowhere is this possibility greater than among deprived or disadvantaged children. Nowhere can these children be found in greater concentration than in the inner cities. As an example, Kenneth Clark and his researchers were able after one month of daily reading instruction in the summer to observe up to two and three-fourths years gain among Harlem children.

Educational planners can, through adequate portrayal of creative teaching opportunities in the city schools, reverse the flow of experienced city teachers that currently is toward the suburbs.

Whether in Baltimore or in other cities, distinctions ought to be made between (1) Negroes occupying physical space within the geographical limits of a city, and (2) Negroes being part of the social and civic life of the city. That Negroes can inhabit space in Baltimore physically is illustrated by the more than 100,000 increase in the city's Negro population between 1950 and 1960. Distribution of the city's 325,589 Negro residents — or rather, concentration of these people — is shown in Figure H. What is more important is the extremely limited physical space in which this ten-year growth in the Negro population took place as indicated in the following map (an enlargement of the inner-city areas).

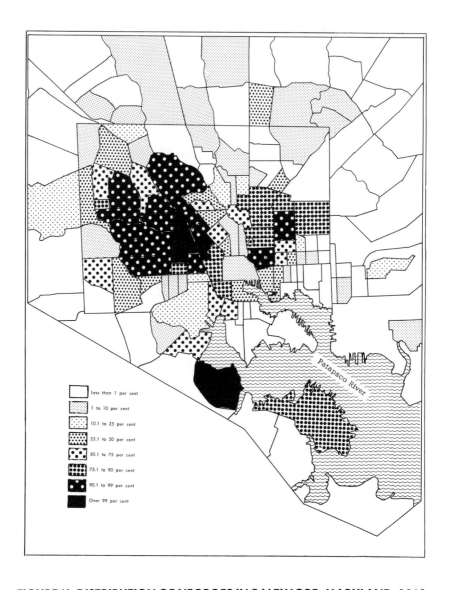

Less than 1 per cent
1 to 10 per cent
10.1 to 25 per cent
25.1 to 50 per cent
50.1 to 75 per cent
75.1 to 90 per cent
90.1 to 99 per cent
Over 99 per cent

Patapsco River

FIGURE H. DISTRIBUTION OF NEGROES IN BALTIMORE, MARYLAND, 1960.

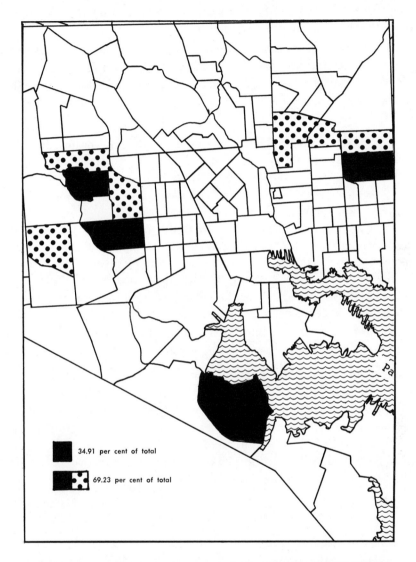

AREAS OF MAJOR INCREASE IN THE NEGRO POPULATION OF BALTIMORE, MARYLAND, 1950 TO 1960.

To be part of the social and civic life of a city implies participation in all aspects of the workings of the city, or at least the *freedom* to participate in those workings. That Negroes have been denied

133

such freedom seems to be the major contention that is being voiced by a third of Baltimore's population.

Traditional American values suggest nothing undesirable, nothing bad, nothing wrong about a city being populated primarily by Negroes or by members of any other ethnic group. Statistical bases have been examined here, on the other hand, which suggest that Baltimore is rapidly becoming populated by people

1. who hold some values that conflict with those ordinarily held by many Americans (e.g., values relative to legal marriage, legitimate marriage, and family "togetherness");

2. who, because of economic circumstances, cannot pay the expenses of operating a large city;

3. who place a disproportionate burden on public educational and welfare systems (Buffalo, New York, exemplifies this — whereas the total population in Buffalo has decreased by about 100,000 since 1930, the public school population has decreased by only 5,000);

4. who are not skilled for the trades and professions that modern urban living demands; and

5. who are, for the most part, crowded into the less desirable areas of the city.

Educators need also to recognize that Negroes in Baltimore (1) lack effective leadership and organization (although these may develop in the near future); (2) *can* control the key to political power in the city through bloc voting; (3) are victims moreso than perpetrators of the statistical conditions described above; and (4) are fed up with second-class citizenship in a first-class society. Effective school planning cannot ignore these conditions.

PART II

DECISION-MAKING IN THE
URBAN SCHOOL SYSTEMS

Case Studies

ROBERT L. CRAIN and DAVID STREET

Robert L. Crain is Senior Study Director at the National Opinion Research Center—where he has been
involved in studies of city politics,
including the study of school desegregation reported here—and Assistant Professor of Sociology at the
University of Chicago. David Street
is Assistant Professor of Sociology at
the University of Chicago. He has
been involved recently in a study of
public school administration.

SCHOOL

DESEGREGATION

AND SCHOOL

DECISION-MAKING

IN MANY WAYS THE school desegregation issue is an ideal
context in which to examine the general question of how
school systems make policy decisions. First, it is an issue of some
importance, so that the decision-making process uncovered can be
assumed to be a nontrivial one. Second, it is a relatively new issue,
so that the system can make decisions without much reference to
traditional decision-making rules; this means that the social scientist need not be greatly concerned with the impact of prior historical
accidents. Finally, the issue has arisen in nearly every large city
with only minor differences among cities in the way in which it has
been raised and with such idiosyncratic factors as the taxing power
of the system being of minor importance. This means that the setting is almost ideal for comparative analysis.

This paper principally discusses some of the conclusions of a
comparative study of integration in eight northern large city school
systems carried out by the National Opinion Research Center in
1965.[1] Data were gathered by teams of graduate students who

---

1. This research is reported in Robert L. Crain, Morton Inger, Gerald A. McWorter,
and James J. Vanecko, *School Desegregation in the North: Eight Comparative Case*

spent ten man-days in each city interviewing school administrators, school board members, civil rights leaders, political leaders, members of the civic elite, and other informants. The cities were selected by a modified random sampling design from the cities having a population between 250,000 and 1,000,000 of which at least 10 percent was Negro. The findings are supplemented by observations made in the course of research on the social organization of the large city school system carried out principally in the Chicago schools.[2]

The Issue

Very little research has been devoted to the school desegregation issue as a problem in policy-making. Consequently, almost everyone, including most social scientists, have been dependent upon the popular media for information about the issue. This has produced a widespread acceptance of some important misconceptions. Perhaps the most common is the view that intense conflict over school desegregation is unavoidable because civil rights leaders want major concessions which the white voters are too prejudiced to give. This statement contains, we believe, three errors: First, our findings indicate that in some circumstances intense conflict is avoidable. In the eight cities studied, three (Newark, Baltimore, and St. Louis) have at least temporarily resolved their conflict with the civil rights movement. In three other cities (Pittsburgh, San Francisco, and Buffalo), the controversy has cooled down and shows promise of being resolved. In the two remaining cities the controversy is still raging. Second, our data indicate that most civil rights leaders will be satisfied (or at least call off their attacks) if they receive even minimal concessions. Third, survey data have indi-

Studies of Community Structure and Policy Making, Chicago: National Opinion Research Center, Report #110A. The research was sponsored by the U.S. Office of Education.

2. This research was supported by the Russell Sage Foundation. Major findings will be reported in David Street, *The Public Schools and Metropolitan Change*, forthcoming publication.

cated relatively little opposition to school desegregation in national samples of white voters.[3]

In short, the school system has some freedom to establish a policy which will prevent conflict. This is not the same as saying that the school system has the power to develop a policy which will actually alter the basic nature of the schools' treatment of Negro students; indeed, we doubt that any big city school system can do this. Thus, it will be necessary to divide our discussion into two sections: first, viewing school desegregation as an issue of symbolic politics, and then looking at the actual outputs of the school system —the extent of school integration and the extent to which educational opportunities can in fact be equalized.

Symbolic Politics: The Demands of the Civil Rights Movement

Traditional civil rights groups have pressed for school integration in all eight cities studied in the NORC research. To these groups the integration issue means two things: (1) the prevention of discrimination in allocating students to schools; and (2) the acceptance on the part of the school system of the principle that integration is desirable. Beyond these rather minimal goals, the civil rights leaders would prefer, of course, a maximum amount of actual integration, but most of them view true integration as a nearly unattainable goal.[4] If the school system can be persuaded to make racial integration one of its major goals, the civil rights groups will have achieved an important victory, for this commitment exerts normative pressure on the total community to accept the principle of racial equality and to define the efforts to segregate Negroes as illegitimate. Thus, for the traditional civil rights movements, the written policies and pronouncements of the school system are important regardless of their impact. (Of course, if the

---

3. For a general review of these and other survey data, see Paul B. Sheatsley, "White Attitudes Toward the Negro," *Daedulus*, 95 (Winter, 1966), 217-238; and Harriet B. Erskine, "The Polls: Race Relations," *Public Opinion Quarterly*, 26 (1962), 137-148.

4. It is for this reason that we have chosen to use "desegregation" rather than "integration" in the title of this paper.

system took no efforts to implement the policy, the civil rights leaders would raise the cry of hypocrisy.) The civil rights groups would probably endorse the definition of integration given by the Pittsburgh Urban League: "We regard a community as integrated when opportunities for the achievement of respect and the distribution of material welfare are not limited by race."

One is tempted to draw parallels between the school desegregation issue and labor–management negotiations. The major difference is that the corporation is required by law to negotiate with a labor union, while the school board is not. The school board is in the position of the corporation of four decades ago, when management had to decide whether it was wise or morally proper to negotiate with labor unions. The Northern school board is not required to recognize the civil rights movement as legitimate, and indeed many whites who appear otherwise unprejudiced do not consider it so. But another problem is that even when the school system decides that negotiation is proper, the question remains of whom to recognize as the true spokesmen for the civil rights movement. For these two reasons, actual back-room negotiations with the civil rights movement are not common. In our eight cities, only two school systems have been able to maintain this sort of communication with the civil rights groups. This means that we will have to analyze the school systems' policy-making as taking place with only limited private face-to-face communications between the "negotiators."

The First Stage of the Desegregation Decision:
The School Superintendent as Decision-maker

We shall see that the policy decision on desegregation is made by the school board, not the superintendent. However, in each case the board attempted to avoid making a decision for as long as possible. The typical school board seems to operate in a highly pragmatic, fire-fighting fashion. It has limited time, resources, and information with which to make policies, and the result is that it seems not to have a clear policy perspective but primarily makes *ad hoc* decisions as issues become "hot."[5] In the case of desegregation, none of the eight school boards took action when the issue was first raised, and this placed the burden of decision-making on the superintendent. Of ten superintendents who served in the eight cities during the racial controversy, seven can be said to have acted autonomously without board direction to reject demands made by the civil rights movement, while three urged the board to take a liberal position. This comes as no surprise. It is now fashionable to accuse superintendents as a group of being narrow-minded and arrogant in their dealings with civil rights leaders. As our data indicate, superintendents do not uniformly reject civil rights demands, but enough do to require us to discuss this point.

The statements of school superintendents frequently stress three themes. The first is that the appropriate stance should be "color blindness"—the refusal to pay any attention to race. This sometimes leads to statements that racial census of school children is illegal or at least immoral. Coupled with this concern with color blindness is the stress placed on a narrow definition of the function of the school as "educational" rather than "social." The third theme which recurs (although with somewhat less frequency) is an extreme defensiveness and an intolerance for "lay" criticism. Lay persons are dismissed as unqualified to make recommendations, and their criticisms are frequently answered with flat disagreement or with vague, overly detailed, and off-the-point replies.

Of course, these reactions are common to all organizations which must meet criticism, but the educators go further than most public officials in reacting defensively to political demands. Educational administrators are insistent on defining themselves as professionals and have an entrenched ideology that grants lay control but stresses the importance of the teaching certificate and "educational experience" as the boundary between the expert and the layman. In part, the response to the demands for integration is only another instance of the professionals' tendency—developed through generations of conflict over political interference, progressive education,

---

5. Support for this hypothesis is provided by L. L. Cunningham, "Decision-making Behavior of School Boards," *American School Board Journal* (February, 1962).

charges of communism in the schools, and other issues—to perceive any criticism as an "attack upon education."

Further, civil rights demands also strike deeply at one of the most firmly held tenets of the ideology of the large city superintendent: universalism. In the development of the large city schools, insistence on equality of programs for all populations in the city marked a dramatic accomplishment as it gave the schools protection from the pleas for special treatment from various political and ethnic groups. Without this universalism, Northern schools would be more segregated than they are; even after World War I, biracial high schools still discriminated against their Negro students in extracurricular activity participation.[6] Yet, demands by the civil rights movement give the lie to the assumption of universalism, thereby provoking a defensiveness around a highly salient theme and, often, the administrators' counterattack that civil rights demands are themselves a case of special pleading. The defensive response may also be increased by the superintendent's knowledge that even if he were wholly committed to making integration a prime value of the schools, many of his personnel are too traditionalistic, too prejudiced, or too recalcitrant to make the needed adjustments without great resistance.

Thus, we can understand the superintendents' initial defensive response. But in most cases, the school board has little difficulty taking control of the decision from the superintendent. Why is this? The answer seems to lie in what areas the superintendents can make believable claims to expertise. On many issues—for example, curriculum construction, textbook selection, or design of facilities—the superintendents' judgments generally go unchallenged, not only because they usually fall into areas of indifference but also because the superintendents' accumulation of detailed information, his technical background, and his appeals to standard or good practice argue well for honoring his professional claims. On such issues, the superintendent in effect runs the schools. Any criticism in these

6. J. H. Tipton points out that in the late 1940s Negro students were not allowed to use the swimming pool in one high school in Gary, Indiana. See his *Community in Crisis*, New York: Columbia Teachers College, 1953.

areas may cause the superintendent to accuse the board of interference with his administrative role.

But it is only in the extreme case of Benjamin C. Willis in
Chicago that a superintendent has been willing to take the stand
that he must have autonomy or he will resign over a racial issue.[7]
This is understandable, for there is not truly marketable expertise
on racial integration anywhere, and there is certainly little claim
possible in this area from within the education profession. Therefore, the superintendent, after his initial negative response, often
finds his upstaging by the board to be the least awkward exit.

In addition, the origins and backgrounds of the large city superintendents generally do not provide them with a sensitivity to urban
social change and problems and to the current revolution of rising
racial expectations in the large cities which would lead these men
to play a leadership role in the absence of professional claims.
Evidence bearing on this point comes from the biographies of the
eleven big city superintendents contained in *Who's Who*. Of the
ten whose birth date was given, the mean age was fifty-seven. Nine
of the eleven began as teachers, and only one finished graduate
school before beginning his career. Six of the ten American-born
superintendents were from very small cities or farms, and none
of the eleven attended a first-rank undergraduate college. Seven
of the eleven began their teaching in small towns, and much of
the administrative experience of all but four had been outside
the large cities.

While many of these men had been administrators in smaller,
suburban, and often vanguard or experimental school systems, their
experiences in the large cities have not stimulated their desire to be
experimental. The financial problems of the large city systems, the
sheer administrative problems of size, scale, and change, and the
often inert middle-level personnel and principals (who frequently
are political appointees left over from an earlier era) tend to move
these superintendents toward an emphasis upon a traditionalistic

------

7. Willis' temporary resignation was apparently triggered by a taxpayer's suit charg-
ing that he had arbitrarily changed a voluntary transfer plan designed by the board to
further integration. The incident is described in Joseph Pois, *The School Board
Crisis*, Chicago: Aldine Press, 1964, pp. 109-114.

philosophy of education that stresses the three R's, the standard neighborhood school, and "sound programs." When racial and other social changes place new demands on the schools, these super-intendents generally are unable to articulate a leadership ideology dealing with integration and broadened welfare goals.

The Second Stage of the Controversy:
The School Board Takes Over

In the typical city studied, the civil rights movement first approaches the board cautiously over a period of a year or two, making statements and testifying at hearings. In general, the school system does not respond to this; the issue is still below the level of saliency. The integrationists then step up their campaign, and their demands are rejected by the school superintendent at this point. When the movement replies to this with demonstrations or threats of demonstrations, the school board begins to take the issue seriously and responds in a variety of ways. At this point, the second stage of the controversy has begun. The board has taken over racial policy-making. In six of the eight cities it is possible to find a point at which the superintendent's recommendations were ignored or a point when he was instructed to alter his policy. In the other two cases, the system changed superintendents without changing its policy, so that we must assume that the board supplied policy continuity to the system.

The first response made by the school system during this second phase we call the "key response," because it sets the tone for the remainder of the conflict. This key response by the board seems to be made with almost complete autonomy. One might expect the community political and civic elites to exert great influence, but we have only one clear case where this was done successfully. In two cases, the school board seemed to ignore the recommendations of the mayor; in another case, the community's most prominent industrialist was flatly rebuffed. It is not possible to describe all the actions taken by various actors in this short paper, but in general it seems clear that there is less direct influence exerted on the board than one would expect and that attempts to influence the board usually are not very successful.

The most complex question is: To what extent can the civil rights movement control the outcomes of the school desegregation decision by their use of power? The evidence seems to indicate that they have surprisingly little influence. The civil rights movement can force the school system to deal with the issue, of course; few if any of these systems would have done anything about civil rights if they had not been pressured by the movement. Generally, the movement is successful in part—that is, the system will usually desegregate schools to some limited extent, and all of the eight cities have adopted a policy statement advocating integration. But concessions may be minimal and may come so late and be given so grudgingly as to be nearly meaningless.

Apparently, there is little that the civil rights leadership in a typical city can do to prevent this. Once the key response of the board is taken, the process is "locked in." If the key response is conciliatory, continued low-keyed civil rights activity will extract additional concessions; if the key response is negative, the civil rights movement will retaliate with demonstrations, but this usually leads to an escalation of the conflict and the school board's subsequently becoming more reluctant to negotiate or make additional concessions. The only way in which the movement can control the outcome is by introducing a new authority—for example, the state government may step in to order desegregation, and this is sometimes very effective.

Altogether, the findings mean that the school board usually is nearly autonomous in its policy-making on racial issues. It generally is not effectively influenced by political or civic leadership, by its superintendent, or even by the behavior of the civil rights movement, despite the fact that the decision on race is probably the issue of greatest immediate importance to the largest number of actors.

In order to demonstrate this conclusion, the research staff of the eight-city study ranked the cities on four variables: the level of civil rights activity prior to the key response, the level of civil rights activity after the key response, the degree to which the key response indicated a willingness to acquiesce to the civil rights demands, and the final level of acquiescence of the board to the demands made. Acquiescence is based on the number of demands met and the general public tone taken by the schools with respect to the civil rights movement. Put another way, the research staff attempted to rank the cities according to the degree to which a typical civil rights leader would feel satisfied with the response of the school system. The eight cities varied greatly in their acquiescence. In Pittsburgh, for example, the school board reacted very early to civil rights demands with a transfer plan which integrated two previously all-white schools. When demands for integration reappeared later, the school board committed itself, in a long and candid statement, to integration; adopted some short-range integration programs; and began planning for large scale educational parks as the long run answer to the integration question. In Baltimore, a demand for the elimination of overcrowding in Negro schools led to a summer of negotiation between the civil rights leaders and the school board, resulting in a decision to transport 4,000 Negro students and eliminate all double-shift schooling in the system, effective only six months after the issue was first raised. These two school systems are scored at the top of the acquiescence scale. At the opposite extreme, two school boards have refused to meet any of the demands for integration made, despite repeated demonstrations and pressure from other governmental officials. These two systems are located at the bottom of the scale.

Figure 1 diagrams the rank-order correlations between the initial level of civil rights activity, the acquiescence of the key response, the level of civil rights activity following the key response, and the total level of acquiescence of the school system. The correlations indicate that the key response is not dependent upon the level of civil rights activity directed at the board, and also that the key response predicts quite accurately the final amount of acquiescence of the school system. If the rank correlations are accurate, they indicate that the civil rights movement principally responds to the behavior of the school system rather than being a cause of the character of the school system's behavior.

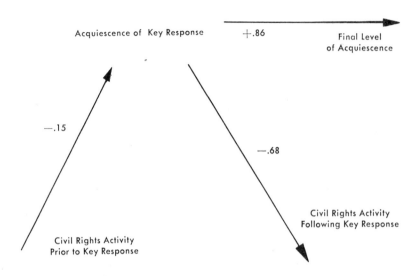

Figure 1. Rank-Order Correlations between Civil Rights Activity and Acquiescence of School Boards to Civil Rights Demands.

This is only indirect evidence that the boards can be quite autonomous in their decision. We also have some direct evidence of this. In Figure 2, the eight boards have been ranked by a combination of two closely correlated variables: the percentage of the board members having high socioeconomic status (men from large businesses, corporation lawyers, or professionals) as against the percentage who are professional politicians or related in other ways to the political parties in their city. (High-status men are, of course, generally independent of the parties.) This single variable predicts quite well the final level of acquiescence of the school system. Since the variable is clearly independent of the actual decision situation, this seems to be strong evidence.

The autonomy of the nonpolitical board is not so surprising. However, the five boards which are partly or wholly made up of political appointments are also largely autonomous. Two of these boards are elected boards in cities where political power is quite decentralized. In a third city, the mayor's recommendations seem to have been largely ignored. In another, the mayor's appointments

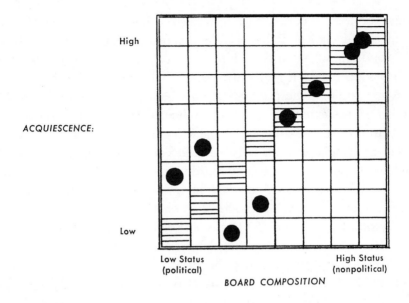

High

ACQUIESCENCE:

Low

Low Status
(political)

High Status
(nonpolitical)

BOARD COMPOSITION

(**Note:** The two boards in the upper right are tied on both rankings.)

Figure 2. Status and Political Activity of School Board Members and Acquiescence to Civil Rights Demands.

have disagreed strongly with each other and have involved the city in a lengthy controversy. In the fifth city, the mayor seems to have maintained control over the school system, and here the board has been persuaded twice to change its position on a racial issue.

It is usually assumed that political leaders wish to maximize their power and, therefore, detachment from school politics may seem surprising; but the mayor who tries to run the schools would be taking a great risk for a very small reward.

Before considering the implications of these findings, we also should consider why it is that the civic board is more acquiescent than the political board. The answer is a simple but empirical one: On our measures, the civic board members are more liberal on racial issues and the political board members are more conservative. This is not a trivial statement, because it is certainly not necessary that

147

there be a high correlation between the personal attitude of government officials and their public actions. In fact, a similar study of Southern school boards indicates that there is at best a weak correlation between racial attitudes and behavior regarding school desegregation.[8] The presence of this high correlation in the North indicates the extent to which the school desegregation issue is unstructured. In the absence of clear legal guidelines for action, of efficient communication between the contesting parties, and of a coherent educational ideology to draw upon, the school board members are "on their own" in deciding what to do. Board members are very conscious of this; more than one has publicly appealed for a decision by a local or Federal court to clarify the situation. Buffalo, New York, furnishes a striking example of what this kind of clarification by an authority can do. The state commissioner of education, James E. Allen, demanded that the board desegregate the schools, and immediately the board became a cohesive decision-making body even though it had been torn by internal conflict for well over a year prior to his intervention.

The lack of structure and clarity in the civil rights arena is, we think, also reflected in the fact that heterogeneous school boards and boards with a history of internal conflict have the greatest difficulty in meeting civil rights demands. Only two of the eight boards have contested elections for membership (five are appointed while another is *de facto* appointed by a slating committee); these two boards were the least acquiescent, probably because of their heterogeneity and the pressures on the boards to make their disagreements public. The board with internal conflict cannot acquiesce to the demands made on it for two reasons: First, it cannot agree on what is being asked of it, and what strategies are available to it; second, it cannot prevent public controversy which polarizes the community and further limits the alternatives available to it.

---

8. See Robert L. Crain, Morton Inger and Gerald A. McWorter, "School Desegregation in New Orleans: A Comparative Study in the Failure of Social Control," Chicago: National Opinion Research Center, Report #110B.

The great debate over community power structure hinges about the amount of autonomy which governmental officials have and the extent to which the civic elite are able to influence policy. The findings of this research suggest that it is possible for government officials to have great autonomy and at the same time for the civic elite to have great influence. In the case of the schools, the nature of the local civic elite is a principal factor in determining the composition of the school board, and thus the elite indirectly controls policy, even though it makes little or no effort to influence any single decision (and probably could not do so if it tried). The three most acquiescent cities all have high-status schools boards, and the civic elite in all three cases plays an important role in locating school board members. These three cities have elites which are highly active across a wide range of local policy issues. In the other five cities, the elites are weaker, and the result is that school board members are selected either from the ranks of the political parties, or from the leadership of voluntary organizations or in order to represent various ethnic groups.

Even the degree of heterogeneity and internal conflict in the school board has its roots in the structure of the political parties and the nature of the elite. The conflict-ridden boards which resist desegregation appear in cities with weak political parties, for example. Thus, the school board is autonomous in its decision-making procedure, yet the degree of acquiescence of the school system is determined by the overall political structure of the city.

Symbolic Politics and Real Outputs

To this point we have not discussed the real outputs of the school system's racial policy—the actual changes in quality of education or the actual increase in the number of students in integrated schools. It is not difficult for a school system to adopt a racial policy which will partially satisfy civil rights leaders without actually making a large impact on the operation of the schools. (These symbolic victories may have a considerable impact on the attitudes and behavior of individual Negro students, but this is outside the range of the two studies.) Conversely, it is also possible for the school system to have in operation policies which increase school integration without satisfying the civil rights groups. In two cities, Negro students were routinely bussed into white schools, but the school adamantly refused to state that such integration was desirable, and the board in each case was subject to a great deal of attack.

The actual amount of integration is, of course, small. Among the eight cities, the greatest acquiescence, as judged by the research staff, was in Pittsburgh, Baltimore, and St. Louis. In Pittsburgh, the school system has succeeded in remaining on cordial terms with the civil rights leaders and has committed itself wholeheartedly to integration; but to date, Pittsburgh has done little to increase integration. St. Louis and Baltimore have adopted bussing programs which have successfully relieved overcrowded Negro schools, but less than 5 percent of the Negro students are directly involved. In the eight cities, the proportion of Negro elementary school children attending schools which are at least 90 percent Negro varies from a low of 30 percent in San Francisco to a high of 86 percent in St. Louis; the median for the eight cities is 68 percent. If the largest cities—Chicago, Detroit, Cleveland, Philadelphia, Washington, and New York City—had been included in the study, the picture would look even bleaker.

The school board may commit itself to a policy of integration but find its efforts to implement this policy restricted by a number of factors outside of its control. The superintendent may undermine the design and implementation of the policy through his role in developing technical details of the plan. Voluntary plans for pupil-transfer may have a minimal effect because of a lack of interest among Negro parents, or may even further segregation by allowing whites to transfer out of integrated schools. (This is another example of universalism; transfer plans explicitly based on the race of the pupils involved are quite *avant-garde*.) Or track systems or practices of homogeneous grouping, discriminatory or not, may segregate pupils rigidly within the "integrated" school. And in cities where racial tensions are especially high, such as in Chicago and Cleveland, Negro students attending white schools have been assaulted, and it is often a community prophecy (and in a part a self-fulfilling one) that integrated schools will become all Negro.[9]

More important, the school system cannot control its own personnel. The heart of successful integration is the classroom teacher, and many big city teachers do not feel comfortable teaching Negro students or handling an integrated class. Further, it is a big city tradition that the integrated school is a "changing" school, where teachers transfer out, morale drops, and high-level programs are phased out as no longer appropriate to the clientele.

The difficulties encountered by the school systems in implementing effective integration go beyond the particular personality problems of the individual actors. They are tied to basic inadequacies in the organizational capacities of the large city school systems for adapting to social change. Briefly, these inadequacies include the following:

1. A bureaucratic rigidity flowing from the statutory and quasi-legal restrictions placed on the school systems by states and accrediting associations. These restrictions limit the scheduling of the school year, prescribe certain courses and curricula, bureaucratize teacher recruitment, etc. This rigidity is related to the great emphasis upon universalism, a stress which in large part is a heritage of many cycles of reform. The result is administration by numbers: an attempt at innovation becomes merely an elaborate formula for assigning X numbers of specialists to Y numbers of schools. Another example is the procedure of allowing teachers to pick whatever schools they want on the basis of seniority, a practice which usually undermines the "difficult" school. And a crucial result is the highly standardized curriculum, which exists despite obvious differences in the needs of different schools.

2. The fact that teachers are basically solo practitioners. Unlike most professions, teaching offers relatively little opportunity for collegial contact which could provide the opportunity not only for

---

9. Each of these problems is potentially subject to remediation as shown, for example, in St. Louis's ability to bus approximately 2,600 Negro students into white schools in 1965-1966. The bussing program seems to have an informal "quota"; none of the integrated schools is over 40 percent Negro. After the initial shock, there has been virtually no opposition in this border city, and bussing of Negro students is now taken for granted.

respite but for communication of new practices and the development of new attitudes. In-service training tends to be restricted to short-term workshops which are likely to have a minimal impact on teacher attitudes relevant to racial change. Yet, intensive resocialization procedures are apparently essential because of the conventional perspectives with which persons enter teaching.[10] Further, rewards for the teachers are largely ascriptive, based on seniority and on graduate work which in most schools of education is not oriented to the problems of urban education. As solo practitioners, the teachers frequently are reluctant to have anyone enter their classrooms, including subprofessionals or volunteers who could play a significant role. Principals and middle-level administrators face similar problems of poor lateral and vertical communication except on purely administrative matters.

3. Given these patterns, the large city school systems have very primitive mechanisms of control, which limit them severely in producing change. These systems are overcentralized in the sense that standardized curricula and administration by formula do not provide enough fiscal and administrative autonomy to permit "decentralized" administrators to vary their programs to local needs with any real facility. Yet they are undercentralized in the sense that it is very difficult for decisions made at the top of the organization to alter the traditional operating procedures. This is particularly the case in cities where principals or other personnel have become highly entrenched in their positions; the man who has been principal of the same school for twenty years is not responsive to supervision. Commitment to the status quo is often heightened by inbreeding and by the associations of principals and other personnel which act as mutual protective associations.[11]

---

10. The tendency for even city-bred teacher trainees to have quite negative orientations toward the challenges of "problem schools" in the inner city is described in Bryan Roberts, "The Effects of College Experience and Social Background on Professional Orientations of Prospective Teachers," unpublished dissertation, University of Chicago, 1964. Findings of an experiment conducted by Bruno Bettelheim in cooperation with the Russell Sage project indicate that teachers' difficulties in dealing with Negro children who present behavior problems flow not principally from racial prejudice but from social class views in which the teacher assumes that the children are unlikely to learn. The Bettelheim work also seems to demonstrate that really intensive in-service training can produce a reduction in these stereotypic views.

11. For a discussion of the power of this sort of clique, see W. S. Sayre and H. Kaufman, *Governing New York City*, New York: W. W. Norton & Company, Inc., 1965, 279-280.

4. Also limiting the school system in producing innovations in racial practices and programs for the deprived is their general weakness in research and development. The large systems have numerous special projects for dealing with Negro pupils, and many have generated a sense of success and excitement. But evaluation research is usually poor, and attempts to expand the program to other schools are so haphazardly administered that few survive to become incorporated into standard operating procedure.

Cumulatively, these characteristics of the large city school system imply that more adequate integration of the large city schools will require not only higher levels of leadership in broadening and pursuing educational goals, but also substantial transformations in the organizational format.

Conclusion

It has often been said that in a large and complex organization the leadership does not have control over the operation of the system. These data indicate that there is considerable truth in this. Control over the classroom teacher is limited by the fact that she cannot be supervised directly and by the nature of her contract and the character of her professional organization. Control over individual principals is limited because supervision must be from a distance and by a strict universalism in administration. The board cannot supervise a school superintendent unless he supplies information to them, presents the full range of policy alternatives, and permits the board to believe that it knows something about how to run a school system. Similarly, the men who select the school-board members must defer to them as "experts" once the selection has been made.

On the other hand, we do see a clear line of influence which runs from the top of the system to the bottom. When members of the mayor's staff or members of the civil elite choose school-board members (and in most cities they do choose them), they have in mind an operational image when they say they want a "good man" for the job. It is hardly a surprise that they get the kind of man they want most of the time. These men then control the schools "image" on racial matters and to a limited extent this style can filter down to the classroom. The board selects the superintendent, and some boards have definite criteria in mind; if he does not meet them, he may then be subject to what one board member called a "learning experience." And the superintendent, through his choice of subordinate administrators and his use of policy directives and public relations, can project a "style" into the school system. Granted there is no close isomorphism between this "style" and the actual day-to-day operations of the schools, but at least there is some order in the system.

DAVID ROGERS

*The author is Senior Research Sociol-
ogist at the Center for Urban Education and a member of the faculty of
the Graduate School of Business Administration at New York University.
Dr. Rogers has been conducting field
studies on the politics of school desegregation controversies in New York
since 1964. The following paper is a
summary of his book,* Politics, Schools,
Segregation: The Case of New York
City, *to be published by the Center
for Urban Education.*

OBSTACLES TO SCHOOL DESEGREGATION IN NEW YORK CITY: A Benchmark Case

THOUGH MORE THAN A decade has passed since the historic Supreme Court decision supposedly outlawing school segregation, the extent of segregation has remained almost the same as it was in 1954, in the North as well as in the South. In fact, it has increased markedly in many Northern cities, partly as a result of the demographic and residential changes they have experienced. Yet there have been variations, both in extent of segregation and of receptivity to desegregation plans in large Northern cities.

AUTHOR'S NOTE: *This study was begun under Grant No. 2857 from the U. S. Office of Education. It was completed with the support of the Center for Urban Education. I am especially grateful to Robert A. Dentler, Deputy Director of the Center, for making it possible for me to complete this study. I am also grateful for the help provided by Rosalyn Menzel and Faith Kortheuer, my research assistants. Ronald Milavsky, Kenneth Lenihan, Ivar Berg, and Theresa Rogers provided helpful criticisms of earlier drafts. The views expressed in this paper are those of the author and do not necessarily reflect those of the Center for Urban Education.*

Little is known, however, about the "mix" of conditions associated with such differences.[1] One way to find out is through comparative study. Another important way, the one I have followed, is to generate hypotheses about conditions related to action or inaction by school officials from an intensive study of a single case. My case is New York City.

A case study strategy is perhaps especially appropriate at this time, since there haven't been enough studies or codifications of evidence to even suggest what all the relevant variables may be. My purpose is to develop hypotheses to explain New York City's experience, calling attention to the range of variables that should be taken into account in any study of school desegregation.[2]

The Relevance of New York City

Some students of comparative politics see New York City's problems as idiosyncratic. Nonetheless, it is a very strategic case for several reasons: First, its school system has often been a model for those in other cities. It is generally further along in the formulation of desegregation plans and their implementation on a selective, local basis than any other large Northern city. The successes and failures of strategy of its school and political officials and of various civic groups involved in desegregation controversies are taken into account by their colleagues elsewhere and become guidelines for their actions.

Second, regardless of some impediments to change inherent in

---

1. Cf. Robin Williams's *Factors Affecting Reactions to Public School Desegregation in American Communities*, unpublished paper, April, 1964, for the most comprehensive codification to date of studies in this field. Unfortunately, there were no published studies on the school desegregation experience of very large Northern cities for Williams to include in his codification.

2. My data include informant interviews with school and city officials, leaders and activists deemed most influential on the issue; observation at meetings and public hearings; and a content analysis of press clippings, studies, and public statements of the board and involved civic groups. My purpose was to trace through the positions taken by every influential party to school desegregation controversies since 1957, when the issue first was contested publicly in New York City; delineate the many coalitions and factions; ascertain the extent of access of various interest groups (school staff as well as civic groups) to decision centers on the issue; and suggest the effects of such patterns of influence on the speed and scope of the board's desegregation efforts.

its fragmented and highly bureaucratized governmental institutions, New York City has long been a center of cosmopolitan values, of progressive politics, and of innovation in many fields.[3] Its present lay board reflects this, dominated as it is by people with a long record of support for progressive labor and civil rights causes. They share an egalitarian, social reformist outlook that has been a hallmark of the city's political life. If school desegregation is not taking place in New York City, then, it would be important to know why, since conditions are more favorable there than in many other cities. Yet the fact is that even in New York City not much desegregation has taken place.

Indeed, despite many plans and programs (e.g., rezonings, Open Enrollments, Princeton Plan Pairings, feeder pattern changes), formulated long before most other Northern school officials were ready to move, and despite the liberal traditions of the city and the school board, there was minimal implementation. In fact, New York City's Board of Education has not arrested the trend toward segregation. It may even be moving the other way.

Ethnic Distribution

The board's data on ethnic changes in the city's schools show the following clear-cut trends: First, the number of predominantly Negro and Puerto Rican schools (those having 90 percent or more Negro and Puerto Rican pupils at the elementary level and 85 percent at the junior high and high school level) increased from 118 in 1960 to 187 in 1965. In 1960, they accounted for 15 percent of all schools and in 1965 for 23 percent, pointing to an increase in segregation.[4] At the same time, the number of predominantly white schools has decreased from 327 to 237, accounting for a decrease from 42 percent to 31 percent of the schools. Finally, the number of midrange schools (those with between 10 percent and 90 per-

---

3. See Wallace Sayre and Herbert Kaufman, *Governing New York City*, New York: Russell Sage Foundation, 1960, especially Chapter 19.

4. Cited from *Ethnic Distribution of Pupils in The Public Schools of New York City*, New York City Board of Education, Central Zoning Unit, March 24, 1965.

cent Negro and Puerto Rican pupils at the elementary level and 15 percent to 85 percent beyond that) increased slightly during this period from 337 to 387, accounting for 43 percent in 1960 and 46 percent in 1965. The data thus suggest a mixed picture with more segregation among Negro and Puerto Rican pupils and less among whites.

This becomes clear if one traces the trend for Negro–Puerto Rican pupils and whites considered separately: In 1960, 41 percent of Negro–Puerto Rican pupils were in segregated schools compared with 49 percent in 1965. And although the proportion of midrange schools may have gone up slightly, the proportion of Negro and Puerto Rican pupils in such schools actually declined from 56 percent to 48 percent. Where there was more desegregation, it was only for whites.

Furthermore, two artifacts in the data may well play down the actual trend toward increased segregation for Negro pupils. First, Puerto Rican and Negro pupils are lumped together in the statistics. Since more Puerto Rican pupils attend midrange and predominantly white schools than do Negro pupils, reflecting the wider dispersion of the Puerto Rican population throughout the city, lumping the two groups together only obscures the trend toward segregation for Negroes. Second, by breaking down the midrange, integrated category of schools into smaller subgroups, the distribution becomes bimodal, with most of the Negro pupils at one end, in schools with from 70-90 percent Negro–Puerto Rican, and most of the whites at the other. This picture contrasts sharply with the situation in 1960, when many more white and Negro–Puerto Rican pupils were in the middle of the distribution in schools with 30-70 percent of each ethnic category. In short, there has been a substantial increase in segregation in the last five years.

A standard interpretation for such a trend is that it is a result of a change in the entire population of the city as well as a hardening and extension of housing segregation. The continued out-migration of the white middle class, the continued withdrawal from the public schools of whites who stay in the city, the increase in young, low-income Negro and Puerto Rican families whose birth rates are much higher than those of whites, and the mushrooming of low-income housing projects in ghetto areas, further ghettoizing them and spreading the ghetto out across the city, all make the task of increasing racial balance in the schools a difficult one.[5]

The increased housing segregation is a special obstacle. It limits the number of "fringe" areas, correspondingly limiting the prospects for securing a desegregated pupil population short of massive transfer programs involving long-distance traveling. Even the more militant of the civil rights leaders generally accept the argument that housing segregation has contributed, in part, to school segregation. They just are not willing to give it the same weight as the board does.

Even if the housing pattern allowed for more school desegregation, so the argument continues, there are chronic scarcities of trained and committed staff, of building space, and of funds as further obstacles to the board.[6] All these factors, then, constitute a formidable array of social forces generally outside the control of school officials, yet limiting their capacity to desegregate on any meaningful scale.

There can be no question about the importance of such conditions. Their impact seemingly serves to corroborate the view that the board is being held responsible and accountable for changes they have not the authority and influence to implement. However, my data do not completely bear this out. In fact, they suggest quite the contrary: namely, that the board failed to exercise leadership

---

5. The withdrawal of white pupils from the New York City schools shows few signs of leveling off. The percentage of white pupils decreased from 66.8 percent in 1956-1959 to 54.5 percent in 1964-1965. Of those white families staying in the city, the typical pattern is for upper-income populations increasingly to send their children to private schools and for low income populations to send their children to religious or parochial schools. Many upper-middle-class, civil rights activist white *and* Negro parents have withdrawn their children from public schools in large numbers. They claim they have left the public schools because of their deteriorating quality. More evidence is obviously needed to delineate their true motivations and interests. Since many are dedicated in a number of ways to civil rights causes, it would not necessarily be accurate to say that they are running away from the Negro or integration.

6. One can argue, of course, that though such scarcities do exist, a number of structural characteristics, codes, and operating procedures within the board of education — its overcentralization, poor communications between headquarters and the field and across divisions and other units, and the absence of long-range planning — have all contributed to substantial malfunctioning and inefficiencies, and that the scarcity argument can be overdone. My data support this view. See the section below on the board.

and power in many situations where desegregation might well have been forwarded. I will give several examples in a later section.

To summarize, I would suggest two preliminary propositions. The first is that school segregation is deepening and lines are hardening in New York City, as is supported by the above figures. The second is that this trend cannot be attributed only or even mainly to constraints such as housing and demographic patterns or scarcities of personnel, funds, and space. Political constraints, as well, have prevented board action. The remainder of the paper will be devoted to a preliminary documentation of this second proposition.

A "Political" Interpretation of Increasing School Segregation

The most compelling evidence for the assertion that political forces have served to prevent board action is the wide and growing gap between the board's many policy statements and their implementation. Some of the most "advanced" policy statements ever written on school desegregation (going back as far as 1954 when it was not yet "fashionable," at least in the North) were advanced by New York City's Board of Education. And they recommended basic, not diversionary, strategies, e.g., site selection, changes in feeder patterns, rezoning, and establishing educational complexes and parks. Yet, after more than a decade of such policy statements, there has been little implementation.

A few examples may suffice to make the point. The first major desegregation plan, Open Enrollment, resulted in only the most limited numbers of pupil transfers. Fewer than 10 percent of those pupils to whom the plan was applicable actually transferred. As the authors of the Allen Report on the city's desegregation prospects stated: "The [Board of Education's own] Commission on Integration recommendations on the redistribution of pupils through 'permissive zoning' and busing were not implemented."[7]

7. "Desegregating the Public Schools of New York City," report of the State Education Department's Advisory Committee on Human Relations and Community Tensions, May 12, 1964, reprinted in full in *Integrated Education* (August-September, 1964), p. 16.

The board's interpretation for Open Enrollment's limited success is that Negro parents did not want to have their children transferred out of their local schools. Undoubtedly, this was the sentiment of some and it will always be true of some. On reviewing the history of how Open Enrollment was introduced, however, it is unfair and inaccurate to place the responsibility on Negro parents for the small numbers who took advantage of the program.

This is how it generally went: The board did not take initiative in informing the public. It did little to prepare parents, students, staff, and communities participating in the program. And when people were informed, it turned out that local school officials and many headquarters personnel were by and large opposed to the plan. There is no available evidence to suggest, for example, that the board and school officials had pointed out with much conviction the possible advantages of participating in Open Enrollment. And there is evidence to suggest otherwise.

The first pamphlets encouraging parents to take advantage of the plan were prepared by officials of the Urban League with the help of the American Jewish Committee and other civic organizations. The board refused to help distribute them. Later, when other city agencies did cooperate and much publicity was given this fact, the board of education joined in. In effect, the board followed rather than led public opinion on the issue.

Extensive records and files furnished me by some civic leaders and school officials suggest a widespread pattern of sabotage by principals, teachers, and field superintendents and a very limited publicity campaign from headquarters. The practice of not informing Negro parents in ghetto schools of the new opportunities open to them to send their children to underutilized white schools was so widespread, in fact, that headquarters took over more and more of this function. The further practice of lecturing to Negro parents on the many "costs" of transferring their children out, engaged in by many principals and teachers, and the rather strong urging that parents keep their children in their local schools, undoubtedly contributed to the low percentage who participated in Open Enrollment.[8]

Field sabotage took place in "receiving" as well as in sending schools. More often than not, principals in receiving schools, anxious to preserve homogeneous classes, would end up placing incoming Negro pupils in segregated situations. Likewise, the limited preparation of students, parents, school officials, and communities (in receiving schools) for incoming students also served to discourage Negro parents. The limited resources headquarters allocated for such preparation and its failure to sanction principals and teachers who scuttled the plan further contributed to its minimal implementation. To top it all off, sabotage at one end could build on sabotage at the other. Principals in sending schools referred to segregated conditions in receiving schools in urging parents not to transfer their children.

The board's policy statements, however, went well beyond such voluntary plans. They included, as I mentioned, rezoning, changes in feeder patterns, and fundamental changes in the construction program, with schools to be built in "fringe" areas wherever possible. On balance, they simply were never implemented. For example 39 of the 106 projects in the board's 1964-1965 building program were for local school areas where the estimated ethnic composition of the school was 90 percent or more Negro and Puerto Rican pupils. In short, over one-third of the schools planned were guaranteed to be segregated, though many might have been located in fringe areas to prevent that. The board's most recent construction budget calls for over 55 percent of its funds for segregated schools.[9] To quote the Allen Report once again:

The school building program as presently set forth reinforces

---

8. One reason so many principals from "sending" schools objected to open enrollment was that it might seem to reflect adversely on the quality of their program. If too many Negro parents transferred their children out, some principals feared it might suggest to the board that there was much parent dissatisfaction. Others were against it because they wanted to keep at least a few potentially "high achievers."

9. "Study of the Effect of the 1964-1970 School Building Program on Segregation in New York City's Public Schools," City Commission on Human Rights of New York City, unpublished paper, 1964. The main findings and conclusions of the study were released to the press and never publicly refuted by the board.

substantially the historic pattern of building on sites within the most segregated areas. This is the case chiefly in Negro residential areas, but it is also true in some mainly White neighborhoods, and thus helps to intensify both forms of segregation.[10]

The consistent board practice has been to "build the schools where the children are," despite continued pressure from civil rights groups and continued encouragement from the State Education Commission to do otherwise. Indeed, the construction program is a key to the whole segregation problem. Civil rights pressures have continued unabated in this field but to no avail. In sum, the board's actual school construction and site selection decisions are at wide variance with its stated desegregation policies.

Why is it then that even in New York City, though they, at least, get to the policy-making stage, there is so little implementation? Why has the board tended to zone and build schools in a way that followed rather than ran counter to the segregated housing pattern? And why have they even zoned in some areas to counteract an integrated housing pattern? To answer these questions is to suggest some of the political forces that have contributed, and I think substantially, to the increased segregation of New York City's schools.

My research suggests the following political forces in New York City preventing much implementation of school desegregation plans: the development of a strong opposition — the result of an unplanned alliance of some school officials, white parents, and real estate interests (supported by key politicians) around the "neighborhood school" slogan; a strategy of caution, vacillation, and ineffective planning by the board of education; a politically ineffective integrationist coalition — due in large part to lack of unity among integrationist groups, their inability to mobilize much grass roots support, their limited resources, and their particular political strategies; an unwillingness of powerful "moderate" groups to support many desegregation plans and their successes at scuttling them; the structure and operating codes of the school system itself — leading to poor communications, schisms, and an inability to co-

---

10. "Desegregating the Public Schools...," *op. cit.*, p. 17.

ordinate their actions, let alone innovate, at key points in the system (e.g., conflicts between the lay board and superintendent, between the board and professional staff, between field and headquarters, across divisions, bureaus, and other functional units as to respective spheres of influence and responsibility); and the fragmented structure of New York City government, preventing any meaningful city-wide educational planning through a coordination of housing, urban renewal, transit, industrial development, and poverty projects with the board's desegregation program. I will discuss briefly the role of each factor, pointing up how they relate to one another. It is obviously difficult in a case study of this nature to assess which of these factors was most significant. At the same time, it is possible to suggest how the degree of leadership and initiative exercised by the board and city officials (e.g., the degree to which they passively reflected or tried to shape public opinion) affected the course of school desegregation controversies in recent years.

The "Neighborhood School" Coalition

One of the biggest obstacles to school desegregation, in New York City as elsewhere, has come from within the education profession itself. The "neighborhood school" tradition, propounded almost three generations ago by the profession to suggest organizational forms especially appropriate for urban school systems, has become the clarion call around which a variety of *status quo*-oriented interests have united. The concept was originally developed to counter the impersonality, decline of primary group ties, and anomie of urban life. It resulted in a number of policies: building schools very close to home, zoning in a way to minimize travel time, gerrymandering to preserve ethnic and class homogeneity, constructing smaller schools. All these policies were assumed to have innumerable benefits: quality, economies, security and safety for children, and close school-community relations.[11]

---

11. See Allan Blackman's excellent summary of the neighborhood school doctrine, "Planning and the Neighborhood School," *Integrated Education* (August-September, 1964), pp. 49-56.

Regardless of how one evaluates such benefits by today's conditions, it seems abundantly clear that powerful professional interests inside the school system (teachers, principals, field superintendents, divisional heads, key headquarters personnel), local parent associations and home-owner, civic groups, and many public and private real estate interests have supported the concept. And although the doctrine is increasingly viewed as an essentially "fundamentalist" one, given the recognized need for consolidation in fragmented, big city school systems, it has rallied a large number of followers, even in as cosmopolitan a city as New York.

Thus, a loosely joined coalition in defense of the *status quo* and having tremendous political resources and influence developed in New York City as school desegregation became more of an issue. It frequently mobilized strong white parent support by raising the spectre of "mandatory, long distance busing," something that the board never intended. The coalition thus formed was not that motivated and planned. Rather, it was an unintended consequence of the pursuit by each of a number of interests of its own inner agendas. What are they?

White parents in New York City most affected by school desegregation plans tended to feel increasingly crowded by expanding Negro populations and embraced the neighborhood school symbol as a socially acceptable expression of a need to preserve the essentially white, middle-class, and "private" character of their schools. Recent studies in New York City suggest the following profile of interests of white parents supporting the neighborhood schools.[12] They represent lower- and lower-middle class populations recently migrated from central city slums and decaying areas. They want to keep their new neighborhood "respectable" by preserving uncrowded, "good" schools and safe living conditions. They are an ethnocentric and highly status-conscious second generation, proud of the way they rose from a proletarian existence through their own

---

12.   Kurt and Gladys Lang, "Resistance to School Desegregation among Jews," *Sociological Inquiry* (Winter, 1965), pp. 94-123; an unpublished study by David Caplovitz and Candace Rogers, Bureau of Applied Social Research, Columbia University, 1965; and David Rogers and Bert Swanson, "White Citizen Response to the Same Integration Plan: Comparisons of Local School Districts in a Northern City."

efforts. They say that if the Negro had any ambition, he could do the same. Many of these whites are home-owners anxious about declining property values if Negroes move into their area. As parents, they are concerned about the upward mobility and occupational achievement of their children which they see as threatened by forced desegregation and, they reason, a decline in quality of education.

All of these interests predispose them to embrace the neighborhood school concept. They constitute a large, mass base for resistance to desegregation and have been especially susceptible to demagogic appeals in Queens (Parents and Taxpayers), Brooklyn (Joint Council for Better Education), and the Bronx, areas of expanding Negro and Puerto Rican populations. They are especially resentful of the fact that upper-middle-class "white liberals" and civil rights leaders have placed them on the firing line while sending their own children, in many cases, to private schools.

There was a rather striking similarity in social outlook between these white parent populations and many school officials, both at headquarters and in the field, who resisted any implementation of the board's desegregation plans with every conceivable strategy they could muster — both private and public. Many of the same arguments against "forced" integration plans were used by teachers, principals, field superintendents, and some headquarters officials, who came from the same kinds of ethnic origins (Irish, Jewish, Italian), and had the same kinds of latent and not so latent prejudice against lower-class minority group children.[13] Their resistance illustrates how insulated public school educators have become in

---

13. For a sample of the sentiments of some of the supervisory staff within the New York City school system, see "The Integration Crisis," reprinted in *Integrated Education* (June-July, 1964), pp. 30-35. This was a statement issued by the Council of Supervisory Associations, a group representing 3,000 high school, junior high school, and elementary school principals, department chairmen, administrative assistants in high schools, assistant principals, board examiners, assistant superintendents, and other supervisors. They opposed pairings, feeder pattern changes, and the abolishing of group IQ tests. Their stand even appalled one of the city's most powerful "moderate" organizations who hadn't given much support to the integration forces. See UPA press release, April 20, 1964, in which they referred to the "negative attitude recently advanced in the statement of the Council of Supervisory Associations." My data on staff prejudice come from interviews and observations. See also Kenneth Clark, *Dark Ghetto*, New York: Harper & Row, Publishers, Incorporated, 1965, Chapter 6.

recent years, especially in metropolitan centers experiencing such rapid demographic and social changes. They have acted as though they were still dealing with a predominantly white, middle-class clientele, and still training low-income populations for jobs that are disappearing in an automating economy.

Thus, the personal and career interests of many public school officials in New York City converged with the interests of the white parent opposition. Principals' associations, district superintendents, and some headquarters personnel staged heated campaigns, in the press and in private, to forestall nonvoluntary desegregation programs. Desegregation meant a number of changes in their working conditions — in curriculum, in staffing and training requirements, in ethnic composition of schools and classrooms, and even in grade and divisional organization. Many understandably felt much more secure and comfortable following older traditions, even if they were dated. And they were especially enraged with civil rights demands for nonvoluntary desegregation plans, since such plans violated the most "sacred" tradition of all, that of the neighborhood school. It was the tradition that many school officials, especially an older generation, had been taught had so many benefits and virtues.[14]

Finally, a variety of public and private real estate groups, perhaps in a number of unplanned ways, reinforced and gave structural support to the twin goals of maintaining segregated residential areas and neighborhood schools. Though not oriented directly toward educational matters, private developers, local home-owner groups, slum landlords, and even city housing agencies, acting in their perceived economic interests or in accordance with housing codes, tended to perpetuate and expand a segregated housing pattern. The housing politics of Queens, Brooklyn, and the Bronx, for example, are replete with examples of the successes of local home-owner groups in white, middle-class areas in keeping low-income housing projects out of their neighborhoods. Slum landlords have successfully resisted some efforts to renovate or demolish tenements in ghetto areas. Private developers have frequently been insensi-

---

14. Junior high school principals were especially opposed to the board's desegregation plans because they included a grade reorganization that would abolish the junior high school division.

tive to the pleas of the board of education to take into account the school and housing integration implications of their decisions. Finally, Federal moneys for low-income housing projects have only been rendered if the projects were located in decaying slum areas. This has served to perpetuate and expand segregated housing patterns.

All these real estate and housing pressures need not necessarily be viewed as some form of "conspiracy." Rather, they may mainly have been a consequence of the pursuit by a number of public agencies and private home-owner and business groups of their economic or political self-interest, divorced from any self-conscious considerations of school segregation. The result, however, has been very clear; namely, the growth and proliferation of ghetto neighborhoods.

The Board's Strategy

A second factor serving as an obstacle has been the board of education's strategy for dealing with the desegregation issue and with civil rights demands. It can only be understood within the political context just discussed. Their strategy has been one of caution, hoping not to alienate the large block of white parents and school officials fearful of compulsory segregation plans; of vacillation (as a reflection of cross-pressures from civil rights and opposition groups); and of ineffective planning and preparation for the policies it finally implemented. Faced with demands from conflicting publics, each asking for services in a situation of perceived scarcity and limited supply, the board's response is understandable. This is not to say that it could not have been quite different. And it certainly contributed to polarizing civil rights groups and the opposition as well as to the long stalemate on the issue.

A key indicator of the board's caution was their posture of insulation from protest groups, as evidenced by periods of virtually no communication with local civil rights leaders and officials and their refusal to allow for any "outside" mediation in the period just preceding the civil rights-sponsored boycotts of February, 1964.[15] Board President James Donovan dismissed the boycott in a public statement as "Fizzle #1," rather than coming to terms with the fact that all civil rights groups had united to support it and that 445,000 pupils stayed out of school. Indeed, it was only after some outside parties did intervene and force the board to resume meetings with civil rights groups that they did resume communications.[16]

Another indicator was the manner in which they handled the controversy over Princeton Plan Pairing. Board members and headquarters officials developed a plan for as many as twenty pairings for implementation in September, 1964. They did not decide which of the twenty pairings to implement. Instead, they invited selected parent groups along with district superintendents, principals, and local school boards to private meetings to help the board decide not how but whether pairings would be implemented in their local areas. Civil rights groups were not invited nor was the opposition. The case made by local parent associations, with the help of the research staff of their parent organization, United Parents Association (UPA), helped defeat sixteen of the twenty.

The tone of the private meetings was significant. Civil rights groups were denounced for their demands, and in the course of a few months of such meetings, Princeton Plan Pairings were effectively scuttled in New York City. Since civil rights leaders, as well, gave up the pairing idea by the time the board finally came out with its plan for four pairings, it seems unlikely that they will ever be tried on any scale, large or small. Civil rights groups came to an agreement that it was more important to restructure the school system along the lines of the Allen Report recommendations than to continue with pairings. The board's own evaluation of the four

---

15. The Commission on Human Rights had played an important mediating role in August and September of 1963, forestalling a boycott for the opening of school. Through the fall, however, the board refused to meet with Commission officials, accusing them of acting merely as another civil rights group and not as a "sister agency." The board turned down suggestions for other mediators.

16. There were, however, some private meetings between Board President James Donovan and the militant opposition. It should be noted, in passing, that the Board President had considerable power and exercised it constantly throughout the period of greatest controversy (fall, 1963 through June, 1965).

pairings, completed a year ago, has not been published at the date of this writing.

It is important to note, in passing, that the board did not maintain a posture of insulation from all civic groups. The UPA and local parent associations had obviously been given access before major decisions were made. So too had other moderate organizations and even, in a few isolated cases, had the oppositionist Parents and Taxpayers. The general pattern was that the more moderate the organization, the more access it had.

A final example of the board's caution was its response to the Allen Report, which contained recommendations for a number of fairly sweeping structural changes to effect more desegregation (e.g., a 4-4-4 grade organization, educational complexes and, eventually, parks, and changes in the building program).[17] Although the board issued a statement as early as June, 1964, seemingly accepting the Allen Report recommendations, it was then silent on the issue until the following March. Even its present grade reorganization and building plans constitute a fragmentary first step. For example, most of the middle schools it plans to build in the next few years have been sited in the segregated areas. There are, of course, many political pressures to make sure that this segregated building pattern will continue.

On hindsight, it is possible to trace the effects of the board's caution, limited leadership, and initiative on the course of the controversy. As the board refused to keep open communications with civil rights groups and refused to move ahead on pairings, it strengthened the support for the most militant civil rights leadership, and it thus helped contribute to the first boycott. At the same time, the board dealt equally cautiously with many white groups as well. In the early months of 1964, for example, before the board had finalized its pairing decisions, rumors, feelers, and leaks through the press were quite common, stirring the already heightened anxieties of white parents in local areas assumed to be possible sites for desegregation plans. Yet these groups could not get any official word on the state of the board's deliberations. A leadership and

17. "Desegregating the Public Schools...," *op. cit.*, pp. 14-34.

information vacuum thus existed, contributing in some degree to the increased organizational strength and militancy of the opposition. As anxious white parents could get little information from school officials on actual plans, opposition leaders were able to exploit the situation and feed on parent concerns in typical demagogic fashion, thus spawning a powerful opposition movement.

As the opposition engaged in demonstrations, protests, and boycotts, this further activated already existent tendencies toward similar public protests and direct action tactics by militant civil rights groups. The two sides soon became polarized. The holding of numerous public hearings further fanned the conflict and polarized the sides as each had more publicly sanctioned opportunities to square off against the other, even as neither was quite sure what the board was going to do.

The process did not stop there, however. As the board's intentions and plans were still not clear, groups within the integrationist "camp" became divided and fragmented. Latent divisions among civil rights groups and between them and "white liberal" groups got magnified. With so little to respond to from the board itself, they filled the vacuum and conducted heated discussions within their own ranks, eventually magnifying their own minor strategy differences. An inevitable stalemate followed.

It would seem reasonable to conclude, then, that the board's style of relating to the community did a lot to exaggerate a conflict and some internal divisions that would have occurred anyway but to nowhere near the degree that they did. This became a classic illustration of a generalization suggested by Williams in his codification of studies and community experiences with school desegregation. As Williams noted:

> An impression of vacillation and indecision on the part of boards of education or of educational administrators, no matter how it may be communicated to the public at large, tends to increase the likelihood of resistance to desegregation (and thereby, the likelihood of conflict).[18]

---

18. Williams, *op. cit.*, p. 51.

As insulated as the board tried to be, its strategies and actions were not formulated in a vacuum. They were conditioned themselves by political forces within the city. One such force, and a third factor, was the weakness of the integrationist coalition. The main groups within this camp — civil rights organizations, both national and local (NAACP, Urban League, CORE, City-Wide Committee for Integrated Schools, Parents' Workshop for Equality, Harlem Parents, EQUAL, Conference for Quality Integrated Education, and various ad hoc groups); Puerto Rican organizations (Commonwealth of Puerto Rico, Puerto Rican Forum, Puerto Rican Committee on Civil Rights); "white liberal" groups (American Jewish Congress, American Jewish Committee, ADL, Protestant Council, ADA, Catholic Inter-Racial Council, Reform Democrat groups, ACLU, Liberal party, a few unions); a scattering of city and school officials; some activist academicians; and some militant local parent associations in ghetto areas, other than those above. These groups have rarely been solidly united on any school desegregation issue for any extended time in New York City. Divergent loyalties, status affiliations, leadership clashes, organizational imperatives, and constituent pressures have quite consistently prevented much united action except in periods of extreme crisis or extreme clarity as to the board's intentions and actions.[19] Though not necessarily planned that way, it was to the board's advantage to maintain a degree of uncertainty and confusion as to its intentions and policies.

The civil rights movement has been split between militant, locally based groups (Rev. Galamison's Parents' Workshop, Harlem Parents, EQUAL, local CORE and NAACP chapters) and established national organizations (especially NAACP and Urban

---

19. Some cases in point for this generalization are the following: Integrationist groups became much more united in the summer and fall of 1963, after Commissioner Allen made a request that all local school boards throughout the state report to him on the extent of "racial balance" in their districts and what they planned to do to increase it; they reunited again in May, 1964, after the Allen Report was issued. They divided when the board hesitated and delayed in implementing open enrollment, pairings, and the Allen Report.

League). The divisions were not so much over goals or even, in many instances, over appropriate strategy but rather they were reflections of leadership struggles, organizational priorities, and limited funds. One important structural condition that helped contribute to the split, for example, was the fact that New York is the headquarters city for all national civil rights organizations. Their boards and large donors are frequently from the "white liberal" New York City community. They stress the need for legal and negotiating strategies and for emphasizing other goals (e.g., attacking discrimination in housing and employment and voter registration drives). This has resulted in national civil rights organization's taking a more moderate stand on school desegregation in New York City than many local groups.

Civil rights groups, in turn, have been divided time and again from "white liberal" organizations that have participated only in the most limited way in protest actions and have had considerable difficulty mobilizing much support from their ranks for nonvoluntary desegregation plans. The best examples of this were the decline of two coalitions of Negro and white organizations that attempted to bridge the differences. One such coalition, the Inter-Group Committee, was formed in the early 1950s and composed of over forty city-wide and local organizations. It dissolved in 1959, partly as a result of many leadership struggles. The other was the Conference for Quality Integrated Education, formed in March, 1964, for the purpose of maintaining unity between Negro and white organizations and to give support to the civil rights movement from the white community. It too dissolved after little more than a year of operation.

The board capitalized on and attempted to exploit such differences. Overtures were made to national civil rights leaders in the hopes of getting them to go along with a board plan, so that they could be (and were) quoted to militant local leaders. The same kinds of overtures were made to leaders in white organizations. They were generally, though not always, rebuffed. Though not necessarily done for conventional "conspiratorial" reasons, they sometimes had the same effect, namely dividing the coalition. The board understandably felt it had to use some "strategies of defense" during the period of most intense civil rights pressure, and this was one of them.[20]

Another source of political ineffectiveness for civil rights and white integrationist groups was that they, unlike the opposition, had the most limited mass base. For example, Parents and Taxpayers were able to build a grass roots support on already existing home-owners, taxpayers, neighborhood improvement groups, but civil rights organizations had to deal with a more atomized local population. And they did not have the resources and perhaps the foresight to build grass roots support for their point of view. National civil rights organizations that had most of the money are quite limited in their funds, relative to the national problems they address themselves to. And as I mentioned above, pressures from within prevented them from committing more of their scarce resources to this problem.

One of the results of limited grass roots mobilization was that Negro parents from ghetto areas expressed themselves at times in public hearings as favoring an up-grading of schools and replacements in their local areas, rather than to have their children transferred out. A tightly knit family structure within the Puerto Rican population, accompanied by a similar failure of grass roots mobilization, led to an unwillingness to have their children travel. White parents, even those of a more liberal cast, had grave apprehensions about the effects of desegregation on quality. White liberal organizations had great difficulties in gaining acceptance for desegregation plans from their local chapters and constituents.

Integrationist leaders and activists were in actuality just a handful of people conducting a "liberal monologue" with one another. They were truly "leaders without followers." The board began to sense this and guided its actions accordingly. It should also be said that the board exercised little effort to educate and persuade the community in the benefits of desegregation. Its

---

20. Interviews with several civil rights leaders confirmed this. There are some parallels between the board's strategies of relating to civil rights groups and those of many business-men to rival labor organizations in the early organizing stages of the labor movement. The strategy of quoting and playing off key leaders against one another was similar to the "whip-sawing" tactics of business in labor management controversies.

public relations, and community relations programs were quite limited, despite the recommendations of many commissions and civic groups that it do more in this field.[21]

Even though the opposition was well mobilized and integrationist groups only partially and sporadically so, there might well have been more movement, given New York City's progressive traditions, had the city's powerful "moderate" organizations provided some pressure and support for the board's desegregation efforts. But moderate organizations, holding the balance of power on the issue, did little to forward the school desegregation cause. The most important of these organizations were: (1) the United Parents Association (UPA), representing as many as 430 local parent and parent teacher associations and 440,000 mothers and fathers throughout the city; (2) the Public Education Association (PEA), representing through its Board and Coordinating Committee some of the most influential professional and civic groups in the city (Citizens' Budget Commission, Men's and Women's City Clubs, NYC Bar Association, Citizen's Union, League for Industrial Democracy, NY State Congress of Parents and Teachers); and (3) the Citizens' Committee for Children (CCC), an organization of professional and lay experts in various fields of child care and development with close ties both to Mayor Wagner and his administration and to civil rights and "liberal" organizations (among them: Reform Democrats, labor movement, The New York Post).

Such professional and civic organizations with a social reformist,

---

21. A few illustrations are the sabotage on open enrollment by principals and limited publicity it got, and the board's handling of school officials and parents in areas to be paired. On the latter, it was the consensus of virtually all the teachers, principals, and district superintendents interviewed in the board's evaluation study that their schools and communities had not been adequately prepared. The board only came out with its decision on pairings in May, 1964. There was little time for staff preparation. A "critical incident" illustrating the board's limited community relations efforts took place a week before the opening of school. One civil rights leader suggested that the board hold some intervisitations of parents and pupils in schools to be paired and have an open school week. The board responded favorably. One cannot help but wonder why they didn't have the idea themselves.

"Good Government" outlook have gradually come to the position that while desegregation may be important, it entails more costs than benefits if pursued on any scale or too rapidly. They see a decline in quality and a further intensification of white parent opposition and withdrawal from the school system as inevitable results of rapid, city-wide desegregation. Their position is that other goals (quality, increased funds, teacher training, neighborhood school centers, administrative reorganization) should have priority. They favor compensatory programs for ghetto schools (Operation Head Start, More Effective Schools, Special Service Schools, All Day Neighborhood Schools) as the strategy to follow. And they represent some of the same real estate, education, and local parent interests as does the opposition, though they express their views in a more reasoned and respectable way. Perhaps more to the point, they have the "ear" of city officials.

All moderate organizations, but especially UPA and PEA, reflect a pattern of middle-class control of the New York City school system. They have privileged access to the board and high level city officials of a kind that has generally been denied to civil rights and integrationist organizations.[22] Both PEA and UPA have become highly politicized organizations and have built up their private access to top board officials through years of experience. Both were called on in a "consultative" capacity before public hearings and before the board decided on its final desegregation plans. Through informal relations with key board officials they shared in such decision-making. And their views of desegregation were, of course, part of the public record.

They essentially "straddled" and related obliquely to the issue by emphasizing diversionary matters. They would never discuss the merits of the board's particular plans, e.g., pairings or educational parks as desegregation techniques for New York City. In-

---

22. Corroborated in interviews with many school officials and civic leaders and from observation. For a detailed study of PEA, documenting some of these points, see Sol Cohen, *Progressive and Urban Social Reform*, Bureau of Publications, Teachers College, Columbia University, 1964. As Cohen notes: "The PEA enjoyed privileged access to school officials. And as Truman observes, once a political interest group has established access, it will exert tremendous efforts to retain the structural arrangements that have given it advantage."

stead, UPA issued a statement that it was against "mandatory, long-distance busing," and PEA officials would debate with civil rights leaders on the same issue. Long-distance busing was not the issue, however, either in the board's actual or projected plans. UPA's general response was to emphasize an orderly implementation of the board's desegregation plans and to maintain quality in desegregating schools. They never came out as an organization for or against any particular plans. Privately, however, they functioned effectively to water down and curtail any grandiose plans the board might have had in mind.[23]

It was easy for PEA and UPA to denounce public protests by civil rights or opposition groups since they had informal access on a daily basis in key headquarters decisions. While it all sounds much like a "conspiracy" interpretation of New York City public education, this was the way it worked out. To speak of a pattern of middle-class control of the New York City school system, as up to 50 percent of its pupils are from low-income Negro and Puerto Rican families, is quite accurate. The reasons for such control relate to the tremendous inequalities in political resources of moderate groups as compared with civil rights organizations. Most integrationist organizations, including civil rights groups, are multipurpose organizations, with many commitments and priorities other than school desegregation. Their education staff covering New York City are either volunteers or working on the problem in New York City on a part-time basis.

In sharp contrast to that pattern, UPA and PEA are primarily concerned with public education in New York City. Both are affluent enough to have full-time staff professionals who spend their entire working time on these issues. And both have been involved in "watch dog" activities in the public education field since the turn of the century. Their professional staff are experienced in dealing with the board; they know much about the system's operation and are especially cognizant of the many strategies that board officials

---

23. The moderates were an important source of citizen support and money-raising activities for the board. Board officials needed the moderates' support to maintain some stability and both sides knew it. Had the board moved further to the left, supporting civil rights demands more than it did, it feared a withdrawal of the moderates' support.

use when confronted with citizen groups like themselves, making demands on the system for more services. In sum, they have money, personnel, experience, grass roots support, powerful city organizations' support, and many informal relationships with board and city officials. It is no wonder, then, that they are much more powerful than civil rights organizations.

But why have they been so opposed to much desegregation? Part of the explanation lies in their ties to local parent groups and "establishment" organizations that exert pressures for moderate or *status quo* positions. And much of it lies in the fact that they have as organizations become a part of the decision-making and policy-making apparatus of the board of education and have a vested interest in its preservation. The changes the Allen Report recommends threaten that interest.

The Structure and Operating Codes of the Board

If these forces alone did not serve to stack the cards against change, there were two others that just about closed out any prospects. One pertained to organizational characteristics and codes within the school system over and above commitments to the neighborhood school doctrine. The other related to the articulation and dovetailing of decisions and projects of other city agencies with those of the board.

The most relevant characteristics and codes of the board of education that prevented much implementation of desegregation plans were the following: an overcentralized, authoritarian structure, accompanied by many levels in its administrative hierarchy and a principle of "bureaucratic" rather than "collegial" (professional) authority; consequent feelings of distrust and alienation of field personnel toward headquarters and traditions of noncompliance with headquarters directives, leading, in turn, to a wide and continuing gap between "advanced" policy statements and their implementation; much specialization on multiple and sometimes contradictory bases, accompanied by a fragmentation of units and informal "power blocs" at headquarters, seriously limiting pros-

178

pects for developing a strong enough coalition for innovation (as groups could veto one another's ideas); poor communications between headquarters and the field and across divisions and other units, leading to a minimum of dovetailing and coordination of functions and inefficient implementation of new ideas; an examination system that has led to an inordinate amount of "in-breeding" and to the promotion to high headquarters posts of some people with a minimum of daring and innovativeness; insulation of professional (headquarters and field) staff from lay review and controls, reflected and rationalized by a "technocratic" mythology that education should be kept separate from "politics," and reflected further in continuing conflicts between the board and superintendent about appropriate spheres of authority; and an almost complete absence of long-range planning.[24]

In sum, the combination of an unwieldy bureaucracy and of particular personalities and personality clashes (e.g., Superintendent Gross and Board President Donovan) was another important factor preventing much desegregation. It is important to note, however, that this was a bureaucracy that had long resisted innovation. Powerful, "inbred," professional groups (principals' associations, district superintendents, divisional heads) had delayed, watered down, or sabotaged innovation for decades. School desegregation was just the latest of a long series of changes they had resisted.

New York City Government

If power and resources for change could not be mobilized from the populace or from within the school system, one of the only other sources was the mayor and city government. But the fragmentation and pluralism of interest groups in the community and at the board were paralleled by similar patterns in the political structure of the

---

24. Space does not permit elaboration of these many points. Many were documented as long ago as 1951 in a study directed by George D. Strayer and Louis E. Yavner, *Administrative Management of the School System of New York City*, Mayor's Committee on Management Survey, (2 vol.). There have been many similar reports since then. All these points are elaborated upon with many "critical incidents" in my forthcoming book. See also the article by Dr. Marilyn Gittell in this volume.

city. The proliferation in numbers and expansion in size of city agencies with few mechanisms for interagency coordination has resulted in drift, a web of bureaucratic entanglements, and a stifling of city-wide educational planning and innovation. On the school desegregation issue, the board of education's options were seriously limited by urban renewal programs, the spread of low-income housing projects, and the use of desirable sites for industrial rather than educational parks.

The board and numerous citizen groups have recommended many times over the creation of a superordinate body to coordinate school, housing, urban renewal, poverty, and mass transit projects to create a more integrated, open city. This has never come about. Traditions of agency autonomy, a preference of city officials for a perpetuation of the informal bargaining that characterizes inter-agency transactions, and especially the refusal of the mayor to promote it led to inaction. His role in school desegregation controversies, in turn, was very consistently one of withdrawing as much as possible from any direct or indirect participation.

Federal Aid to Inner Cities

On a more general note, one important precondition affected the playing out of this controversy and shaped its parameters. That precondition was scarcity. The school desegregation controversy in New York, as in every other Northern city, involves a direct confrontation of civil rights groups going through a period of "rising expectations" with white populations possessed of a "scarcity psychology" in municipalities facing a diminishing fiscal base and crying out for more funds. Ultimately, the balance between the nation's international and domestic commitments, especially its economic programs for the cities, may well shape the forms this controversy is likely to take in the future. Experience from New York City and elsewhere suggests that when desegregation is accompanied by increases in staff, services, and facilities there is less opposition from the white community and less fear that desegregated schools will suffer from a decline in quality of education. The Federal government is obviously the major source of funds for such additional services. Such funds would be better used, however, if there were more coordination of city agencies and more provision for city and perhaps metropolitan area-wide educational planning.

Some Implications

But what implications does the New York City experience have for interpreting that of other cities? Much of the New York City experience has a familiar ring. A "mix" of conditions, some demographic, some structural, and some behavioral (strategies followed by various key parties) are related to the limited desegregation of schools there. One proposition indicated by my study is that the more the pluralism and fragmentation of interest groups and governmental agencies in a city, the more likely it is to become polarized and then stalemated on such a highly contested issue. One reason is that fragmentation and pluralism frequently result in caution and at times vacillation (weak leadership) from school and city officials, caught as they are in a cross-pressure situation.

Actually, the relation between fragmentation and weak leadership is a reciprocal one. Each reinforces the other. As city officials fail to put forth clear and unambiguous plans for change and press firmly for their implementation, the opposition becomes more mobilized, change-oriented groups become more polarized from them, they become divided from within between "moderates" and "revolutionaries," confusion mounts, and a divided community becomes even more so. This process contributed directly to New York City's stalemate on school desegregation.

Other propositions, relating characteristics of the school system, city government, the civil rights movement, and the moderates to the extent of innovation in this field, are also suggested from my study. On the board of education, for example, its high degree of bureaucratization, especially its militaristic structure, had militated against all kinds of innovations (decentralization, elimination of many headquarters units and of layers in the administrative hierarchy) before desegregation became such a contested issue. Its

181

insulation from lay review and controls, as indicated by the continued weakness and lack of influence of the city board and local boards, and by a perpetuation of the power of entrenched, "inbred" interests within the system, worked in the same direction.

The board's relations with the mayor and various city agencies also prevented any implementation of innovations to up-grade quality and foster desegregation. The diffusion of authority and responsibility for major board decisions across so many city agencies (e.g., on school construction and its capital budget) had led to interminable delays and an exercise of so many particularistic, local pressures that there was little opportunity for meaningful planning on a city-wide or at least borough-wide basis. In addition, the unwillingness of the board and other city agencies to join together to coordinate their projects, even as education, housing, poverty, transit, industrial development, and urban renewal decisions were all so interrelated, had also contributed to an absence of meaningful innovation.

The mayor obviously has a key role to play in all these matters — in encouraging and mandating administrative reorganization and planning both within the board of education and in city government. Though there are many political "costs" in his becoming involved in such activities, perhaps the alternative "hands off" policy that New York City mayors have followed in the past is no longer in order, given the increased citizen demands for an expansion and more equitable distribution of vital city services. An infusion of more state and Federal funds without major efforts at consolidation and planning may only solidify traditional (fragmented and pluralistic) structures and magnify the city's many problems.

A change in strategy, alliances, and outlook among civil rights and moderate groups would further contribute to some needed innovations. The civil rights movement has allowed its internal divisions to get exploited by the board and other high-level city officials. It has also followed a kind of "conflict strategy" in pressing for racial balance in the city's public schools without pointing up how desegregation could and did relate to other goals (quality, economies) that potential opposition groups thought were closer to their interests. Though pressure for school desegregation through some form of "consensus politics" — and that does not dilute in any way the goals of the civil rights movement — civil rights groups may not activate to the same degree the anxieties and opposition of many white populations. In other words, civil rights groups could be a much more effective change agent than they have been.

Finally, the most powerful civic groups of all, various moderate organizations, may hold the key to any prospects for desegregation. Given their present outlook and commitments to maintain the *status quo* in which they have such a vital interest, any increase in support from them for desegregation on a much broader scale seems unlikely.

Perhaps the most significant levers to social change, though, lie in the intervention of outside parties who have not played as big a role as they might. There are three such parties — the mayor, the State Education Department, and the Federal government. It seems quite clear from the history of the school desegregation struggle in New York City that there will not be too much movement on the issue without the strong and direct intervention of these parties. All have been subject in the past to political and economic constraints that have limited their participation. The mayor faced a highly organized voting bloc of irate white populations. The State Education Commissioner faced pressures from a coalition of upstate legislators and big city "neighborhood school" advocates as well as from other agencies of state government. And the Federal government has not had the legal powers or the fiscal role (Federal funds had only constituted a small part of the board of education's moneys) to exert much pressure. Unless these parties are able to shake loose from such traditional constraints and intervene more directly in this controversy there may be no desegregation.

Perhaps the key theme of all, running through my discussion of social forces that have prevented desegregation in New York City, is that of pluralism and fragmentation. This relates directly to the role that outside parties can play in fostering change. The mayor can press for consolidation of city government, to effect more city-wide educational planning. The State Education Commissioner can press for similar changes within the board of education. And the Federal government can give or withhold funds, depending on how much coordination and planning actually takes place. Such structural changes within the board and in city government can help to eliminate the chaos that so frequently accompanies the implementation of even the most limited desegregation plans. It can also help create some unity in a change-oriented coalition of city and board officials and integrationist groups, thereby diluting the power and effectiveness of the moderates and opposition.[25]

The argument will be made, of course, that the demographic changes of New York City, like those of most other large Northern cities, are so inexorable that no such intervention will help effect more desegregation. And some will argue that it may even hasten the withdrawal of whites from the city and the school system. Perhaps it has to be tried and fairly soon, however, to test the validity of these assertions. The continued deterioration in quality and hardening of lines of segregation in New York and all other large Northern cities indicate that the long-term benefits of such intervention will probably far outweigh any temporary, short-run costs.

---

25. These propositions parallel those of Amos Hawley in his studies of community power structures and urban renewal success. Hawley found a direct correlation between the extent of concentration of power in cities and the extent of innovation in urban renewal. See Amos Hawley, "Community Power and Urban Renewal Success," *American Journal of Sociology* (January, 1963), pp. 422-433. On the unwillingness of big city mayors caught in cross-pressure situations to take risks in supporting controversial proposals for change, see Edward C. Banfield and James Q. Wilson, *City Politics*, Cambridge, Mass.: Harvard University Press and M.I.T. Press, 1963, pp. 121-125.

ALAN ROSENTHAL

Alan Rosenthal is currently at The
Eagleton Institute of Politics, Rutgers
—The State University. This article
was written while the author was at
Hunter College of the City Univer-
sity of New York.

PEDAGOGUES AND

POWER: A Descriptive

Survey

OR SOME YEARS NOW conflict between school employees
and school managers has been on the rise. Not long
ago, for example, the president of the National Education Association
(NEA), in an address to public education's foremost establishment,
spoke forcefully about the right of teachers to participate in the
formulation of public school policy. In laying it on the line to the
nation's school administrators, he disclaimed any intention by
teachers to seize control but was unequivocal in demanding for
his classroom colleagues full partnership in the educational enterprise.[1] Words and action both signify a new militancy which characterizes teachers as they are organized today. Unlike the docile
pedagogues of the past, the current armies manning the battlements
of elementary and secondary education are in "a state of ferment

AUTHOR'S NOTE: This aspect of general research on the roles of teacher
organizations is part of a study of large city educational systems being
conducted by the Metropolitan Studies Program of Syracuse University.
The entire program is supported by a generous grant from the Carnegie
Corporation. My own efforts have been further assisted by a New York
State Legislative grant and the cooperation of the Urban Research Center
of Hunter College of the City University of New York.

1. Richard D. Batchelder, speaking before the 98th annual meeting of the American
Association of School Administrators, Atlantic City, N.J., February 15, 1966 (NEA
press release).

bordering on rebellion." [2] One spokesman for the militant American Federation of Teachers (AFT), and president of the United Federation of Teachers (UFT) in New York City, has commented on the new movement in the following way:

> Teachers are demanding more and more decision making power. Power is never given to anyone. Power is taken, and it is taken from someone. Teachers, as one of society's powerless groups, are now starting to take power from supervisors and school boards. This is causing and will continue to cause a realignment of power relationships.[3]

This argument, as well as those made by numerous others, maintains in essence that (1) educational power now is held largely by school boards and administrations, with teachers powerless by comparison, and (2) teachers are now demanding more power, primarily in order to achieve a significant voice in the processes of educational decision-making.

To explore the bases of these contentions, this paper will examine the views of leaders of teacher organizations in five large cities. These cities, which have seen varying degrees of teacher militancy and conflict, are New York, Boston, Chicago, San Francisco, and Atlanta. Four of the teacher groups whose leadership views have been surveyed are affiliated with AFT: New York's United Federation of Teachers (UFT), the Boston Teachers Union (BTU), the Chicago Teachers Union (CTU), and the San Francisco Federation of Teachers (SFFT). Three others are tied to NEA: the Chicago Education Association (CEA), the San Francisco Classroom Teachers Association (SFCTA), and the Atlanta Teachers Association (ATA).[4] Two have no national affiliation: the Boston Teachers Alliance (BTA) and the Teachers Association of San Francisco (TASF). In late 1965 and early 1966, questionnaires were mailed to members of the executive boards of these

2. These words are quoted from Allan M. West, Assistant Executive Secretary for Field Operations and Urban Services, NEA, "What's Bugging Teachers," *Saturday Review* (October 16, 1965), 88.

3. Albert Shanker, "Teacher-Supervisory Relationships: A Symposium," *Changing Education*, I (Spring, 1966), 23.

4. The cooperation of one teacher organization in Atlanta could not be obtained.

nine groups.[5] Completed questionnaires have been received from
185 of the 270 board members (a response rate of 68.5 percent),
and these individuals constitute our leadership sample for the
present analysis.[6] On the basis of responses to structured items in
the survey instrument, we intend to describe and compare leadership perceptions of power and attitudes concerning power with
regard to several domains of educational policy-making. Underlying this design was a suspicion that perceptions and attitudes
would differ considerably, depending upon whether the relevant
policy domain was general or, more specifically, salary, personnel,
curriculum and instruction, or the organization of the school system.[7] At a later time, we plan to complement survey data with
information obtained from interviews, link leadership attitudes to
organizational behavior, and explore the correlates and effects of
teacher militancy. At the moment, however, our aims are simply
to describe educational power as teacher leaders perceive it and
profile the strategies and objectives of different organizations in
several large cities.

The Distribution of Power

Until recently, few observers of the educational scene thought
very much of, or even thought at all about, the potency of teachers
or their organizations. Hardly any would have described them as
very effectual in the grand affairs of educational decision-making.
A decade ago, one expert characterized their influence rather

---

5. Mailings also went to the professional executive secretaries or directors of several
nonunion groups, whose views are included here. These people, like the full-time
presidents or business managers of unions, have major influence within their own
organizations.

6. By organization, the response was as follows: UFT, 39 of 47 (83%); BTU, 28
of 40 (70%); BTA, 8 of 17 (47%); CTU, 18 of 40 (45%); CEA, 19 of 32 (59%);
SFFT, 24 of 33 (73%); SFCTA, 22 of 26 (85%); TASF, 7 of 8 (88%); and ATA,
20 of 27 (74%).

7. In emphasizing specialization, our treatment of the educational arena is patterned
after recent investigations which have shown power to be differentially exercised in a
community according to the type of issue being decided. See, for instance, the following:
Edward C. Banfield, *Political Influence*, New York: Free Press of Glencoe, 1961; Robert
A. Dahl, *Who Governs?*, New Haven: Yale University Press, 1961; Roscoe C. Martin,
et al., *Decisions in Syracuse*, Bloomington, Ind.: University of Indiana Press, 1961; and
Wallace S. Sayre and Herbert Kaufman, *Governing New York City*, New York: Russell
Sage Foundation, 1960.

briefly: "Teachers as a group," he wrote, "have little or no say in the formulation of school policy." [8] This may be something of an exaggeration, but it must be admitted that the collective impact of teacher organizations on matters other than salaries and related benefits had been slight indeed. Due largely to the militant assertiveness of teachers today, we might reasonably expect power to have shifted in their favor. Doubtless, teachers, particularly those in urban areas, exercise greater influence now than previously. But just how much this is when compared to that of other major participants in educational policy-making remains to be seen.

Our initial task is to describe how the leaders of teacher organizations perceive the distribution of power in their city school systems. While we are well aware of the conceptual and measurement difficulties which challenge students of "power," [9] it is nevertheless striking that when leaders comment casually on the power of various participants, they seem to be speaking the same language. Terms like "power," "influence," "control," "voice," and "say" all have wide currency and meaningful elements in common. For present purposes, they are presumed to be roughly equivalent and relate to educational choices or decisions. Items in the leadership questionnaire solicited assessments of whether potentially influential participants, such as the mayor and municipal officials, the board of education, the superintendent, the bureaucratic chiefs at headquarters, school principals, and teacher organizations had "much," "some," or "little" power in deciding various kinds of educational policy. Responses relating the relative power of core participants were then aggregated for each city and each policy domain by means of a simple index. [10] These aggregates serve as a basis for the following discussion.

8. Daniel Griffiths, *Human Relations in School Administration*, New York: Appleton-Century-Crofts, Inc., 1956, p. 106.

9. See especially the summary analysis of conceptual approaches and measurement procedures by James G. March, "The Power of Power", in David Easton (Ed.), *Varieties of Political Theory*, Englewood Cliffs, N.J.: Prentice-Hall, Inc., 1966, pp. 39-70.

10. The "power assessment" index, which we have employed, is the average of core participants in each city. Responses were scored so that designations of "much" power received a rating of 2, "some" received 1, and "little" received 0. Scores given each

Before proceeding, several caveats should be mentioned. Both as a result of earlier scrutiny of public school politics and in order to maximize the number of respondents, we decided to limit evaluation only to those who might usefully be considered core participants in educational policy-making.[11] Except for the mayor, whose role is of special interest, all the others are either legally or professionally involved in the local government of public education. Notably absent are community groups ("satellite contestants," to use the terminology of Sayre and Kaufman), such as business and labor organizations, civic and neighborhood associations, and civil rights groups, as well as presumably influential agencies of the nation and states located beyond local municipal boundaries. A more important limitation applies to reputational analysis, on which our classifications are based.[12] Procedures used in this investigation resemble those used in many "community power" studies, all of which involved some variation of asking individuals to assess the relative power of other individuals. But here, of course, reputation hinges solely on the perceptions of teacher leaders. Power distributions seen by teachers may differ from those seen by others in the same city, and either one or several sets of perceptions may be well out of line with reality. Therefore, although subsequent discussion rests mainly on teacher leadership evaluations of policy-making power, some attention will also be paid to corroborative evidence furnished by other participants and observers.[13] With

---

participant by individual teacher leaders were cumulated and averaged. It should be noted that middle-range scores can reflect one of two response patterns: (1) consensus that the participant has "some" power or (2) a division of leader opinion between "much" and "little," averaging out to "some" power. Because of space limitations, index scores are not reported here. They are summarized in Table 1.

11. The concept of "core" participants is adapted from Sayre and Kaufman, *op. cit.*

12. A few good examples of the literature on reputational analysis are William V. D'Antonio and Eugene C. Erickson, "The Reputational Technique as a Measure of Community Power," *American Sociological Review*, XXVII (June, 1962), pp. 362-376; Nelson W. Polsby, *Community Power and Political Theory*, New Haven: Yale University Press, 1963; Robert Presthus, *Men at the Top*, Fair Lawn, N.J.: Oxford University Press, 1964; and Raymond E. Wolfinger, "Reputation and Reality in the Study of 'Community Power,'" *American Sociological Review*, XXV (October, 1960), pp. 636-644.

13. The assessments of five research associates, who participated in the Syracuse study, have been used to check teacher views. Each associate spent about two years investigating the educational system of one of the cities. Generally, their evaluations agree with those of teacher leaders.

these qualifications in mind, an overall portrayal of patterns in the distribution of educational power can at least be suggestive. Table 1 summarizes index scores by presenting the rank order of various participants and categorizing their power as "high," "medium," or "low." This tabular presentation should serve as a convenient tool for following the analysis of how power is distributed in five cities and several policy domains.

American educators have inveighed loudly and campaigned strenuously against political interference in the management of local public education. In so far as these five cities evidence tendencies by municipal officials to intervene, the fears of educators appear to be highly exaggerated. Except in Atlanta, teachers attribute some power to their city's mayor over educational policy in general. This apparently reflects the mayor's potentially critical role in fiscal matters, particularly in the determination of teacher salaries.[14] In New York City and Boston, for instance, the chief municipal official is considered to be the principal architect of salary policy. But in Chicago and San Francisco, his influence is thought to be considerably less than that of school boards and superintendents. And in Atlanta, according to teacher leaders there, it is quite negligible. Even on matters pertaining to the organization of the school system, where we might imagine municipal intervention in response to a persistent array of community pressures, mayors in all five cities allegedly have little power. As one moves into even more esoteric matters of policy, such as personnel or curriculum or instruction, these political officials play an extremely small part. In the area of personnel, for example, only 14 of 179 organization leaders responding to the particular item characterized the power of the mayor as "much." And in the area of curriculum, only 1 of 177 described his power similarly. In sharp contrast, half of the leadership sample felt the mayor had considerable influence in the determination of teacher salaries.

These perceptions accord with some rather obvious behavioral evidence, a few examples of which follow. In New York, former mayor Robert Wagner's characteristic strategy had been to avoid

---

14. It may also indicate the mayor's role in other areas, such as school construction, about which we lack comparable information.

TABLE 1

The Distribution of Power:
Rank Orders and Power Categories*

Policy Domain and Participant	New York RO	New York CY	Boston RO	Boston CY	Chicago RO	Chicago CY	San Francisco RO	San Francisco CY	Atlanta RO	Atlanta CY
Policy in General										
Superintendent	1	H	2	M	1	H	1.5	H	1	H
Board of Education	2	H	1	H	2	M	1.5	H	2	H
HQ's Bureaucracy	3	M	3	M	3	M	3	M	3	M
Mayor and Officials	4	M	4	M	4	M	4	M	6	L
School Principals	5	L	5	L	6	L	5	L	4.5	L
Teacher Organizations	6	L	6	L	5	L	6	L	4.5	L
Salary Policy										
Superintendent	4	M	3	M	1	H	2	M	1	H
Board of Education	3	M	2	H	2	M	1	H	2	H
HQ's Bureaucracy	5	L	4	M	4	L	5	L	4	M
Mayor and Officials	1	H	1	H	3	M	3	L	6	L
School Principals	6	L	6	L	6	L	6	L	5	L
Teacher Organizations	2	M	5	M	5	L	4	L	3	M
School Organization										
Superintendent	1	H	2	H	1	H	1	H	1	H
Board of Education	2	H	1	H	2	M	2	H	2	H
HQ's Bureaucracy	3	M	3	M	3	M	3	M	3	M
Mayor and Officials	4	L	4.5	L	4	L	5	L	6	L
School Principals	5.5	L	4.5	L	5	L	4	L	4	L
Teacher Organizations	5.5	L	6	L	6	L	6	L	5	L
Personnel Policy										
Superintendent	1	H	1	H	1	H	1	H	1	H
Board of Education	2.5	M	2	H	3	M	2.5	M	2	M
HQ's Bureaucracy	2.5	M	3	H	2	M	2.5	M	3	M
Mayor and Officials	6	L	5.5	L	4.5	L	5	L	6	L
School Principals	5	L	4	L	6	L	4	M	4	L
Teacher Organizations	4	L	5.5	L	4.5	L	6	L	5	L
Curriculum & Instruction										
Superintendent	1.5	H	1	H	1	H	1	H	1	H
Board of Education	3.5	M	3	M	3	M	3	M	3	M
HQ's Bureaucracy	1.5	H	2	H	2	H	2	M	2	M
Mayor and Officials	5	L	6	L	5.5	L	6	L	6	L
School Principals	3.5	M	4	M	4	M	4	M	4	M
Teacher Organizations	6	L	5	L	5.5	L	5	L	5	L

* Column headings RO and CY are abbreviations for rank order and category. Categories are: high (H), medium (M), and low (L), which are based on the "power assessments" of teacher leaders in each city (see footnote 10).

involvement in the sensitive arena of public education. With the notable exception of teacher salaries, affairs in which union tactics had impelled him to intervene and find additional public funds, the mayor succeeded in remaining remarkably aloof.[15] Whether because of personal choice or political necessity, Wagner exercised little control over vast areas of public education. Boston differs only slightly in this respect. Here, too, the mayor controls the school budget, in that if the budget is more than it was the previous year, he must approve the excess. Since salary requests regularly exceed these limits, the mayor in consequence has great authority. But on many other matters, with the possible exceptions of school construction and racial balance, Boston's John Collins has shown no disposition to meddle in the business of the politically strong, elected School Committee. In Chicago, as well, where Richard Daley's political machine has managed effectively to endure so long, public education has truly been independent since the school scandals of the 1940s. Members of the Chicago board are appointed by the mayor, but the board and the school system are basically autonomous, fiscally and in other policy respects.[16] In all five cities, municipal officials show little desire to enter the thickets of education or compete for control with school boards and administrations. Doubtless, they all exert some pressure on school authorities to keep budgets down and within the bounds of political and financial feasibility. But only in New York and Boston and perhaps indirectly in San Francisco[17] do they actually exercise major influence over teacher salaries.

In most of the policy areas, however, the bulk of power, in the view of teacher leaders, is shared by the board, the superintendent, and the upper echelons of the administrative bureaucracy at school headquarters. Generally, as Table 1 indicates, superintendents and boards dominate. The former have more to say than the latter in Chicago, Atlanta, and New York. In San Francisco, they share control about equally. Only in Boston does the lay board seem to

15. Marilyn Gittell reaches the same conclusion in her forthcoming study of educational decision-making in New York City. The reluctant role of ex-Mayor Wagner in school integration is suggested by Bert E. Swanson, *School Integration Controversies in New York City*, Bronxville, N.Y.: Institute for Community Studies, Sarah Lawrence College, 1965.

16. Joseph Pois, *The School Board Crisis*, Chicago: Educational Methods, 1964, p. 64.

17. In San Francisco, teacher salary increases, although determined finally by the board, often resemble rather closely raises given classified personnel by the mayor and municipal officials.

have slightly more influence than its hired professional expert. At the middle levels of power are the various administrative bureaucracies, comparatively stronger in Boston and New York and weaker in the three other cities.

In view of the proclivity of school boards to stress money matters, we might conceive the superintendency to be relatively uninvolved in salary policy. This appears to be so. In Chicago alone the chief administrative officer predominates on salaries, as he evidently does on any other type of issue. Atlanta's board and superintendent share authority on these questions, while in San Francisco the layman, representing community influentials, have the largest voice in making decisions. Boston's School Committee battles the mayor on salaries, and here, too, the superintendent plays a lesser role. In New York, as salary negotiations reach a critical phase, the teachers union deals with the mayor or his mediators, while both the board and its executive have relatively little to say. On other kinds of issues, however, the superintendent is the central figure. In every city, the way the school system is organized depends upon decisions by superintendents and to a slightly lesser degree by boards of education. There is little question among Chicago teachers that on problems of school organization the superintendent has been the kingfish. He apparently has the edge over the board in New York, San Francisco, and Atlanta as well. Personnel policies like recruitment, assignment, and promotion are largely decided by superintendents and administrative chiefs with boards taking a smaller part. On the most esoteric matters, such as curriculum and instruction, power is almost completely monopolized by professional administrators. In New York City, deputy and assistant superintendents at school headquarters share control with the top administrator. In Boston and Chicago, differences between the power of superintendents and bureaucratic leaders are slight. Only in San Francisco and Atlanta does the superintendent have no peer in the higher ranks of the central office bureaucracy on decisions concerning curriculum and instructional policy.

That mayors play a greater role on salary matters and superintendents and administrators dominate in areas of personnel and curriculum might well be expected. Nor should it occasion surprise that power distributions vary from one city to another. On the basis of teacher leader perceptions, as buttressed by the reports of others, we can venture a few generalizations. As far as most important educational issues are concerned power resides at establishments like Livingston Street in New York, Van Ness Street in San Francisco, and Beacon Street in Boston. Professionals tend to control, but a few lay boards take a substantial part in educational policy-making too. Nor does it seem to make much difference to board strength whether members are elected, as in Boston and Atlanta, or appointed, as in New York, Chicago, and San Francisco.

Chicago's superintendent has ruled almost absolutely, with neither board nor administration seriously challenging his reign.[18] Joseph Pois, a former member of the board there, has outspokenly described the dominance of Benjamin Willis. According to Pois, it is due not only to Willis' control of information and his ability to deluge the board with trivial but also to "the reluctance by board members to do anything that might even inadvertently or by implication undermine the general superintendent's leadership." [19] With respect to the superintendent's preeminence, Atlanta closely resembles Chicago. Although power is more dispersed within the higher echelons of school government, Superintendent John Letson ably manages both board and bureaucracy. The relationship between the board and Superintendent Harold Spears in San Francisco strikes an even balance, although here as in Atlanta and Chicago the central office bureaucracy wields less influence. From all indications, Spears' role is the major one, but usually his educational proposals—seldom very radical to begin with—are carefully tailored to suit the predispositions of board members. Comparatively speaking, the strongest public representatives serve on the school committee in Boston. William Ohrenberger, relatively new to the superintendency, has to share power with the committee on policies concerning school organization, with the bureaucracy on curriculum, and with both groups on personnel. New York City's

---

18. It is true, however, that recent pressures from civil rights groups helped to hasten the retirement of the Chicago superintendent.

19. Pois, *op. cit.*, p. 89, also pp. 45-49, 56. For the primacy of Willis in the fields of personnel and curriculum, see Pois, *op. cit.*, pp. 51, 55, 149, 167, 197, 198, 202.

new superintendent, Bernard Donovan, commands a position stronger than that of his Boston counterpart, but it does not appear to compare in strength with the positions of either Willis or Letson. The board responsible for governing the nation's largest school system is probably weaker than most, while chieftains in the huge administrative bureaucracy seem to be somewhat more powerful than administrators elsewhere.[20]

On the peripheries of power, far less weighty than boards, superintendents, and administrators are school principals and teacher organizations. By whatever comparative standards, teachers fare poorly indeed. According to the perceptions of their own leaders, their minimal shares of power are slightly greater in New York and lesser in Chicago than in the other cities. With regard only to salaries are they thought to play a substantial role, and in this area groups like UFT, ATA, and BTU feel at least some potency. On these matters, of course, all nine of the organizations have concentrated their efforts. In New York through collective bargaining, in Boston, Chicago, and San Francisco by means of presentations before administrations and school boards, and in Atlanta through negotiating on a study committee, teacher groups have influenced decisions on salary and related matters.[21] Outside of this arena, however, they appear powerless. Even the United Federation of Teachers, which many New Yorkers regard as a powerful group, allegedly carries little weight when it comes to deciding most policy matters. Perhaps leaders of the New York City union underrate the group's influence. From a less subjective point of view, its successful interventions on aspects of personnel and school organization policies appear to entitle UFT to more political clout than its own leadership might think. In the four other cities, however, there is little discrepancy between what

---

20. Gittell, *op. cit.*, attributes great power to headquarters deputy and assistant superintendents. Her evaluation is based primarily on the administrative bureaucracy's part in budget-making and curriculum. UFT leaders agree on curriculum. Our survey, however, has not treated budgeting separately.

21. As of late 1965, BTU had begun bargaining collectively in Boston and SECTA had started to participate as a member of a negotiating council in San Francisco.

leaders and other observers see as regards the limited influence of teacher organizations except on salaries and personal benefits. In any event, it seems fair to say that among core participants teacher organizations are still some distance removed from the command posts of public education.

The Pursuit of Power

A furious competition now rages between NEA and AFT, each of which seeks to represent the nation's teachers in their struggles to gain material benefits and improve their status. One group advocates professional negotiations, the other calls for collective bargaining. However the two may differ, both vigorously encourage affiliates, and particularly those in cities, to increase their influence in the decision-making processes of public education. In view of pressures from these national bodies as well as the escalating effects of local rivalry, we would expect that teacher leaders are dissatisfied with the low-power estates of their own organizations. This is more or less the situation in the five cities under discussion.

An expansion in the power of teacher organizations can come about in a number of ways. If the influence of other participants remains stable while that of teachers grow, the result would be a net gain for teachers. A similar result would ensue if the influence of all core participants expands, but not as greatly as that of teachers. Alternatively, a decrease in the influence of boards, superintendents, and bureaucracies coordinate with maintenance on the parts of teacher groups would lead to a like outcome. The greatest change would probably occur given a diminution of the power of all other participants and a simultaneous enhancement of the power of teacher organizations. In light of these possibilities, we endeavored to discover how teacher leaders feel about a redistribution of power in the various policy-making domains of each city. Our method resembles the one used previously in assessing the distribution of power. By way of prescription, respondents indicated whether they believed that participants, ranging from the

196

mayor to school principals, should have "more," "the same amount," or "less" power than they presently had.[22]

Leaders in the total sample substantially agree on two points only: Their own groups should have more power, and mayors and municipal officials should have less. The belief pervading professional doctrine and cherished by administrators and teachers alike is that education should be kept entirely separate from politics and that school departments should be completely autonomous of other local agencies. It is predictable, then, that leaders of the nine teacher organizations, subscribing to traditional tenets, want public officials in their cities to have less influence in school affairs. Two-thirds of them, in fact, expressed the view that mayors should have less to say about educational policy in general, while only one-third wanted to leave the meager power of municipal officials intact. Similar proportions concurred in advocating the reduction of mayoral influence in the particular policy domains of salary, personnel, curriculum and instruction, and school organization. Nor does it matter in most cases whether the mayor was perceived to have had power in the first place. In Atlanta, where his influence was thought to be minimal, members of the ATA executive board overwhelmingly desired that it be reduced further. Where his influence was apparently greatest, leadership opinion was divided. Boston leaders almost unanimously favored a shift in fiscal authority from the mayor to the school committee. On the other hand, UFT leaders, who in the past had benefited from intervention by City Hall, generally agreed that no change in the mayor's role was necessary.

As we mentioned earlier, the loci of educational power are the central offices of the school departments. Depending upon the type of issue and the particular city, school boards, superintendents, and administrative chiefs share in fashioning educational policies. Should these dominants have more or less to say on various kinds of matters? There is little consistency in the patterns of response revealed by the leadership sample. Certainly no overall desire on

---

22. A "power prescription" index was constructed, with scores of 1, 0 and —1 assigned for each "more," "same amount," and "less" response. Although scores are not reported in this paper, they provide a basis for part of the ensuing discussion.

the parts of teacher organizations to curb the powers of the powerful emerges from these data. Nor is there a correlation, either positive or negative, between the ways in which leaders would allocate power among dominants and the manner in which they think it is presently distributed. In Atlanta, executive board members are pretty well content with the current allocation. In Boston, leaders of both groups tend to favor a somewhat greater authority for the committee, superintendent, and bureaucracy. The discernible difference here is that the union would prefer the school committee and the independent association would prefer the superintendent to have more of a voice in salary determination. Despite the obvious predominance of Chicago's superintendent, leaders in this city show little disposition to restrict his powers. The AFT affiliate, however, would strengthen the board, while the NEA local would strengthen the bureaucracy. Of the three teacher organizations in San Francisco, two of them, one linked to NEA and the other independent, evidence no dissatisfaction with the present distribution of power at the central office.

Seven teacher groups, therefore, would likely shun a strategy designed to reduce the policy-making prerogatives of either board, superintendent, or administrative bureaucracy. Apparently, they make little linkage between their own power and that of key participants. The two remaining organizations, however, take a more militant posture, presumably relating their own aspirations to the overwhelming influence of the educational establishment. Leaders of UFT and SFFT prescribe lesser amounts of power for all other core participants. Perhaps because it has not yet achieved comparable status, the San Francisco union takes an even firmer stance than UFT. In all four policy areas, SFFT's executive board splits, with about half the members advocating less, another half the same amount, and scarcely any favoring more power for the board or administration. The prescriptive views of UFT executive board members vary to a somewhat greater extent. Leaders of this entrenched organization seem least unhappy about the superintendency and most discontent with influence exercised by deputy and assistant superintendents at school headquarters.

On one element of prescription, there is naturally a high degree of consensus. Hardly a leadership respondent believes that the power of his own organization should be diminished. Yet the cohesiveness of leaders, in terms of their commitments to pursuing power, does vary from one organization to another. As Table 2 clearly shows, teacher groups differ substantially, ranging from those where leaders are unanimous or nearly unanimous in desiring greater power to those where about half are satisfied with the current status of their organization. If we exclude the two independent

TABLE 2

The Pursuit of Power:

Percentages of Leaders Desiring More Power for Their Own Organizations

POLICY DOMAIN

CITY	ORGANI-ZATION*	Policy in General	Salary Policy	School Organization	Personnel Policy	Curriculum and Instruction
New York	UFT	97	77	92	92	92
Boston	BTU	82	93	79	89	82
	BTA	88	100	75	88	88
Chicago	CTU	65	83	67	78	61
	CEA	50	72	39	61	50
San Francisco	SFFT	100	91	88	100	96
	SFCTA	55	59	64	64	68
	TASF	86	86	71	86	86
Atlanta	ATA	45	55	30	45	30
	NEA Locals	50	62	45	57	50
	AFT Locals	89	85	83	90	85

* The number of responses for each organization is reported in footnote 6. Total number of NEA leaders = 61; total number of AFT leaders = 109. The actual number of responses varies slightly by policy domain.

groups (BTA and TASF), a consistent organizational pattern emerges. NEA associations and AFT unions diverge sharply in their aspirations for increased influence. Aggregate percentages in Table 2 demonstrate that, with regard to educational policy generally or any single domain, union leaderships are solid, while association leaderships are divided in desiring power for their own groups. Specifically, the four union locals (SFFT, UFT, BTU, and CTU) rank higher from one policy domain to the next than do the three

199

associations (SFCTA, CEA, and ATA). In fact, with the exception of salaries where the rankings of individual organizations shift somewhat, the order is almost the same whatever the policy area being considered. Among the unions, the ones in San Francisco and New York, which are most desirous of curtailing the influence of other participants, appear also to be the most militant regarding the enhancement of organizational power. Union leaderships in Boston and Chicago are less cohesive in this respect. Among the associations, all of which rank lower, those in San Francisco and Chicago are notably more prone to pursue power than is ATA in Atlanta.

Intercity comparisons likewise prove interesting. Generally, leaders in New York, San Francisco, and Boston are more concerned with group power than are their counterparts in Chicago and Atlanta. In the latter cities, as well as in Boston, teacher organizations of whatever affiliation seem most intent on enhancing their influence over salary policy. Fewer leaders in these places care much about group power in the domains of personnel, curriculum, or school organization. In contrast, salary power is less important in New York and San Francisco. This is understandable, since UFT already carries considerable weight here and San Francisco teachers earn salaries which compare quite favorably with those paid in other large cities across the nation.

Teacher organizations understandably want more power. But how much, particularly when compared to that held by educational dominants? This question leads us to examine the roles teacher organizations seek to play in the arenas of educational policy-making. Today especially, professors of school administration and superintendents abstractly agree that teachers should be involved in deciding matters of import. "Teacher participation" has become a new shibboleth of American education. What it really means, however, is unclear. One aim of the present study is to see how teachers themselves view participation. What do local leaders think their organization's proper role should be? In this inquiry we have posited for each domain five possible levels of participation in the formulation of school policy. Respondents were asked to denote a preference as to whether teacher organizations (1) should have more to say than the board and/or administration; (2) should have a voice equal to that of the board and/or administration; (3) should be consulted and have their advice weighed heavily; (4) should be kept informed, but not necessarily called upon for advice; or (5) should not be involved.[23]

On the basis of the pronouncements of national officials as well as the responses about power cited above, we would hypothesize that union locals aspire to more decisive participation than professional associations or independent groups. Totals for AFT and NEA in Table 3 suggest that this is indeed the case. Depending upon

TABLE 3

Participation in Policy-making:
Percentages of Leaders Desiring High Participative Roles

POLICY DOMAIN

CITY	ORGANI-ZATION*	Policy in General	Salary Policy	School Organization	Personnel Policy	Curriculum and Instruction
New York	UFT	77	82	71	74	66
Boston	BTU	57	52	29	32	46
	BTA	13	38	25	00	25
Chicago	CTU	22	33	22	28	28
	CEA	05	21	00	06	00
San Francisco	SFFT	83	83	75	67	88
	SFCTA	41	32	27	27	33
	TASF	29	14	14	29	57
Atlanta	ATA	10	20	00	10	30
	NEA Locals	20	25	10	15	22
	AFT Locals	64	66	53	54	59

* The number of responses for each organization is reported in footnote 6.
Total number of NEA leaders = 61; total number of AFT leaders = 109.
The actual number of responses varies slightly by policy domain.

the policy area, from one-half to two-thirds of the union leadership subsample opts for a major or equal voice in decision-making. The proportions of NEA leaders choosing the same roles are much lower, ranging from about one-tenth to one-quarter. In places where sev-

---

23. Questionnaires included these items for educational policy in general and for each of the four policy domains. For present purposes, we have dichotomized responses, with choices of (1) or (2) signifying "high" participative objectives and (3), (4), or (5) signifying "low" participative objectives.

eral organizations exist, intracity comparisons reveal that in every instance higher percentages of union than of other leaderships desire to participate significantly in the several areas of policy formulation. Naturally, the agreement among leaders on organizational objectives varies from one domain to another. In general, teacher leaders are likelier to desire major participation on salaries and curriculum. Proportionately fewer insist on a comparable level when policy concerns personnel or school organization. Specifically, in Boston and Chicago, salaries and then curriculum evoke greater desires for high participation on the part of teacher groups. In San Francisco and Atlanta, the order is reversed.

If the participative roles prescribed by leaders are any indication, we might easily conclude that UFT in New York and SFFT in San Francisco rank as the most militant organizations. This conforms with other evidence previously presented. BTU trails well behind, while either CTU, the most conservative union, or SFCTA, the most militant association, comes next. As far as participation in policy-making is concerned, leaders of CEA in Chicago and ATA in Atlanta seek not a major or equal voice but rather a consultative role for their own groups.

Power, Participation, and Militancy

Many, if not all, discussions of the new militancy stress its behavioral features—aggressive activity, hard conflict, open warfare. An appreciation of the militancy of teacher organizations, we believe, requires that several dimensions be taken into account. From the standpoint of teacher leaders, we have considered three: how power is distributed; how it should be redistributed; and what role teacher organizations should play in educational policy-making. Leadership perceptions of influence may not be entirely accurate, but they do conform closely to the views of other observers of school politics in these five cities. In any event, it is important to realize how leaders feel when comparing their own influence to that of school boards and administrators. Given low self-images, teachers inevitably desire enhancement of their own power holdings. Otherwise, there is no discernible relationship between the distri-

202

bution of influence on the one hand and leadership advocacy of its redistribution on the other. While they want more for themselves, most leaders of most organizations are relatively content with the power allegedly possessed by boards, superintendents, and bureaucratic chiefs.

If a common strategy involves gaining increased power (while not depriving others of their present shares), a principal goal is regular participation in the policy-making processes of public education. Conceivably, some groups could desire far greater power than they had and still be satisfied with a passive role in deciding policy. Others could desire somewhat less and yet seek an active role. Our explorations, however, demonstrate a close relationship between the pursuit of power and the desire for a significant voice in the processes of policy-making. Rank order correlations, using Kendall's tau, between power aspirations and policy-participation objectives are all positive: educational policy in general, .81; salary, .62; school organization, .81; personnel, 1.00; curriculum and instruction, .81. With the exception of salaries, the San Francisco Federation of Teachers, the United Federation of Teachers, and the Boston Teachers Union consistently rank highest and, with only one additional exception, the Chicago Education Association and the Atlanta Teachers Association rank lowest on both types of ordinal scale.[24] Thus, where leaderships are solidly committed to increasing group power, their intention is to convert that power into a full partnership in educational policy-making.

Our descriptive survey admittedly has ignored many crucial questions. Whatever their evaluations of influence, their power ambitions, and their objectives, the militancy of teacher organizations hinges also on their willingness to fight. Unless groups are disposed to act forcefully in pursuing their goals, the militant label should

24. The reversed rankings of UFT and BTU with regard to salary on the power and participation scales are probably attributable to two factors. First, at the time the questionnaire was sent, BTU had just won a collective bargaining election. It was about to enter into negotiations, the major element of which concerned salaries. Hence, its desire for greater salary power. Second, UFT already has, and is conscious of having, a considerable say on salary matters. Thus, although leaders agree on a high level of participation, they are less inclined to feel the need for even more power to achieve their objective.

not be applied.[25] Combative dispositions do not necessarily lead to actual conflict, however. Nor does open conflict necessarily enable teacher organizations to succeed in attaining their objectives. Thorough understanding of the militancy and achievement of teacher organizations in large cities demands that careful scrutiny be given to at least three broad categories of factors.

First, we must explore further the characteristics of teacher organizations themselves. In profiling leadership attitudes, this study has made a modest beginning. Attention must also be paid to the stage of an organization's development, since groups with small, fervent memberships may operate differently from those with large, passive memberships. Rank-and-file satisfaction with the educational status quo, organizational resources in terms of skills and finances, and competition between or within groups must be considered.

Second, the attitudes and behavior of other core participants presumably affect the way teachers feel, what they do, and just how much they accomplish. Superintendents and boards of education have a choice when responding to teacher demands. Through adamant opposition, benevolence, or plain weakness, they may either encourage or discourage militancy.

Finally, cultural, political, and situational variables must be taken into account. State legislation regulating employer–employee relationships, community folkways, and patterns of political practice all appear important and all vary among cities. Strikes or strike threats may be viable tactics in New York but self-defeating in Boston. Open conflict may be legitimate and productive in Chicago, but personal diplomacy may prove better suited to Atlanta. In one city, a particular issue can be salient and furnish the spark for collective action; in another, no such catalyst might appear.

Only after probing into these uncharted areas will we add substantially to our knowledge of the characteristics, roles, and impact of local teacher organizations. Along the way, we may be able to shed further light in general on the educational politics of large city school systems.

---

25. In our investigation we have found that teacher organizations ranking high in the pursuit of power and on policy-making participation also are most disposed to engage in combat.

MARILYN GITTELL

The author is Associate Professor of Political Science at Queens College of the City University of New York and Director of their newly-formed Institute for Community Studies. She is the Editor of Urban Affairs Quarterly. *Dr. Gittell has served as a consultant to the Education Task Force of the (New York) Mayor's Temporary Commission on City Finances. The following article is based, in part, on a monograph (published by the Center for Urban Education), research for which was supported by a grant from the Office of Economic Opportunity.*

DECISION-MAKING IN THE SCHOOLS:

New York City,

A Case Study

FOR TOO LONG, American school systems have been insulated from public and expert scrutiny. Although education policy has been removed from political controls, school boards and school administrators — spending public funds and making public policies — are engaged in activities that are inherently political.

While studies of power and decision-making proliferate, there has been a reluctance on the part of social scientists to scrutinize school officials as politicans.[1] Professional educators are, therefore, the primary source of evaluation of the system they have created. Their studies invariably are based on the a priori conviction that

---

1. There are two notable exceptions, Dahl selected education as one of his areas of analysis in New Haven, identifying the professionals as major decision-makers. Robert Dahl, *Who Governs?*, New Haven: Yale University Press, 1962. The Syracuse study is a thorough analysis of politics and financial support. Stephen Bailey, Richard T. Frost,

educators are apolitical, that their decisions must therefore be objective and that, consequently, all policy-making should be within their province.[2]

Decision-making studies and analyses of local power structure in cities have much to offer to our understanding of the operation of school systems. More intensive studies of decision-making and the distribution of power in school systems can, in turn, contribute significantly to our knowledge of how cities are governed. Almost every study of power in large cities points to functional specialization, the dispersion of power to specialists in particular areas, and the increased role of the bureaucracy in decision-making. Few have concentrated their analyses on a center or island of power to describe the influences, relationships, and the character of policy-making in that particular area. The following study of decision-making in the New York City school system concerns itself with the distribution of power within one of these centers, testing the hypothesis of functional specialization and, hopefully, expanding on its implications.

New York City As a Case Study

The New York City school system, as a basis for analysis, offers a good case study. It is nominally a dependent school district (that is, the school district does not have independent taxing power), and

Paul E. Marsh, *Schoolmen and Politics*, Syracuse: Syracuse University Press, 1961. There are twelve monographs in the series. A poor attempt to review the relevancy of decision-making studies in education which in effect assumes the priority of the Hunter reputational analysis approach is Ralph Kimbrough, *Political Power and Educational Decision-Making*, Chicago: Rand McNally & Co., 1964. Several studies of state involvement have identified the general political framework of State government as an integral part of educational policy. Notably, Nicholas A. Masters, Robert H. Salisbury and Thomas H. Eliot, *State Politics and the Public Schools and Explanatory Analysis*, New York: A. Knopf, 1964. See also, Michael D. Usdan, *The Political Power of Education in New York State*, New York: Institute of Administrative Research, Teachers College, Columbia University, 1963.

2. Some solutions tend to be even more extreme, Liberman recommends that professional associations take over the function of local school boards. Myron Liberman, *The Future of Public Education*, Chicago: University of Chicago Press, 1960.

the City schools and school policy have often been described as dependent upon local political influence.[3]

Concern in New York City with the failures of the education system was brought to a head by legislation, introduced in the 1964 session of the Legislature, to establish a fiscally independent school system.

The mayor requested the Temporary Commission on City Finances to explore the feasibility of such a plan and review the general character of the administrative structure in education with special attention to the role of the board of education. This study was prepared to review critically the operation of the school system as a means of evaluating proposals for increased independence. This analysis of decision-making in education in New York City was developed to project the impact of fiscal independence on the existing structure. Since no previous study had fully explored the sources and procedures of policy formulation there was little evidence of how the school system functioned under its present structure. Using five key areas as a basis of study, participants and participation in school affairs were studied in depth.

Rather than analyze individual decisions, which might prove deceptive, given the nature of the decision and the element of time, five *areas* of decision-making were selected for study. The basis of selection was diversity in the subject dealt with, allowing for the widest possible range of participation, as well as relevance of the policy selected to the overall education function. Generally, exploration of a continuum of policy was considered superior to a single policy decision. Historical data and institutional analysis was utilized in all of the areas in which it was relevant.

Selected for intensive study were: (1) Selection of the Superintendent, (2) increases in teachers' salaries, (3) budgeting, (4) school integration, and (5) curriculum development. Other areas of policy were reviewed in a more cursory way to broaden the scope of the analysis.

---

3. Wallace Sayre and Herbert Kaufman, *Governing New York City*, New York: Russell Sage Foundation, 1960.

Within any school system the potential participants in school policy-making are essentially the same, although actual participation may vary according to the relative power of each in given circumstances. Legal power is usually divided between a board of education and the superintendent. As regards the bureaucracy, distinction must be made among the central administrative bureaucracy and field administrators, top supervisory staff and middle management. Organizations representing these groups are common in the larger school districts and their activities can be significant. Teachers and teacher organizations, parents and parent organizations are potential participants. Specialized education interest groups (ad hoc and permanent) have been active in many communities and their role can be a vital one.

In the general community there are other potential participants, local, state, and Federal officials, civic groups, the press, business organizations, and individual entrepreneurs seeking the rewards of the school system. Interrelationships between these potential participants, the relative power of each, and their role in particular decisions provided the basis for study. The role of the participants and their interrelationships were analyzed with respect to the five areas of policy, distinguishing, where feasible, between initiation, promulgation, and implementation of policy.

Over a period of a year and a half, the author analyzed all newspaper items, in two daily newspapers, recording all public statements and reports on education policy. These items were categorized by participant and issue, providing a general picture of the public roles and concerns of all participants. A series of detailed, selective interviews with professional staff and board members were conducted. Data was cross-checked in interviews with participants outside the school system, including staff members of the Public Education Association, United Federation of Teachers, and other civic groups. Lawyers and educators, knowledgeable in school affairs, were also consulted. A special survey questionnaire was developed for longer interviews with half the field superintendents in the system. The files of civic groups were researched for relevant data on specific issues. For comparative purposes, a search was made of all professional and popular literature for accounts of decision-making in other school systems.

General conclusions drawn from the study are relevant to the analysis of education decision-making in other large urban centers, as well as to the general trends in other areas of decision-making.[4]

Findings

In the last two decades, education in New York City has become amazingly insulated from political and public controls. One could accurately describe the situation as an abandonment of public education by key forces of potential power within the City. Bureaucratization and professionalization have been conditioning elements. Weber's theory of the emergence of a specialized bureaucracy monopolizing power through its control of expertise, characterizes the role of the education bureaucracy in New York City. The claim that only the professionals can make competent judgments has been accepted. Contributing to and perhaps an outgrowth of this attitude is the change in the mayor's role to one of non-involvement. Civic and interest groups have responded ambivalently; on the one hand they accept the notion of the professional competence of the bureaucracy, but at the same time, express a hopelessness regarding their ability to change the system. The result is narrow or closed participation in large areas of decision-making, restricted to an inside core of top supervisory personnel in the headquarters staff of the board of education. Policy alternatives are rarely discussed or offered and the inclination to support the *status quo* is reinforced.[5]

---

4. An area omitted which later proved worthy of further exploration was school site selection and construction. The study did review this area only as it related to the integration issue and budgeting.

5. Lowi's study of appointments in New York City (Theodore Lowi, *At The Pleasure of the Mayor*, New York: Free Press of Glencoe, 1965, p. 199) as well as the Sayre and Kaufman study (*op. cit.*, p. 716) suggested that the system (referring to the City-wide power structure) is more favorable to defenders of the *status quo* than to innovation.

Participants and Participation

Participation in school policy formulation was directly related to consensus, or lack of it. Types of participation can be viewed in four categories: (1) *closed,* only the professionals in the system were participants; (2) *limited,* professionals, the board of education and/or the mayor were included; (3) *expanded,* involved other specialized interests, such as Public Education Association, United Parents Association, and the United Federation of Teachers; and (4) *wide,* potentially open to all kinds of groups not generally involved in school policy. The greater share of school policy falls within categories (1) and (2).

In a few instances, participants voluntarily widened the scope of participation when it was to their advantage, or the scope was widened as a result of conflict. The Union, for instance, widened participation on the salary issue to include the mayor, because it recognized that it would gain by his participation. The integration issue was not resolved internally in the system and participation was thrown into an open arena. In some respects the issue itself could be said to influence participation, but if decisions are not visable, those interests which might potentially become involved, do not.

State and Local Officials

Although this study did not attempt to evaluate fully the state's role some obvious conclusions are noteworthy. State minimum standards for education are not an overwhelming influence on a large city like New York, which tends to make even greater demands on itself. The leading influences are the State-aid formula, largely determined by the Governor, Regents' policy, and the administrative rulings of the State Education Commissioner. Recent studies in other states have emphasized the increasing importance of the state bureaucracy in local educational policy, particularly, the role of the commissioner.[6]

210

The State Commissioner was involved in two major policy decisions affecting New York City in recent years. He was instrumental in the removal of the entire board of education in 1961. Subsequently, he recommended the change in procedure for selection of the new board. In 1958, his condemnation of *de facto* segregation in New York City was a catalyst to the initiation of board policy on school integration and he continued to influence City policy in this regard by the publication of a series of reports. In addition to these more overt actions, the commissioner's influence is felt in his informal contacts with the superintendent and the staff.

Legislative policy affecting the schools is primarily related to the State-aid formula.[7] City groups have been notably ineffectual as a force in Albany. One study attributes this failure to the splintering of City educational interest groups. The New York State Educational Conference Board is the strongest and most influential coalition of interest groups in the determination of state education policy. City interests are meagerly represented on the Conference Board and the state has been able to ignore City education needs without serious political consequences. The general deficiency in leadership in public education in New York is reflected, in part, in its failure to influence state policy significantly.

The City

The most significant trend in education in New York City has been the isolation of school administration from City government. In each era, complaints of undue City interference have resulted in the delegation of increased responsibility to the board of education. In the 1940s, the National Education Association condemned Mayor LaGuardia for direct interference with the school system,

---

6. Masters, Salisbury and Eliot, *op. cit.*, reviews the role of state educational officers in local school policy in Michigan, Illinois, and Missouri. James Conant's concern with the monopoly of the professional educators is particularly relevant. The professionals run the local school systems, control government policy in state administrative posts and direct the teachers colleges.

7. Bailey, Frost and Marsh, *op. cit.*, and Usdan, *op. cit.*

particularly, in personnel policy; the institution of a strict merit system and internal controls over promotions and transfers prevented future mayors from engaging in similar practices. In 1951, the Strayer-Yavner Report concluded that education policy was controlled by the Board of Estimate, the mayor, and the Budget Director of the City because of the line item budget,[8] subsequently the lump-sum budget was adopted, giving the professionals complete control over allocation of funds.[9] Complaints about a political board were satisfied by the institution of the civic selection panel.[10] Overriding these specific changes in the structural framework is increased bureaucratization and overblown professionalization of the school system. The professional bureaucracy has manipulated its resource of expertise to discourage opposition and alternative policies. The acceptance of technical expertise as the most relevant, if not the only, basis for sound judgment furthered the depoliticalization of education policy.

The depoliticalization process was a two-way street. Contributing significantly to it was the mayor's stated desire to delegate complete responsibility for the City's schools to the board of education.

Detailed review of newspaper items over the last five years substantiate the mayor's intention to remove himself from educational policy-making.[11] His public statements were always general, in support of more and better schools, and specifically avoiding particular policy positions on any school issues. On school integration, he repeatedly stated his desire to leave the matter to the board of education and the professional staff. "I subscribe without reservation to the goals of quality integrated education in our schools and of equal opportunity for every child. But the plan, the means, the how, where and what — the timetable, the specific approaches and programs — that is for the educators and for the

---

8. George D. Strayer and Louis Yavner, *Administrative Management of the School System of New York City*, Volume I, October, 1951.

9. *Local Law*, No. 19 passed by the City Council on April 6, 1962.

10. *Education Law*, Section 2553, subdivision 1, 2, amended L. 1961.

11. In combing three years of school news stories in two prominent New York City papers, the mayor's public statements reflect direct responses to public pressures.

Board to determine." During the most heated periods of controversy, he felt compelled to meet with protest groups, but repeatedly refused to intervene.

Requests to the mayor in 1964 for $45.3 million in additional funds for a More Effective Schools program drew the mayor to the fringe of the integration issue. The proposal called for obtaining additional funds and services for ten More Effective Schools in ghetto areas. Ultimately, after consultation with school officials and staff members of educational interest groups, his decision favoring a smaller appropriation was reached.

An aide to the mayor verified that the mayor had unquestionably shifted responsibility for education policy to the board of education, "the mayor did not want to get involved with school problems, particularly school integration problems." Only in instances, where there was an obvious conflict between the board and another City agency which had to be reviewed and resolved before the Board of Estimate, did the mayor become directly involved. Although someone on his staff was designated as educational assistant to the mayor (on Board payroll), he was certainly not functioning in that capacity. No one questioned was aware that the mayor's assistant was ever engaged in education matters, and many of the participants in educational affairs could not even identify his name.

The mayor and the Board of Estimate are major instruments of financial policy, determining overall budgetary appropriations. Their review of the education budget, however, has always been concerned with the total amount to be alloted. Major increases in financing during the year have been presented to the mayor for his approval and for additional funds.

The mayor's continued involvement in fiscal matters is apparently due more to the fact that the school politicians themselves want to shift responsibility to him, than his own desire to participate. Although the board of education is charged with legal responsibility for determining salaries and has the discretion to increase salaries with the total of alloted funds, it has not been adverse to relinquishing this responsibility to the mayor — freeing

213

the board from the painful necessity of complying with its own budgetary limitations.[12]

The mayor, through his negotiators, has twice made direct settlements with the Union — in 1961 and 1965.[13] Financial commitments were then met by an additional City appropriation and transfers of funds within the education budget. After the 1965 contract settlement, the superintendent expressed dismay at the settlement, which far exceeded his planned budgetary allotment for salary increases.

The union, on its part, sees an obvious advantage in shifting the decision to the City arena. In an interview, the head of the union stated his opposition to any procedure which would deny the union recourse to the mayor. He indicated that the union was in a more viable position in negotiating with the mayor than it was with the board.

The mayor's policy of non-involvement was reinforced by two major changes in procedure instituted during his administration. The lump-sum appropriation of school funds and the panel selection of board members.

Under a local law first passed in 1962 and re-enacted each year since then, and by way of a memorandum of understanding with the mayor, the board has the power to determine its own allocation of funds. Budget preparation, the allocation and transfer of funds, and post-audit control are internal operations controlled largely by the top supervisory staff. The board of education is the only city agency with such budgetary independence of the municipal government.

Prior to 1961, board appointments were made directly by the mayor. Under the new procedure, the mayor appoints the nine members of the board from a list of candidates screened by a selection panel composed of the heads of eleven educational, civic and professional organizations. The change in procedure was

12. A member of the board disagreed with this interpretation, suggesting that the mayor had taken the initiative. The same person, however, confirmed the author's view, that the mayor did not interfere with the board in education policy. The United Federation of Teachers' officials verified the author's interpretation.

13. In 1961, the press gave credit to the superintendent for his successful negotiation on salaries but neglected to explain why the mayor was involved in the final settlement.

established in an effort to deter "political" appointments. It followed six years of hearings, scandal, and removal of the board by the State Legislature. Traditionally, the mayor's appointments had reflected careful consideration of proper interest balance, as well as political favor. The balance of interest was reflected in an implicit religious formula of 3:3:3, and the appointment of either a Negro or Puerto Rican or both. Geographic distribution demanded by the by-laws assured borough representation. The religious and racial balances, interestingly enough, are contained in the current selection process (see Table 1).[14] There was little question, prior to 1961, that the mayor would exercise some measure of control over the board, and the board members, in turn, could use their political influence with the mayor. Strong board presidents who were politically oriented served as the channel for communication with the mayor.[15]

TABLE I
Composition of the Board of Education

Religion	Old Board		New Board	
	1947	1957	1961	1965
Catholic	2	3	3	3
Protestant	3	3	3	3
Jew	3	3	3	3

The screening panel procedure strengthened the role of the civic groups and reduced the discretion of the mayor. Members of the board nominated by civic groups are less likely to be intimates of the mayor and they are less likely to consult with him on school problems. People outside the formal school structure, inter-

14. Expectations based on the religious formula was pointed up by an item appearing in the *World Telegram and Sun* of May 29, 1963, reporting criticism expressed by the Catholic Teachers Association of Mayor Wagner's failure to appoint a Catholic to replace a retiring member, Brendan Byrne. Months later, when a Jewish member of board retired, a Catholic was appointed to replace him, thereby reestablishing the 3:3:3 balance.

15. In the period from 1945 to 1961, the three board presidents later moved on to political office. Maximilian Moss was elected Surrogate in Brooklyn, Arthur Levitt was elected State Controller, and Charles Silver became a personal advisor to the mayor. This would indicate not only their closeness to the mayor but their active participation in the Democratic party.

viewed during the study and asked about the new appointment procedure, expressed dissatisfaction with the lack of political "know-how" of board members. They pointed out that board members lack personal influence and no longer can play the poltical role expected of them by school groups. It has been said of the new board that, it is the "greatest heard of Board, never heard from."

In two general areas, the mayor was forced to take part in school policy. First, on issues in which conflict between major participants could not be compromised — this occurred most frequently in arguments between the Planning Commission and the board on site selection. Secondly, in areas where key participants gained significantly by his direct involvement, as was true on the salary issue.

One of the obvious questions which arises in connection with the mayor's role is whether the precedents established under the Wagner administration, over a twelve year period, have become so integral a part of the structure that they cannot be changed. Mayor Wagner's role fits Banfield's definition of the mayor as mediator of conflicts, rather than as an initiator of policy.[16] A reform mayor who cannot rely on party backing, is less likely to accept this role and, in fact, must use his power to initiate policy in order to encourage new political support. The precedent of non-involvement of the mayor has been based on the acceptance of professionalism. Mayor Lindsay, in his short tenure in office, has already faced the charge of "political interference" in an attempt to initiate policy in the creation of a civilian police review board. Other efforts have been similarly criticized by members of the various bureaucracies who felt their own powers threatened.

The emotional commitment to professionalism, although not inviolate, tends to challenge any suggestion of change or alternate course of action as under "political interference." The effort of the new mayor to reassert his policy role represents a direct threat to those who have held almost complete power in decision-making in these areas.

---

16. Edward Banfield, *Political Influence*, New York: Free Press of Glencoe, 1963.

The control of policy by the bureaucracy has been considerably enhanced by the voluntary self-removal of other potential participants, particularly the civic groups. There is no question but that the development of the bureaucratic structure had to result in the accrual of power to the professionals, but the extent to which they would be forced to consider alternative policies or be influenced by them, is determined by the respective roles of these other forces.

Considering the close-out of the public and civic agencies from education over the past decade, any mayor who decides to become more directly involved in education policy will face serious criticism, not only from the education establishment, but from other groups as well. Any movement toward an increased policy role for the mayor will also involve structural changes. Possibly, a revitalized interest by the mayor as a policy initiator can reactivate civic reformers and public interest sufficiently to expand participation as a basis for reviewing the instruments of policy.

The Board of Education

The board of education is the official policy-making body for the school system and its nine members are responsible for long-range educational planning. Since 1961, board members have been nominated by a screening panel of civic agencies and appointed by the mayor. The membership still represents a balance of borough, ethnic, and religious interests. The current board lacks well known personalities and strong leadership types.

In a review of the backgrounds of board members, only one person on the board was of City-wide reputation and that, perhaps, because of a renowned family name. One member, had a long career in education interest group participation and considered herself to be the spokesman for "liberal causes." Another member, prided himself in his concern with professional education matters; gathering educational materials and attending conferences was his major preoccupation. One member was a distinguished college educator. Few of the other board members could be considered especially knowledgeable in education matters.

217

Board members operate through a committee system which provides the basis of board decision-making. Each committee makes judgments in its special area of concern and the board generally accepts these policies as its own. Board members generally become involved in these specialized areas and devote an inordinate amount of time to administrative details on questions related to their committee assignments. On questioning, board members indicated that they viewed this as their primary role.[17] The board committees and their independent staff have been regularly criticized as competitive with the superintendent and the headquarters staff. As a gesture of good faith, the newly constituted board abandoned that procedure in 1961. Early in its controversy with the last superintendent, however, the board threatened to reinstitute the committee system over his strenuous objections.[18] This action was delayed, but early in the 1965 school year, the board appointed a high-salaried coordinator of the board's new committees (a former executive director of United Parents Association) to its own staff, suggesting its inclination to move back to its earlier stance.

The board's role has been largely one of balancing conflicting pressures and interests. It, too, has become a mediator rather than an initiator of policy. As the spokesman for official policy, the board nominally participates in all major decisions. It spends a great deal of its time, however, on sensitive issues where the balance of power in the board has failed to produce a consensus. These are not necessarily major areas of policy. Site selection controversies appear to occupy an undue amount of board time. The board reviews all questions of site selection where there is disagreement. This is a rather frequent occurrence, particularly since the question of school integration has become so significant. Other seemingly unimportant policy issues have taken up much board time. In 1951, the board was deadlocked for four months in a 4–4 vote on including the United Nations in the social studies cur-

---

17. Strayer and Yavner, *op. cit.*

18. In recent statements on large city school systems H. Thomas James of Stanford strongly supported the need for the development of independent staff for boards of education as a means of increasing the information available to board members.

riculum and raising the UN flag at the schools. Ultimately, the issue was resolved in the affirmative; the opposition was not strong enough to resolve it without debate, and public debate gained the necessary support for approval. The board necessarily concerns itself with issues in which group interests conflict and cannot be settled within the system. School policies which relate to integration generally fall within this frame of reference.

In the policy areas selected for study, the board's role varied from superficial participation in the budget process to formulation and promulgation of policy and failure to achieve implementation in school integration. Selecting the superintendent was the area in which they exercised most direct power. Historically, the selection of the superintendent has been a board function, greatly influenced by its president and subject to the support of high-ranking administrators and education interest groups. In earlier years, the mayor had on occasion controlled the appointment, but in more recent years he has not shown as much interest. The selection is influenced by the bureaucratic pressure for appointment of an "insider." Three of the last five superintendents were chosen from the supervisory bureaucracy; the fourth was a former deputy mayor and local college president.[19] The education interest groups, particularly the Public Education Association, have always been concerned with the choice of the superintendent. Lowi points out that the interest groups in New York City have generally concentrated their attention on appointments and their involvement in the selection of the superintendent and board members in education fits that general pattern.[20] In the past, the Public Education Association supported the appointment of "outsiders" with high academic credentials, without too much success. It has always requested a screening panel of educators to assist the board in screening the field, but in the final analysis the board president

---

19. *New York Times*, April 25, 1962; July 2, 1962. The High School Administrative Assistants Association, the Association of Assistant Superintendents and the Junior High School Principals Association reminded the board that "home grown talent should not be over-looked." The three superintendents chosen from the bureaucracy were Benjamin Wade, William Jansen, and Bernard Donavan; the fourth mentioned is John Theobald. Of the five, Calvin Gross was the only "outsider" appointed Superintendent.

20. Lowi, *op. cit.*

controlled the choice. The Public Education Association has become more influential in the last two appointments than it had been previously. In 1961 the board accepted the recommendations of the professional panel, selecting a highly regarded "outsider." His failure and dismissal resulted in a return to selection of the highest ranking person from within the system.

In budgeting, the board has tended to rely on the budget presented by the superintendent and his staff. It makes few adjustments in the final document. Individual board members have periodically questioned expenditures, but also have referred to their lack of information in dealing with intricate budget detail. Generally, the board views its role as one of assuring City financial support for the total budget, and satisfying staff requests and public pressures.

In school integration policy the board has exhibited a lack of effective follow-through. Although it set a general policy favoring school integration in 1957, and debated questions of rotation of teachers, and rezoning — resolving them in the affirmative — implementation by the staff was never forthcoming and the board failed to press the fulfillment of their established policy. In interviews conducted with board members they noted the practical problems related to implementation of their policy as well as staff inaction, as a cause for delay. A member of the board stated that were she not on the board she would probably be out on the picket line, but dealing with the tough problem of ironing out procedures and seeing their effects had taken the edge off her dedication to implementation. In a detailed case study of school integration in New York City, David Rogers cites the lack of leadership and determination of the board in its equivocation after the integration policy was made, as a key factor in the failure of that policy.[21]

On the two major salary increases in recent years the board has participated in negotiations but has been satisfied to shift responsibility to the mayor or his mediators for final decision-making.

If a trend in the board's participation could be observed, it

---

21. David Rogers. Unpublished manuscript on school desegregation.

was to suggest a diminished role under the new board. The board never fulfilled its obligation for long-range planning and the new board has not been any more successful in that area. Lack of reliance on the superintendent as chief executive officer appears to be a continuing problem, as indicated by the rebuilding of the board staff. Under the old appointed board, contracts were often handled by the board president, this procedure has been shifted to staff under the present board, hopefully eliminating personal favoritism.

It might be more accurate to say, that individual members of the board, as it was formerly constituted, were more involved in policy-making as a result of their own political stature and their association with the mayor. As the school system has grown larger and more complex and policies demand more specialized knowledge, the board has had to withdraw from an effective policy role. The bureaucracy and special interest groups have gained power through their control of the resource of expertise while the board has lost power for their lack of it.

Local School Boards

In 1961, the board of education was empowered to appoint local school board members for twenty-five district boards.[22] For each vacancy, district selection panels submitted two or three names to the district superintendents who, in turn, passed the list on to the board for appointment. The activation of local school boards was, in part, a recognition of the inadequacy of the City-wide board and an overcentralized system to respond to local needs. The local boards, however, were given no real authority in the determination of school policy. Generally, they have acted as a community buffer, holding hearings and discussing narrow local issues, without authority to resolve local problems. Many of the local boards view themselves as preservers of narrow local interests, particularly in integration policy. Officially, the boards rarely act as a body; members are more prone to voice personal

22. *Education Law*, Section 2564, amended by L. 1961.

The board of education was reluctant to delegate any extreme powers to local boards for fear that they would encroach upon its own authority. District superintendents were also hesitant to enhance the position of the local boards, because they might interfere with local school administration. The compromise was to assign the local boards the function of holding hearings, which was harmless enough.

Under a 1965 reorganization plan, the twenty-five boards were increased to thirty-one to conform with the expanded thirty-one local districts. The new plan was to include greater emphasis on decentralized policy-making, utilizing the district superintendent and the local boards more effectively. There is no indication, however, that the plan provides for basic prerequisites for redistributing power in the system locally. Budgeting and personnel policy will continue to be centralized and there is no provision for flexibility in initiating new programs. In an interview, the superintendent indicated that the budgetary limitations in themselves would prevent any effective decentralization of the City School system, and policy formulation will remain a headquarters responsibility so long as these conditions are unchanged.[23]

The Superintendent and the Bureaucracy

One of the most confusing aspects of school administration in New York City is the growth in the power of the administrative staff, at the same time that the superintendent has remained a relatively weak chief executive. In part, the strength of the bureaucracy has undermined the role of the superintendent. Several other factors have contributed significantly to the overall result. The short tenure in office of the last four superintendents has undoubtedly taken its toll. In the last two decades, four superintendents have held the office, none with enough time to enhance that office's powers. (Evidently the high attrition rate of superintendents is characteristic of large cities.[24]) Open conflict with

---

23. The superintendent recently admitted the need for delegating budget and personnel power to local district superintendents. *New York Times*, February 20, 1966.

24. Allan Talbott, "Needed: A New Breed of School Superintendents" *Harpers Magazine*, February 1966, pp. 81-87.

the board was evidenced in two of these administrations, one resulting in dismissal. The last two board presidents have proudly claimed that they devoted at least 45 hours a week to their jobs, indicating their day-to-day involvement in school affairs that properly could be left to the superintendent, and their general lack of reliance on the superintendent for policy recommendations. The abandonment of education by civic groups has been another loss to the superintendent, who might otherwise use this outside support for developing his own role.

The superintendent lacks the most essential power of a strong executive, the power of appointment and removal. The supervisory staff is developed completely through inbreeding and promotion from the ranks. Tenured supervisors bind top policy-making jobs, allowing for little flexibility in appointments. No superintendent can rely on his own team of trusted advisors. Appointments from outside the system are almost nonexistent. Loyalties developed within this environment are strong and are based on how one has received appointment. Top-level deputy, associate, and assistant superintendents have moved up in divisions of the system and their loyalties are based on these associations. Some of them, undoubtedly, think they should have been superintendent. This results in much backbiting and petty jealousies. On reviewing the backgrounds of the twenty-five top supervisory staff members, it was found that they followed a pattern of having served as principals or assistant principals, were brought into the board on special assignment and/or had served on special committees (usually as a result of contacts already established at headquarters). Assignment to headquarters staff by school division reinforces the loyalties of staff members to that division and the supervisory staff in that division. In all school reorganization proposals, these loyalties have repeatedly fostered defense of the *status quo*.

The superintendent must cope with these potentially competing interests of his own supervisory bureaucracy.[25] He cannot

25. Personal contact with board members by the staff is not uncommon. Two years ago the situation was so bad that the superintendent issued a statement on policy halting memos from the supervisory staff directly to board members. *World Telegram and Sun*, November 15, 1963, p. 47.

freely develop his own advisory staff and is encumbered by the appointments and promotions made by his predecessors. Any views on issues. Local boards do not have the information or facility, much less the authority, to follow through on matters. superintendent from outside the system, and not himself subject to these loyalties, would find his task all the more difficult. A recent magazine article stated: "I am told Calvin Gross could have made a real dent on the New York City schools if only he had a handful of trusted special assistants."[26]

Directives and policy statements issued by the superintendent on key policies have been attacked by his own supervisory staff, both by their professional organizations and, officially, through organized committees on which they sit.[27] In March of 1964, the Council of Supervisory Associations (the overall organization for all of the individual supervisory organizations, such as the High School Principals' Association, Superintendents Association, Junior High School Principals' Association, et al.) issued one of its many reports. It condemned policies of the superintendent and noted his failure to consult with his professional staff before making decisions. The Council recently openly opposed the Princeton plan, school busing, the dropping of IQ examinations, and school pairing after they were adopted as official policy by the board and the superintendent. Invariably, policies which require fundamental institutional change are challenged by the supervisory staff.

The inability of superintendents to use basic administrative powers is notable. They have thoroughly neglected the budget as a management tool to shape personnel or organization policy. Several days spent in the Budget Office at Headquarters indicated that the Budget Office staff did not act in an advisory or policy-making capacity. Budget estimates are based essentially on pre-established ratios of books and teachers to pupils with slight adjustment according to the category of the school. Budget

---

26. Talbott, *op. cit.*

27. Both the High School Principals Association and the Junior High School Principals Association have expressed opposition to the 5-3-4 and 4-4-4 organization plans. Several associations opposed the elimination of the IQ examination, school pairing proposals, and the comprehensive high school plan.

approvals come from division heads and are reviewed in hearings controlled by these same people. The last superintendent met only once all year with *his* budget director.

In all of the areas studied, the superintendent played a secondary role as an initiator of policy. He had no direct influence on curriculum, with the exception of support by one administration for complete revision of elementary school curriculum in the 1950s. Curriculum policy has been left largely to the Curriculum Research Bureau and the deputy superintendent.

The superintendent has been most concerned with budget matters, and even in that capacity has shown no strong inclination to control the preparation of the budget or to utilize it as a means of controlling his staff. On integration policy, the last two superintendents have virtually delegated the responsibility to the staff with the result that implementation has not been forthcoming. Since announced board policy was made, neither superintendent considered his role one of leadership in forcing implementation. It was almost as if the superintendent, like the mayor, and the board had become a mediator of disputes, rather than an initiator of school policy.

The Administrative Staff

The education bureaucracy[28] in New York City must be viewed in at least two separate categories; (1) the headquarters staff, and (2) the operational field staff. The latter includes some 3,000 principals and assistant principals, 31 district superintendents, and 1,300 department chairmen.

The Supervisors at Headquarters

A precise figure on the size of the headquarters staff is difficult to determine; it is estimated to be somewhere around 3,000.

---

28. In a study of U.F.T. executive board members' perceptions about who makes school policy, most of those questioned attributed little power to the Union except in salary matters. In most areas, they cited the board and the superintendent as wielders of power. Allan Rosenthal, unpublished manuscript on the role of unions and teachers organizations in policy-making.

At least 400–500 people at headquarters do not appear on that budget. Although full-time headquarters personnel, they are paid out of school budgets. The group, referred to herein as supervisory bureaucracy, would include some thirty headquarters and staff members; including the executive deputy superintendent, the deputy superintendent in charge of instruction and curriculum, six or seven associate superintendents, the Board of Examiners, twenty of the thirty assistant superintendents, and a group of active directors of special bureaus. With the exception of two assistant superintendents, who had earlier experience in school systems outside of New York City, this group was bred in the system; many as principals, almost all with long experience at headquarters.

In each of the decision-making areas analyzed for the study, the supervisory staff at headquarters were major instruments of policy.

In curriculum planning and development, the headquarters staff, lodged in the Bureau of Curriculum Research, has had to contend only with the recent interest and participation of the deputy superintendent. The bureau is indirectly influenced by general changes in approach to certain disciplines, i.e., the new Math., but for the most part, it follows a regular routine of three- to five-year review of curriculum bulletins, revisions and presentation of new guidelines. The actual implementation of curriculum is dependent upon the action of principals and classroom teachers, and this varies considerably from school to school. Although the Bureau has curriculum assistants attached to its staff on a part-time basis (40 percent of their time is spent in the district superintendent's office), there is no planned program for assuring implementation. In fact, the director of the bureau expressed his reservations about their role in implementation.

In budgeting, the distribution and allocation of funds is determined on a division, bureau, and department basis with the staff person in charge, the major determinant of his own needs. School appropriations are largely allocated on the basis of pre-established ratios, providing a prescribed number of teachers, specialized personnel, text books, *et al.*, according to the number of students and the category of school. The district superintendent exercises no discretion in budgeting or the distribution of personnel. In budget hearings, analyzed by the author, and in interviews with budget office personnel, it appeared that old programs were automatically continued and the adoption of new ones dependent upon the approval of the particular superintendent in charge of the division. As noted above, the superintendent has not used the budget as a management tool, nor has he used the budget office personnel in an advisory capacity. He has relied on the judgment of the supervisory bureaucracy for evaluation of programs and needs. There is no internal audit outside of the rather cursory and technical review of the small budget office staff. There is no procedure for evaluation of performance and elimination of ineffective programs in conjunction with the budget. Members of the board of education have noted their own inability to properly evaluate the complex budget document and make recommendations, and City review of the budget is virtually non-existent.

In another major area of policy, school integration, the supervisory staff has been a major participant, in the capacity of veto group. School integration policy was the only area of school policy explored in the study in which there was wide participation. This was an outcome of the diverse interests and goals of the participants as well as the delicacy of the problem. The supervisory staff, in its inaction and public disapproval of stated board policy, contributed inadvertently to that broadening of participation. The board, itself, demonstrated its own lack of resolve in promulgating general policy favoring rotation of teachers, school pairing, rezoning, and school reorganization, yet waiting upon the bureaucracy for implementation for eight years. The supervisory staff, on its part, has not only ignored board policy, but has publicly disagreed with it in statements of policy by their own supervisory organizations. Several of these organizations have opposed each of the proposed plans, at one time or another. The More Effective Schools program was the only plan which they supported fully, and was the only plan which would not have interfered with the existing structure, it entailed only the expansion of funds and personnel for selected schools.

In the other two areas studied, salary increases and selection of the superintendent, one would assume the supervisory staff would have no direct influence. Actually, they are inclined to fully support higher salaries for teachers, since their own salaries hinge on an index, based on increases proportionate to those received by the teaching staff. The ability of the supervisory staff to gain statutory legislation establishing the index is a significant indication of their strength. As a group, however, they are not participants in salary negotiations. Their supportive position, however, cannot be undermined.

In the selection of the superintendent, the supervisory staff is indirectly and directly influential. First, they represent the most immediate and likely source of supply and most superintendents are selected from their ranks. They have been consulted individually by board members and interest groups for suggestions whenever a superintendent is appointed. Their own preference for an "inside" appointment has been a major contributing factor influencing board decisions. The board is, of necessity, concerned with the ability of staff to relate to the superintendent. The recent unhappy experience with the selection of an "outsider" will more than likely encourage even greater reliance on the supervisory staff in the selection of the superintendent.

Discussions with individual board members suggested their concern with the enormous power of the supervisory staff and some indication of concern with the inbred system of selection but a despair in their inability to change the system.

The Council of Supervisory Associations, with close to 3,000 members, has emerged as the defender of the administrative bureaucracy. It is a professional organization made up of the various supervisory associations, including those for high school principals, junior high school principals, elementary school principals, assistant principals, high school chairmen, the board of examiners, assistant superintendents, and associate superintendents. Through their individual associations, and jointly through the Council of Supervisory Associations, the vested interests of the supervisory staff are strongly projected in education policy.

In other areas studied, tangential to the five decision-making areas, it was evident that the professional headquarters staff, particularly the core of fifty-odd supervisors, were major instruments of policy. Overcentralization has long plagued the school system and several studies have stressed the need for thorough administrative reorganization, yet board support and efforts by the last two superintendents along these lines have been thwarted by the vested interests of the staff in maintaining the *status quo*. In school construction and planning, the assistant superintendent in charge has successfully ignored Planning Commission recommendations, as well as integration policy, and is relatively free of other controls. He has become the expeditor of school construction. In assignment of administrative and teaching staff to schools, the central headquarters staff has recently increased its prerogatives. Much of the power which has been lodged in the central staff has prevented the expansion of the role of the district superintendents, who although nominally supervisory, are an anachronism in the system.

District Superintendents

Because so much evidence in the study appeared to pinpoint power in the professional staff, the author considered it worthwhile to explore more fully the particular role of the supervisors in the field. The district superintendents (thirty of them) are the only means for administrative decentralization in the present structure and the only source of professional liaison with local school needs. Since all phases of the study indicated that in the City as a whole, participation was narrow, exploration of the role of the district superintendents could verify the headquarters monopoly on policy. A detailed questioning of twelve district superintendents suggested that they were not participants in the formulation of school policy. Their ineffectiveness could be attributed to their general lack of budgeting and personnel powers and the inferior caliber of appointments. District superintendents have no discretion in the distribution of funds, and the most limited kind of discretion in the assignment of personnel. Their own staffs are small and largely clerical, although they were increased in 1965. This increase in staff was accompanied by a delegation of greater discretion to the district superintendent in the selection of his own staff.

The district superintendent acts as a buffer for parent dissatisfaction, unresolved by the school principal. Most of the local superintendents interviewed complained that they were not involved significantly in budgeting, curriculum implementation, assignment of personnel, and general formulation of school policy. Very few had meaningful relations with headquarters staff. Their contact with the schools in the area was limited to periodic school visits and meetings with principals, but rarely with teachers. Even if they could pinpoint special local needs, there was the feeling that not much could be done about dealing with them. The study of the role of the district superintendents verified their dependence on headquarters staff, not only for long-range policy, but in day-to-day decision-making. The variety of directives and forms to be completed for headquarters was a source of severe complaint by the district superintendents. Although a part of the professional bureaucracy, they are probably the least influential as a group. Their lack of participation in policy decisions gives added support to the conclusion that the central supervisory staff has cornered the power market.

Maintaining the Status Quo

The Sayre and Kaufman and Lowi studies of power in New York City concluded that the system, characterized by specialized centers of decision-making, is more favorable to the defenders of the *status quo.* Educational policy-making, largely controlled by a core group within the bureaucracy at headquarters, reflects this resistance to change by those in power.

The war cry for school independence is predicated on assuring control of educational decision-making by the professionals. Somehow, the professional is expected to proceed to an ideal in educational policy. In New York City professionals are the base of power, a power exercised, removed from the schools and the children and directed more at preservation of the *status quo,* than in an effort to achieve planned educational goals. They have had the power to shape the character of education in New York City and their failure to innovate is not an accident, but a reflection of their need to maintain the system which protects their interests.

United Federation of Teachers

Because of the power it wields in collective bargaining, the United Federation of Teachers sets major policy. The membership of the United Federation of Teachers in New York City includes over 30,000 teachers. It is the official bargaining agent for the City's 50,000 teachers. The Union contract determines wide areas of personnel practices, expenditures, and teaching time allotments. Because salaries and teachers' benefits represent close to half the total education budget, the Union is directly involved in matters of finance. The potential power of the Union to participate in other policy areas has not been fully realized because of its own choice in concentrating its attention on salary scales and related benefits. The teachers and the Union have been ignored by the school policy-makers and they have made little effort to secure a role for themselves. Few teachers participate in the most obvious area in which their expertise would be extremely helpful, that is in the development of curriculum. With the exception of a few high school specialists, the Bureau of Curriculum Research has not involved teachers in their programs. There was no evidence to suggest that teachers were consulted on integration policy or the problems of ghetto schools. The Union repeatedly voiced its objection to any plan calling for the rotation of teachers and that has remained a voluntary program. Its only constructive plan was the More Effective Schools proposal. Teachers are not at all involved in budgeting or selection of the superintendent either as a group or as individuals.

In 1963, after the first strike in the history of the school system, the United Federation of Teachers negotiated the largest single wage increase ever granted the City's teachers. The United Federation of Teachers gained strength from local union and public support of labor. Its membership expanded considerably as a result of its strike action in 1961 giving it unquestioned priority as collective-bargaining agent for the City's teachers. In its negotiations, the Union appeals to the mayor, the Central Labor Council, and the educational interest groups for support. The Union has seemingly bypassed the board and the superintendent to use its strength where it is most effective — at City Hall.

The Union can be viewed as representing another large "professional" group in policy-making in education. Its membership comprises the largest group of professionals in the system. In the few limited areas (outside of salary scale and fringe benefits) in which they have taken a public position, they have been largely motivated by a desire to maintain the *status quo*. They have supported policies which create rigidities in the system and can hardly be considered proponents of change. Board policy on rotation of teachers was met with an appeal by the Union to the mayor to prevent implementation. The Union has publicly and privately fought transfers of experienced teachers to difficult schools. It also questioned the advisability of 4:4:4 school reorganization because the plan threatened the status of the junior high school teacher.[29] In interviews conducted with Union leaders, it was clear that they themselves saw a conflict in objective education and professional goals and the narrow interest of the membership. In some instances they expressed concern that their own positions of power in the Union might be threatened if they violated those narrower interests.

Local Civic and Interest Groups

As has already been demonstrated, education decision-making is closely circumscribed in the functional specialization characteristic of New York City politics. The professional bureaucracy

---

29. Junior high school teachers represent the hard core of union members.

is answerable only to an organized clientele which reflects the same kind of specialization. Two interest groups in New York City share the responsibility of overseeing education policy, the United Parents Association and the Public Education Association. Board membership in both organizations overlaps and their professional staffs work closely together. The United Parents Association is a central City-wide organization made up of delegates elected by school Parent Associations (who have elected membership in the coordinating agency); the Public Education Association is a composite group, made up of other interest groups in the City. Board members of the Public Education Association represent the major civic groups in New York City.

The United Parents Association membership has been drawn largely from middle-class parents who are primarily concerned with local school problems and facilities.[30] The United Parents Association has directed much of its attention to these ends. In more recent years the site selection controversy and school integration problems have occupied much of their time. In an interview the executive director proudly proclaimed credit for convincing the board that more than half the school pairings planned would be inappropriate. Representatives of local Parent Associations were called upon to testify to that effect. The United Parents Association must maintain a parent orientation and a direct concern with the immediate effects of policy on local school situations. It has at times taken general policy positions on "key issues," and when possible makes use of direct influence with board members. A current member of the board was an officer of the United Parents Association prior to her appointment and still maintains active communication with the organization. The executive-director of United Parents Association was recently appointed as a staff advisor to the board. The United Parents Association has supported the appointment of certain supervisory staff in the board of education and appears to have viable contacts within the bureaucracy.

---

30. The United Parents Association is a recent recipient of a N.Y.C. Anti-Poverty Operation Board grant to encourage parent participation in schools in underprivileged communities. This new interest may influence the activities of United Parents Association and broaden their concerns.

Although it is unlikely that the United Parents Association could stimulate broad City-wide parent group support for certain policies, the threat of its large membership has been used effectively to influence board decisions.

The Public Education Association represents the more professional education interests in the City, outside of the system itself. Its activities have centered on the more long-range educational aspects of school policy. Its strategy has been to study special problems in the system and make public recommendations based on these reports. One of the Public Education Association's reports contributed significantly to re-thinking and re-shaping school policy on vocational schools.[31] The views of United Parents Association and Public Education Association on any issue are never far apart.

In the decisions analyzed for this study both organizations were participants in selected areas of policy in a most limited way. Their role as overseer of educational policy is generally supportive rather than critical. Their inclination is to work within the structure, never suggesting radical change, and focusing on particular problems. Both groups exercised little influence in the area of curriculum. On occasion, one or both, have made general statements regarding the need for inclusion of material in the curriculum, or emphasis in a given field, but neither indicated special concern with curriculum matters. Both have supported increased school expenditures and larger city and state appropriations. Public Education Association has tended to support greater independence for the school system in all areas, while United Parents Association seems to prefer continued reliance on City support. The school budget concerns them only in terms of appropriations for particular programs which they are committed to and large state and city support for the overall budget.

The Citizens Committee for Children, which formerly played a larger role in education affairs, has concentrated its efforts on budget review, with the approval of United Parents Association

---

31. *Reorganizing Secondary Education in New York City*, Education Guidance and Work Committee of the Public Education Association, October 1963.

and Public Education Association. Each year the Committee holds hearings in its own offices with the supervisory bureaucracy reviewing the budget for the next year. Representatives of United Parents Association and Public Education Association are usually in attendance. Few changes in the budget result, rather the exercise serves to solicit interest group support for programs and findings.

The screening panel device for selection of the superintendent has given United Parents Association and Public Education Association a more direct role in the selection of board members. Both groups are represented on the panel and exercise a notable influence in the selection process.

Public Education Association has sought a direct role in the selection of the last four superintendents. A change in its influence was discernable when the new board was instituted in 1961. Prior to that time they had not been successful in their pressure to bring in an "outsider" and their recommendations had been virtually ignored. They were, however, a direct influence in the last two appointments. This involvement with appointments fits the pattern suggested by Lowi, that specialized interest groups are primarily concerned with controlling appointments.[32]

Public Participation

Public participation in policy-making can come through two obvious channels, voting and/or organized interest groups. In New York City there are no public votes on school issues. The assumption that voting in itself automatically assures meaningful public participation has long been denied by political scientists. The existence of a pluralist system within the context of a specialized area of decision-making such as education, must be measured in terms of the role and degree of influence of the various public interest groups and elected officials. As has already been demonstrated elected officials in New York City are of de-

32. Lowi, *op. cit.*

clining importance. Two newspapers in the City report regularly on education matters and both have been generally supportive of the bureaucracy. Criticisms of the system have been mild and infrequent. Ethnic and religious groups have been satisfied with adequate representation on the board. Catholic groups intermittently became concerned with text books and curriculum but rely on the Catholic Teacher Association and personal contact with the board to make their minor demands.

Public participation in school policy formulation is circumscribed by the lack of visible decision-making, the shortage of information available to the public on most issues, and a deficiency in the means for participation. Parent associations are active in individual schools, dealing with highly localized and personalized problems. The highly centralized organization of the school system is a deterrent to communications between parents groups and policy-makers.

The school integration issue is the only area in which public response has been vociferous and active. In fact, the integration issue has attracted the widest participation of any policy decision explored.

Local groups of every shade of opinion have organized to oppose or defend individual plans. Among the most vociferous have been the "Parents and Taxpayers Association" (PAT) and their opposition "Parents and Neighbors United for Integrated-Quality Education" (EQUAL). Civil rights groups have entered the school policy field with the single concern of achieving an integrated system. Local civic groups, chambers of commerce, councilmen, and all candidates for public office have voiced strong opinions on proposals. Many of these groups and individuals have never before been involved in school affairs, and their current concern has been limited to the integration issue or its ramifications. Public involvement in the integration issue indicates that more widespread participation results when there is no consensus among those with power and when decisions are forced into the open and become visible.

Perhaps, the most significant development in school decision-making in the last five years is the effect of the integration issue.

Aside from its social and human implications, it has had an important political impact. For the past two decades, superintendents, boards and school bureaucracies have been free-wheeling with little outside pressure. They have successfully closed off participation in school policy formulation from elected government officials and civic groups. The integration issue has broken open the monopoly of power vested in the small core of school officials. It has raised serious questions regarding the role of professionals, their goals and interests in school policy.

Of all the issues studied, integration policy was the only one which involved wide diversity of views and wide participation. It was the only issue which aroused meaningful public participation. Internal conflict on the board, as well as in the bureaucracy, opened the question to public review, though not public resolution. The failure of school bureaucracies to innovate in response to changes in the school population activated citizen and civic interest. This interest may lead to open discussion of other areas of school policy.

Consensus decision-making, confined to the professionals, limits policy alternatives as well as public participation. Conflict between competing forces, and differences in interests and goals guarantee the visibility of policy-making and in turn encourages public participation. These are the characteristics of a system which are most likely to produce change and encourage adaptability.

Lowi points out that changes in New York City have come from three sources (1) a single unpredictable individual, (2) sources outside the City (the state or Federal governments, and (3) the reform system or minority party.[33] The last is the most frequent source of innovation. This conclusion would suggest that changes in education will depend on the new mayor's leadership and perhaps his ability to enlist greater public support and interest in education policy.

Conclusion

In any policy-making structure the adjustment of differences, compromise, and conflict of goals is the process described. The

---

33. *Ibid.*, p. 200.

groups, themselves, are viewed in terms of their own leadership and membership, their resources and resourcefulness. Their pursuit of goals is based on advantage to be gained. The United Federation of Teachers, for example, has greater resources to draw upon in the City community, in the form of general public support, Union allegiances, and direct pressure on the mayor. They have sought, therefore, to transfer their salary battle to the City level. On an issue, such as rotation of teachers, they favor keeping the issue within the school system. Those groups with power tend to rely upon less visible actions and direct pressure. Boycotts and public protests testify to lack of power and/or conflict with more powerful vested interests within the system.

The resources of particular groups or individuals, and the way they are used, is an essential factor in evaluating power. The usual assumption, that economic wealth is a primary resource, is denied in educational decision-making in New York City. The key resource appears to be professional expertise. The education bureaucracy has become virtually self-contained, sealed by its special training and knowledge. It has expanded its role and limited conflict by its manipulation of issues as wholly dependent upon expert judgment, which they alone are competent to make. The teachers and lower level staff have also utilized this resource successfully, challenging any differences in judgment as naive or inexpert. It would appear that conflicts reported throughout the country between school boards and superintendents are a reflection of the struggle which has ensued from the growing importance of professionalism as a viable resource of the education bureaucracy. The holders of economic wealth and/or their representatives in a city, like New York, have supported ever-increasing expenditures in education, but have removed themselves from all other considerations of policy.

There are no economic notables in New York City, who can be identified with public education, none have served on the Board of Education or the Board of Higher Education. It appears that they have concentrated their efforts on broader areas of Federal policy. The civic do-gooders have worked to alleviate problems which are a product of inadequate educational policy rather than assure the development of sound practices.[34] Public education policy has become the province of the professional bureaucrat with the tragic result that policy alternatives are not weighed or even offered and defense of the *status quo* is overpowering.

The results of this study should be compared to data developed for urban school systems in other parts of the country, to determine the degree to which these findings are characteristic of large school systems or related to particular political characteristics which can be defined. The movement toward "professionalization" of school policy-making extends far beyond the City districts. Its implications have been debated by administrative theorists in other fields for some time, yet there appears to be little discussion of the question among school administrators. Constant emphasis on school independence indicates lack of concern or awareness of these larger issues. If nothing else, this analysis of school policy-making in New York City shatters the educators assumption that fiscal dependence denies professional control. It also questions the defense of professional isolation, given the goals of a flexible school system and an involved public.

---

34. This was clearly demonstrated in the activities of Project Head Start in New York City within the last year. Although the board of education is responsible for more than half the Head Start children and facilities the civic groups virtually ignore board policies concentrating their attention and efforts on the private agency centers.

LOUIS H. MASOTTI

*Dr. Masotti, a member of the political
science faculty at Western Reserve
University, is the author of* Education
and Politics in Suburbia, *to be published early this year, and co-author of
"Communities and Budgets: The Sociology of Municipal Expenditures"
published in the December, 1965 Urban Affairs Quarterly. He is currently
engaged in research on the politics of
urban education and the political behavior of the urban poor.*

PATTERNS OF WHITE AND NONWHITE SCHOOL REFERENDA PARTICIPATION AND SUPPORT:

Cleveland, 1960-64

WHILE THE IMPORTANT and difficult battle over *de facto* school segregation is being waged in most Northern cities, the education decision-makers have found it necessary to carry on the day-to-day business of the school system. One of the major persistent problems they have confronted in attempting to meet the changing needs of large urban school systems is money. In spite of the Federal dollars made available recently for urban education programs and projects, the necessity of going to the voters of the school district for the authorization of operating fund tax rates (renewals and increases) and building bonds is ever present. Asking the public to increase taxes is never easy; doing

AUTHOR'S NOTE: *The author wishes to acknowledge the very able assistance of James Monhart in collecting the data and computing the measures used in this paper, the cooperation of the Cleveland School Superintendent and Board, and the Cuyahoga County Board of Elections. The Greater Cleveland Associated Foundation provided financial assistance.*

240

so in the atmosphere of the racial unrest which pervades American cities, when the motives of school boards and superintendents are suspect (by both sides), provides a formal occasion for registering conflict.

This chapter reports the findings of research on the patterns of racial participation in, and support of, seven school referenda issues before and after a bloody civil rights dispute over the question of *de facto* segregation in the Cleveland school system. The researcher's purpose was to determine if there was a significant difference in the patterns of participation and support between

TABLE 1

Cleveland School Referenda, 1960-1964*

Date	Type	Amount	Outcome
May, 1960	*Operating levy*		Defeated
	renewal	8.6 mills/$1.00	
	increase (1961 only)	2.0	
	increase (1962 only)	3.0	
	Building levy		Defeated
	renewal	1.2	
	increase (1961, 1962)	2.8	
November, 1960	*Operating levy*		Passed
	renewal	8.6	
	increase (1961 only)	2.0	
	increase (1962 only)	2.5	
	Building levy		Passed
	renewal	1.2	
	increase	1.8	
November, 1962	*Operating levy*		Passed
	renewal	8.6	
	increase (1963 only)	4.0	
	increase (1964 only)	5.0	
	Building bonds		Passed
	$55,000,000 for construction and equipping of new buildings, additions and modernization of existing buildings, purchase sites and buildings	1.299 mills/$1.00 for 20 years	
May, 1964	*Operating levy*		Passed
	renewal	13.6	
	increase (1965 through 1969)	2.5	

* The Ohio School Code authorizes Cleveland to levy up to 10 mills without voter approval, of which 4.0 mills is now being used. The millage figures for operating levies in the table represent rates in addition to the 4.0 mills already being levied. Thus, the total levy in 1966 is 21.299 mills/$1.00 of assessed valuation: 4.0 plus 13.6 renewal and 2.5 increase authorized in May, 1964, plus 1.299 from the November, 1962 bond issue.

white and nonwhite voters of the community and what effect, if any, the civil rights struggle over schools in this city has had on these patterns.

Seven school referenda were submitted to the voters of Cleveland in four elections spanning the period May, 1960, to May, 1964. In May, 1960, the Cleveland School Board suffered its first referendum defeat in twenty-one years when substantial increases in both the operating and building tax rates were rejected by the electorate. The same package passed easily the following November after the requested increases had been revised down-ward. A much higher operating levy increase, plus a $55 million building bond, carried easily in November, 1962. The May, 1964, operating levy narrowly escaped defeat when it became the target of concerted effort by civil rights groups protesting what they considered the intentional segregationist policy on the part of the school board.

For the purposes of examining the patterns of racial participation and support in the four elections, the thirty-three wards of Cleveland were categorized into three groups: predominantly white, predominantly nonwhite, and mixed.[1] The white wards consisted of all wards with a population 80 percent or more white according to the 1960 census ($n = 20$, range $=$ 80 to 100 percent, mean $=$ 96 percent). The nonwhite wards were 80 percent or more nonwhite ($n = 7$, range $=$ 82.5 to 98 percent, mean $=$ 87 percent).[2] The mixed wards were those which fell between the 80 percent white and nonwhite criteria ($n = 6$, range $=$ 22.4 to 68 percent nonwhite, mean $=$ 48.8 percent).[3]

---

1. It should be noted that the city of Cleveland and the Cleveland school district are not exactly coterminous. Parts or all of three suburbs are included in the district, and two small areas of Cleveland are in the Shaker Heights and Berea school districts. The number of voters involved in both cases is small, and for purposes of analysis it is being assumed that the boundaries of the city and the school district are identical.

2. The term "nonwhite" is used here because much of the available data on the racial composition of the wards used "nonwhite" rather than "Negro." The 1960 census shows that 99.1 percent of Cleveland's nonwhite population is Negro, and therefore nonwhite and Negro are used interchangeably in this analysis.

3. As is the case in most if not all large cities, the census tracts used by the Bureau of the Census and the ward boundaries do not coincide. Fortunately for both the 1960 and the 1965 special census, the painstaking task of converting tract population data to wards had been accomplished before this project was undertaken. For 1960, I relied on the data found in Cynthia Brown, "School Issues Referenda in Cleveland from 1950 to 1964," typescript, Cleveland: Greater Cleveland Associated Foundation, September, 1964.

This classification of the city wards was used for the analysis of referenda submitted in 1960 and 1962, but two events necessitated a reclassification for the 1964 referendum. In 1963, the Cleveland City Council reapportioned the city to reflect the population shifts indicated by the 1960 census. Twelve of the thirty-three wards were altered significantly, but the other twenty-one remained substantially unchanged. A second relevant event was the special mid-decade census of population conducted in Cleveland–Cuyahoga County in the spring of 1965.[4] Although few of the census findings were made public, those that were publicized included population size and race. This information allowed the wards to be reclassified using the same criteria as before but with data which more accurately reflected the rather substantial changes occurring in the size and racial composition of the Cleveland population between 1960 and 1965.[5]

The reclassification of wards for the 1964 election resulted in an increase in the 80 percent or more nonwhite wards ($n = 10$, range = 83.5 to 99 percent, mean = 91.2 percent) and a decrease in the predominantly white wards from twenty to sixteen (range = 87.2 to 99.8 percent, mean = 97.8 percent).[6] The mixed wards increased from six to seven (range = 23.3 to 75.7 percent nonwhite, mean = 43.9 percent).[7]

---

4. U.S. Department of Commerce, Bureau of the Census, "Special Census of Cleveland, Ohio, April 1, 1965," Special Census, Series P-28, No. 1390, Washington: Government Printing Office, November, 1965.

5. Between 1960 and 1965, the Bureau of the Census estimated that the white population of Cleveland declined by 91,436 while the nonwhite population increased by 25,244. *Ibid.* The 1965 city population of 810,858 represents a 7.4 decrease from the 876,050 residents in 1960. The percentage of the nonwhite population increased from 28.8 percent to 34.6 percent in this five-year period.

6. The 1965 special census tract data were converted to ward data by the Governmental Research Institute of Cleveland. The regrouping of the new wards was adapted from a report entitled "Cleveland 1965 Population by Ward Showing Racial Composition," Report #85, Cleveland: Governmental Research Institute, December 29, 1965.

7. There are some obvious disadvantages in trying to compare the aggregate behavior of units over time when the unit boundaries have been changed. On the other hand, given the high mobility of Cleveland's population and particularly the racial patterns noted in footnote 5 above, this disadvantage may be more than offset by the 1965 special census data. It must be emphasized that it is the racial composition of the wards that is being examined here and not the wards themselves. Furthermore, the 1964 referendum is the only one which has occurred since the school controversy and the influence that this event had on the behavior patterns of white and nonwhite voters is a major focus of the research.

The three ward groups have been compared along three dimensions of electoral behavior in the seven referenda under consideration. Two measures of election participation were used — the size of the turnout and the percentage of turnout not voting on school issues — and one measure of school support was used — the percentage of all those voting on school issues who approved them.

Registered Voters and Voting

Table 2 indicates the distribution of registered voters in each of the ward groups for each of the four elections. The distribution remained almost static between May, 1960, and November, 1962, but a rather significant shift took place between 1962 and 1963. How much of this shift is due to the redrawn ward lines and how much is a reflection of the changing composition of the city's population during this period is not known. Nonetheless, by 1964 the white wards had 13.5 percent less of the registered vote, and the nonwhite wards had 10 percent more. The difference had shifted to the mixed wards.

TABLE 2

Distribution of Registered Voters (in percent)

Date	White wards	Nonwhite wards	Mixed wards
May, 1960	64.0	20.4	15.6
November, 1960	63.0	20.5	16.5
November, 1962	63.8	20.0	16.2
May, 1964	50.2	30.3	19.5

The degree to which the vote potential (measured by registered voters) of the three ward aggregates was utilized has been examined by computing a ratio of the percentage of registered voters in each group to the total number of votes cast on school issues (Table 3). The ratio for the white wards is consistently above, and the nonwhite wards consistently below, 1.0. With the exception of 1964, when their ratio exceeded even that of the white wards, the mixed wards had ratios lower than either of the other groups.

244

TABLE 3

Ratio of School Voters to Registered Voters*

Date		White wards	Nonwhite wards	Mixed wards
May, 1960	Operating levy	1.05	.97	.90
	Building levy	1.04	.96	.89
November, 1960	Operating levy	1.07	.88	.88
	Building levy	1.08	.87	.87
November, 1962	Operating levy	1.09	.87	.82
	Building bond	1.07	.92	.84
May, 1964	Operating levy	1.02	.95	1.03
	Mean	1.06	.92	.89

* These ratios are arrived at by dividing the percentage of the total number of registered voters in each ward group by the percentage of the total vote for each school issue in the group.

For the four elections examined in this study, the white ward voters of Cleveland not only have a greater potential vote — although it is diminishing — but they also, on school issues at least, consistently "overvote" their potential, while the nonwhite and mixed wards tend to "undervote" theirs.

Turnout

Voter turnout of the ward groups was compared, and the results indicate some patterns of participation. The data in Table 3 suggest that the type of election is related to racial turnout. For these four elections, at least, the white ward voters tend to turn out in larger numbers than the nonwhite (as well as those voters in the mixed wards) in general elections, but this pattern was reversed in the primary elections. In both primaries the nonwhites outvoted the whites, and in one of the two they outvoted the mixed wards. The citywide turnout rate used as a bench mark shows that the white ward turnout was considerably below this rate for the primaries and considerably above it for the general elections. Both the nonwhite and mixed voters reversed this turnout pattern, exceeding the citywide turnout in the primaries and lagging in the generals. As is to be expected, the turnout for all three groups is markedly higher for the general elections than the primaries, even though the two primaries under examination could be expected to draw turnouts larger than usual because of the extraordinary circumstances of those elections: a vigorous campaign waged by the Cleveland Chamber of Commerce against the large increase in property taxes proposed by the school board in 1960, and the bloody civil rights episode immediately preceding the 1964 election.

TABLE 4

Voter Turnout (in percent)

Date	White wards	Nonwhite wards	Mixed wards	City total
May, 1960	45.8	49.1	51.1	47.2
November, 1960	87.7	83.3	82.0	85.8
November, 1962	69.9	64.8	59.7	67.3
May, 1964	51.5	55.3	54.7	53.3
Mean	63.7	63.1	61.9	63.4

Because of the differences in the degree of support the school referenda received from the ward groups used in this analysis (discussed below), the turnout patterns of the groups become an important consideration for school policy-makers in deciding when to submit referenda. There is evidence to indicate, for example, that the Cleveland School Board employed the kinds of data used in this paper in making its decision to go to the voters with a $66 million bond issue in November, 1966.

Selective Voting Behavior

It is well known that the American voting public does not turn out in large numbers for school elections or for referenda. However, many school elections are special elections held on dates that do not coincide with municipal, state, or national elections. The reasons for this decision are often related to the apprehension of school officials that educational issues will not be considered on their merits when constitutional and charter amendments are included with candidates for municipal, state, or national office, as well as for school office, and perhaps with a number of nonschool authorization and bond referenda. The special school election is designed to focus attention on the school issue and to attract a reduced electorate interested in schools to vote the issue up or down.

All four of the Cleveland elections under consideration were mixed elections which included a variety of candidates and referenda issues: municipal, county, state, and national. This section of the chapter examines the selective behavior of the ward groups by comparing their participation in the election, i.e., turnout, with their participation in the school issues. In general, the concern was with the patterns of transfer voting behavior, that is, what proportion of those who took the trouble to go to the polls (the turnout) also voted on school issues? Specifically, was there any significant difference between the behavior of the white and of the nonwhite wards in this matter? Merely knowing the election turnout patterns of the two groups tells us little if there is a substantial difference in the utilization these groups make of the turnout potential for school issues.

The degree to which the voting potential of the three voting aggregates was used has been examined by employing two indices of school issue turnout compared with the general rate of turnout for each election. Table 5 reveals the percentage difference between election turnout and the turnout for each of the school issues. For example, in the November, 1960, presidential election, the white ward voters had an overall turnout rate of 87.7 percent, but for the school operating levy the rate was only 76.4 percent (a difference of 11.3 percent), and for the school building levy, 75.9 percent (a difference of 11.8 percent).

An examination of this table indicates an interracial pattern without deviation. As is to be expected, a turnout "drop-off" is found in every ward group as well as for the city as a whole. In every case, the drop-off of nonwhite ward voting on school issues is greater than that for the white wards, the mixed wards, and the city. With one exception (City 1964), the overall pattern of all three groups and the city for the four elections is consistent. The drop-off of the nonwhite group is highest in every case, followed by the mixed wards, the city, and the white wards. The consistency of this pattern is more impressive when it is remembered that the

TABLE 5

Percentage Difference Between Election Turnout and School Issue Turnout

Date		White wards	Nonwhite wards	Mixed wards	City total
May, 1960	Operating levy	3.7	8.4	7.8	5.2
	Building levy	3.7	8.8	8.5	5.3
November, 1960	Operating levy	11.3	20.3	19.2	14.4
	Building levy	11.8	22.4	20.6	15.4
November, 1962	Operating levy	9.0	16.0	13.7	11.2
	Building bond	8.6	11.9	11.5	9.8
May, 1964	Operating levy	3.1	10.3	5.8	5.9
	Mean	7.3	14.0	12.4	9.6

248

general turnout rate of the nonwhites exceeded that of the white wards in both primaries (see Table 4).

A second measure of reduced voter participation in school elections is what we have called the percentage of unused vote.[8] This term refers to the percentage of those who go to the polls on election day but who do not cast a vote in a particular contest. It is arrived at by taking the difference between the election turnout of some aggregate (e.g., a group of 80 percent white wards) and its turnout in a particular contest as a percentage of the election turnout. For example, in the white wards in May, 1960, the election turnout was 96,503 and the operating levy turnout was 88,829, a difference of 7,674. These 7,674 went to the polls in May, 1960, but did not vote either for or against the operating levy; thus, 7.6 percent of the potential vote for the school operating levy remained unused.

Table 6 shows the results of computing unused vote percentages for the three ward aggregates and for the city itself for each of the seven school issues submitted to the voters over the four-year period. Since the basic data employed in this index (election turnout and issue turnout) are essentially the same as those used in the preceding one, it is not surprising that the patterns revealed by the two are almost identical. The nonwhites rank first on every issue except one (November, 1962, building bond) with as much as 27 percent of the turnout not participating in a school referendum (November, 1960, building levy). The lowest unused vote figure for the nonwhites (17.0 percent) is greater than the highest for the white wards (13.4 percent). The mixed wards do not trail the nonwhite wards by very much, and on one issue they have a percentage of unused vote surpassing the nonwhites. The white wards have half the amount of unused votes of the nonwhites overall (10.5 compared with 21.1) and rank last on this measure in each of the separate elections. The unused vote figures for the entire city more closely approximate those of the white wards than the others —

8. The concept of the unused vote as a measure of intraelection indifference on the part of the electorate toward particular offices and issues was developed by the author and Maurice Klain while comparing the voting behavior over a period of years of the poorest and richest precincts in Cleveland.

except for the May, 1964 operating levy election, where the unused vote of the entire city percentage exceeds the mixed wards figure by only two-tenths of 1 percent.

TABLE 6

Unused Vote (in percent)

Date		White wards	Nonwhite wards	Mixed wards	City total
May, 1960	Operating levy	7.6	17.0	15.5	11.0
	Building levy	8.0	19.9	16.7	12.3
November, 1960	Operating levy	12.9	24.3	23.4	16.8
	Building levy	13.4	26.9	25.1	13.9
November, 1962	Operating levy	12.9	24.7	23.0	16.6
	Building bond	12.3	18.3	19.3	14.5
May, 1964	Operating levy	6.1	18.8	10.8	11.0
	Mean	10.5	21.1	19.1	13.7

Based on the general pattern of comparative school issue participation indicated by the two measures used in this analysis, the conclusion one must reach is clear and significant. It is simply this: Although the nonwhite wards may demonstrate a higher overall turnout rate than white wards for some elections, specifically for primaries, the more important figure insofar as the school officials are concerned is the rate at which the two groups participate *on school issues*. The Cleveland data reveal a rather substantial par-

250

ticipation drop-off for the nonwhites, approximating one-fifth of the voters overall, but generally higher for the fall elections than for primaries. The importance of this differential participation level of whites and nonwhites becomes clear when we examine the school support levels of the two groups.

School Support

Thus far we have examined two dimensions of election participation in the white, nonwhite, and mixed wards in Cleveland. The voter turnout data informed us about the comparative level of participation by each of the groups in the election itself, and the rate of voter drop-off from turnout to the act of casting a vote on a school issue revealed differences in the utilization of vote potential by the three groups. As important as these participation patterns are, they can only help us to answer questions about *who* votes for *what*. A more crucial question, particularly from the school officials point of view, is *how* those who participate vote. Therefore, we have investigated the differential *levels of school support* among the ward groups, that is, the percentage of affirmative votes of all votes cast on each issue.

The results are shown in Table 7. The patterns of school support revealed by these data are again clear. For the three elections held between May, 1960, and November, 1962, the nonwhite wards are highly supportive of all six issues on those ballots. On four of the issues, the support level ranges between 85 and 90 percent (November, 1960; November, 1962), with the highest for the $55 million bond issue, which marked a significant departure from the board's pay-as-you-go policy. The lowest level of support during this period, when three of every four voters in this ward group approved the issues, was in May, 1960, when both the operating and building levies failed.

During the same period, the white ward voters were the least supportive of the school issues in every case. In May, 1960, when 64 percent of the registered voters lived in the twenty white wards, the failure of the issues to carry was attributed to the extremely

251

negative vote in these wards. On the four subsequent issues the support level doubled but remained approximately twenty percentage points below that in the nonwhite wards.

In the mixed wards, the voters gave a slim majority to the 1960 defeated issues but supported the others in the 1960–1962 period at a 75 to 80 percent level, about halfway between the nonwhite and white groups in every case. In this sense, the pattern revealed here is very similar to the one uncovered when we examined the unused vote figures: nonwhites high, whites low, and the mixed wards between.

A serious racial conflict over schools occurred in Cleveland between the approval of the 1962 issues and the May, 1964, election. It was most violent in the four months immediately preceding the 1964 primary, including the accidental death of a school protestor less than a month before election day. There was a great deal of concern about what effect this eruption might have on the outcome of the operating levy referendum. Voters in the nonwhite wards were strongly urged to reject the school issue in protest over what were alleged to be prosegregationist school board policies. It was not clear then how the white ward voters would behave in the aftermath of the racial violence of April, 1964. In the eyes of many whites, the school board had gone out of its way to bus Negro children into white schools, and this did not particularly please them.

The figures for May, 1964, in Table 7 give some indication of what occurred. The support level of the nonwhites shows a decrease of over 50 percent from November, 1960 to 1962, and support in the mixed wards (44 percent nonwhite in 1965) decreased 30 percent. Because the white ward support remained at about the November, 1960–1962 level, the operating levy passed but with little to spare.

Although it cannot be demonstrated with the data presented here, it has been argued by observers of Cleveland ethnic group politics that the nonwhite "blacklash" directed at the school officials in 1964 was matched by a white ethnic group "backlash" designed to render the nonwhite protest ineffectual. The blacklash behavior is evident in Table 7; the backlash is not evident and is based on assumptions of how the white voters would have voted in May, 1964, in the absence of the racial flare-up the preceding month.

The overall support patterns based on the means of the seven school issues are not significantly altered by the nonwhites' and mixed wards' voting behavior in 1964. For the four-year period 1960–1964, the nonwhite wards averaged 76 percent, the mixed wards 68 percent, and the white wards 57 percent. The citywide average is slightly higher than the white wards, slightly lower than the mixed wards, and substantially below (14 points) the non-white wards.

TABLE 7

Support Levels* (in percent)

Date		White wards	Nonwhite wards	Mixed wards	City total
May, 1960	Operating levy	38.0	73.6	58.1	47.9
	Building levy	33.2	73.5	55.1	44.3
November, 1960	Operating levy	68.7	86.3	78.7	73.3
	Building levy	67.4	88.0	79.7	72.8
November, 1962	Operating levy	61.7	84.9	75.1	67.5
	Building bond	64.7	89.4	79.9	71.3
May, 1964	Operating levy	67.4	34.0	48.1	53.9
	Mean	57.3	75.7	67.8	61.6

*Those who voted to approve the levies and the bond issue as a percentage of those who voted on the issue.

Conclusion

This chapter has attempted to determine if there have been any patterns of racial voting behavior on school referenda in a major Northern city recently experiencing a civil rights controversy focused on school integration. Although it is not without its shortcomings, principally the availability of only one postcontroversy referendum (and that occurring after the voting districts had been somewhat altered), several patterns of participation and support behavior are indicated.

The Cleveland data suggest that voters in predominantly white wards consistently overvote, and those in the nonwhite wards consistently undervote, their potential based on the percentage of total registered vote in each. Voter turnout tends to be a function of the type of election. The whites outvote the nonwhites in general elections and the nonwhites outvote the whites in the primaries, with the differences being approximately the same in both cases. Using two different measures makes clear that of those who turn out for an election, more white than nonwhite voters will vote on school issues. Perhaps most significant is the marked difference in the levels of school support found in the white and in the nonwhite wards; with one important exception — the referendum following the civil rights conflict — the nonwhite wards give overwhelming support to school issues at a rate approximately 20 percentage points higher than the white wards.

These patterns raise some problems for those whose purpose is to pass bond and levy referenda. Although the nonwhite voters indicate a pattern of high support, they also evidence a pattern of low participation *in school elections*. Furthermore, based on the substantial decrease in the level of support from the nonwhite wards in the first and only referendum test since the school civil rights affair, the outcome of future building bond and operating levy referenda is a matter of some concern. Since the 1964 controversy, the Cleveland School Board has appointed a new superintendent who has moved quickly to restore nonwhite confidence in the intentions of the school system. He has been aided by the election of several top-quality people to the school board and the departure of one member strongly disliked by the nonwhite community.

Nonetheless, the civil rights groups have begun to agitate for "more positive steps toward pupil and staff integration." On June 14, 1966, the Cleveland NAACP picketed the administration building. The cochairman of the NAACP's education committee was quoted as saying that the demonstration was designed "to remind the school board that when its promotion list is announced in July we expect more Negro administrators in West Side schools and more Negro teachers assigned to predominantly white schools. *Support of the* [November school operating levy and $66 million bond issue] *could be withheld* if this is not done, if the neighborhood school policy is not changed, and if the Board does not pledge more support and authority for its human relations department."[9] Whether this overt threat will be carried out and support withheld, as was done in 1964, or whether the nonwhite voters will return to the pre-1964 support pattern is a matter for speculation at this point.[10] It would appear, however, that the nonwhite leaders of Cleveland are aware of the nonwhite support pattern and plan to use it in the on-going struggle to minimize segregation of pupils and staff if not to achieve integration.

---

9. *Cleveland Press*, June 6, 1966.

10. The November, 1966, school referenda were held after this chapter was completed. A cursory examination of the support levels in the three ward groupings used in the 1964 election analysis indicate a clear reversion to the pre-1964 pattern:

		White wards	Nonwhite wards	Mixed wards	City total
November, 1966	4 Mill levy increase	64.6	84.8	72.4	70.2
	$66,000,000 bond issue	61.0	81.1	67.9	66.0

PART III

SOLUTIONS AND GOALS

Achieving Change

WERNER Z. HIRSCH

PLANNING

*The author is Director of the Insti-
tute of Government and Public Affairs and Professor of Economics at
the University of California, Los
Angeles.*

EDUCATION TODAY

FOR TOMORROW

T HERE IS LITTLE QUESTION that we face dramatic changes in urban life—including both new socioeconomic conditions and new possibilities for educational innovations that might help us meet these changes. But are we prepared to face up to the education decisions that we will be called upon to make?

It is the contention of this paper, first, that we are not now prepared to do so; and second, that there are a number of measures that can be taken to make education decision-makers better prepared to meet the three fundamental responsibilities they face:

Policy Consideration: The task here is to scan the horizon, identify new goals and directions for education, and become aware of coming opportunities, problems and potential solutions.

Program Formulation: Once goals, problems, and potential solutions are identified, officials must select those activities which will most effectively meet our needs, and integrate these activities into fully formulated educational programs.

Program Administration: Once programs are formulated, means must be designed to administer them efficiently, including the means for review and revision, as required.

While these three areas overlap in that they may be considered concurrently and the same officials may be dealing with more than one of them, they are distinctly different in terms of handling: They may involve different types of decision theory; they may differ in their reliance on analytical tools, such as benefit-cost estimation; they involve different degrees of certainty; they require different mixtures of capital investment and operating costs; they require different types and levels of information; and so on.

This paper discusses each of these three areas of responsibility and suggests specific approaches intended to help officials fulfill them. It then briefly considers, for illustration, a few aspects of the future which serve to emphasize the importance of developing new approaches of the kind suggested.

Policy Consideration

Systematic exploration of the future to identify coming problems and to establish new goals and directions for education is a rather novel undertaking. To the best of my knowledge, there is little precedence and experience from which we can directly learn how to go about this.[1]

The visionary might try to design a far-out, comprehensive, horizon-scanning information system to provide us with early warning and identification. To do so would require him to have a good understanding of how officials do and should act in certain situations and some good hunches about which situations will become major concerns. In urban education, for example, these concerns would likely include the effects of certain scientific and technological advances; underinvestment in education and ineffective use of education, either across-the-board, or in relation to certain minority groups, age groups, geographic areas etc.; population increase; and affluence and other socioeconomic conditions which will affect demand for education.

One could explore these concerns by developing a profile of the future, based on projections of data now available, in the

---

1. Among those who have contributed valuable insights toward approaches for the "futures problem" are Bertrand de Jouvenel (Ed.), *Futuribles: Studies in Conjecture,* Geneva: Droz, 1963 and 1965; and Dennis Gabor, *Inventing the Future,* London: Martin Secker & Warburg, Ltd., 1963.

light of explicit assumptions about the future. For example, a forecast of expenditures greatly exceeding revenues could mean a potential problem, while a forecast of social benefits exceeding social costs might offer new opportunities.

A more cautious approach would be to try to design an information system that relates to new goals and problems as they become identified on an *ad hoc* basis by experts and engage in studies which verify their likely occurrence and importance. Eventually the profile of the future that would emerge might prove similar to that envisaged in the more comprehensive visionary approach.

We should keep in mind that an analyst might detect a potential education problem that decision-makers will not recognize or may not be able to deal with. While I do not want to suggest that analysts limit their interest to "soluble" problems, I do believe they should emphasize those problems that decision-makers are able to do something about. Often the policy-maker will not be satisfied to be told that a great problem in education is likely to be in the making; he will also insist on getting some estimates on whether identifying the problem and working toward its solution will prove politically advantageous to him.

To scan the education horizon for new goals, problems, and opportunities and to develop potential solutions is a large and exciting venture requiring our best minds. But most school districts are too small and poor to engage in this type of effort. But even if they had the money, the commonality of data and methods would make an area-wide rather than a local approach more economical. Therefore, I propose the establishment of a Metropolitan Education Outlook Station to scan the horizon for possible futures that an area might face and for desirable futures that can be created. Such a station could cover an entire metropolitan area or perhaps a number of them without any major government reorganization. Federal and state funds may help establish and perhaps even operate such outlook stations, offering local education units unified information and a common source of experts advice, which in turn could lead to better coordination of action.

An example of one device that might prove useful for scanning the future is the Delphi technique.[2] This is a way to systematically use the judgment of experts on problems where rigorous analysis is not possible because of the unavailability of hard data, inadequate theory, or other reasons.

The method has two functions: to generate ideas and judgments and to combine into a single position the judgments of panel members with regard to the solution of a given problem or choice of policy.

The Delphi technique replaces expert committee activity with a carefully designed program of sequential individual interrogations (usually best conducted by questionnaires) that are interspersed with information feed-in and opinion feedback. The avoidance of face-to-face discussion—the traditional and perhaps simplest way of arranging cooperation among experts—diminishes the influence of certain psychological factors in the formation of a consensus; for example, specious persuasion by a supposed authority, the loudest voice, the unwillingness to abandon publicly expressed opinions, and the bandwagon effect of majority opinion.

Program Formulation

Once the Metropolitan Education Outlook Station (or some similar entity) has identified new goals, problems, and possible solutions of concern to the area, the relative merits of alternative solutions must be investigated and an effective program or, more likely, several candidate programs should be designed and evaluated before choices are made.

Various evaluations would doubtless be carried out by one or more of the different political jurisdictions involved: the Federal government, state government, and/or local school district.

The Metropolitan Education Outlook Station previously described might play a key role here too. For example, the station

---

2. Olaf Helmer, "The Delphi Method for Systematizing Judgments About the Future," MR-61, Institute of Government and Public Affairs, Los Angeles; University of California, April 1966, 15 pp.

might be used to analyze the possible consequences of alternative program formulations, leaving each local district to use this information to suit its own particular needs and outlooks. Or the station might under contract or other support arrangement focus on the situation of one or more local districts. It might perform analyses, make recommendations, and even help in carrying these out under local authority.

One way for one to decide how to meet a particular problem or strive toward a particular goal is to line up the various solutions or approaches, examine the costs of each and the benefits of each, and choose accordingly—either the most effective means for a given cost or the least costly means to achieve a given objective.[3]

Ideally, such benefit-cost analysis should take into account all costs by whomever incurred and all benefits to whomever they accrue. The benefits are the value of the added output or added satisfaction resulting from the choice of one course of action rather than another; the costs are the resources sacrificed if that action is taken, i.e., their value in their best alternative uses.

If benefit and cost measures were all-inclusive, certain, and commensurable, we would expect to choose the alternative which would yield the greatest present value of such benefits. But, in fact, we cannot obtain complete estimates of the present value of net benefits. We can, however, usually identify and make estimates of many major social benefits and social costs and frequently we can furnish the decision-maker with partial qualitative information and judgments for other costs and benefits which cannot be directly measured.

Benefit-cost analysis also involves the careful, explicit treatment of uncertainties and their implications for planning and budgeting. These arise largely because of the extended time horizon required for rational education decisions. Some of the tools for handling these uncertainties are sensitivity analysis, contingency analysis,

---

3. For a concise and rigorous statement on cost-benefit analysis see Roland N. McKean, "Cost-Benefit Analysis and British Defense Expenditures," *Scottish Journal of Political Economy*, Vol. X, pp. 17-35.

and *a fortiori* analysis.[4] Analysts also are concerned with design-
ing decision strategies and options which offer preferred solutions
under different types of uncertainty; e.g., sequential decision-making, parallel activities, investments in flexible multipurpose projects,
etc.

Let us illustrate the use of benefit-cost analysis in relation to a
simplified problem. Assume we wished to educate urban youth
beyond the present six years of high school. We might consider
two alternatives: to provide every youngster with one year of
junior college education or to provide him with five summers of
two-month summer school before he graduates from high school.

To evaluate these alternatives, we can estimate the cost of each
of these programs in terms of capital costs, operating costs, fore-
gone earnings to the student, and other costs. And we can estimate
the benefits of each in terms of the added income the student could
expect as a result of the additional education.

When this is done, we find that the junior college program
results in a benefit-cost ratio for male students of about 1.95—a
return of $1.95 for every dollar invested.[5] The return for females
is less than half of that for males. The summer school program
results in a benefit-cost ratio of 3.23 for male students and 1.47 for
female students. Thus, judging on the basis of these calculations,
one would tend to choose the summer school program.

Such simple calculations have a number of shortcomings, of
course. Especially, one might want to consider other costs and
benefits and other alternative programs not included in this limited
calculation. Such benefits might include the job opportunities which
arise for others when members of the labor force enter junior college on a full-time basis; the decline in the demand for public
services resulting from social and personal disorders, traceable to
more adequate schooling; and so on. Another consideration stems
from the fact that such a program would probably cost annually

4. For a detailed discussion see Gene H. Fisher, "The Role of Cost-Utility Analysis
in Program Budgeting," in David Novick (Ed.), *Program Budgeting*, Cambridge, Mass.:
Harvard University Press, 1965, p. 74.

5. Werner Z. Hirsch and Morton J. Marcus, "Some Benefit-Cost Considerations of
Universal Junior College Education," *The National Tax Journal*, June, 1966.

about a billion dollars, and this same billion dollars could be used in different ways to improve education.

Closely related to benefit-cost analysis is the program budget, discussed below under Program Administration. This type of budget provides a convenient framework within which to carry forth cost and benefit calculations for individual activities and to integrate them into larger units, ultimately up to the level of complete programs. Thus, entire alternative programs as well as their parts may be compared on the basis of how much they cost and the benefits they produce.

Program Administration

Once a program is selected, it must be administered by a specific jurisdiction, even though it might be financed by more than a single government unit. One shortcoming of urban school-district, college, and university administrations is their reliance on administrative budgets which are laid out along organizational lines. This type of budget does not allow the administrator to relate the specific, required resources (costs) to outputs or goals that the school district would like to achieve. Thus, it does not furnish him with a basis for making choices between one alternative or another. It inhibits the coordination of interrelated decisions and the articulation of alternatives in the light of their trade-offs; and it obscures the full cost over time of many decisions.

Because of these shortcomings, I would like to propose the development of a "program budget." The chief feature of this budget is its output orientation. It allows the activities of several departments to be assembled in terms of specific types of activity or output packages—programs and subprograms of various convenient levels of aggregation. The program budget can be structured in a way to be consistent with the program formulation stage and expenditure information. In it, cost data can be arranged in terms of programs and subprograms, and so can be attached to specific outputs and goals which can be expressed, at least partially, in quantified terms. In a program budget, programs must be clearly delineated, with a minimum overlapping and interaction with other programs, and its components should be in close competition with each other. Program organization and cost should allow disaggregation into operationally useful building blocks, i.e., manpower, material, equipment, etc., which can be conveniently combined and recombined to represent various alternative subprograms.

An urban school district might want to design a program budget composed of the following programs:

PRIMARY EDUCATION

SECONDARY EDUCATION
  College preparatory
  Vocational

HIGHER EDUCATION
  Junior colleges

ADULT EDUCATION
  Refresher and retraining for professionals
  Education for late-bloomers
  Education for full intellectual participation in social and cultural affairs
  Urban extension services

LIBRARY SERVICES

RESEARCH AND DEVELOPMENT

Procedures must be established which will facilitate administration of programs without the undesirable feature of excessive central control. In particular, there must be procedures for review and revision, including reprogramming. For example, a dollar threshold might be established for certain administrative levels, so that any reprogramming involving more than a specified dollar amount would require permission from higher authority. Any such arrangements would be facilitated by linking the program budgeting process to the prevailing annual budget cycle of the school district.

There also exist some powerful analytical methods that should help improve the efficiency with which school and university operations can be planned, including linear programming, queing theory, inventory control mechanisms, progress reporting, variance accounting, and others.

Far-Future Opportunities

Let us begin with hindsight, and consider a few examples of some problems and solutions that have emerged in recent years. We should have been able to predict ten to twenty years ago that a fiscal crisis was going to face education and that massive Federal aid to local school districts would come about some time in the 1960s. Since the end of World War II, it was obvious that demand for primary and secondary education would increase. Equally clear was the fact that the tax base at local and state levels was increasing much more slowly than the demand for education funds. It also seemed clear it would be extremely difficult to find new local and state revenue sources of major magnitude unless the Federal treasury could be tapped.

Once the need for Federal aid became sufficiently great, the church-state issue, which blocked Federal aid for many years, was forced to recede in importance; the Supreme Court decisions on school desegregation and reapportionment improved the political climate in Congress and overcame some of the states rights objections; and a solution to the serious funding problem gradually emerged.

Another example is Federal aid to the culturally and economically deprived children within "the war on poverty" framework. This should have been widely foreseen as an issue for the 1960s. (It was, in fact, predicted by Leon Keyserling, based perhaps more on economic information than on civil rights insights.) Projected wealth increases were sufficiently large to support an attack on poverty in the 1960s. There were also projections of budget surpluses which would have deflationary consequences and the recognition that the gap in income between whites and nonwhites was increasing. Further, the importance of educational opportunity as a means of improving in the long run the lot of minorities was clear. In spite of these various indicators, the "war on poverty" approach, and its implications for educational needs was, and perhaps still is, not fully appreciated.

Still another example concerns Federal support for higher education. Ever since the early days of World War II, the importance of a reservoir of well-trained and highly skilled manpower was clear. The national welfare in the long run required more and better education, and yet state and local governments did not have sufficient funds to support higher education; many low-income groups wanted education but were unable to afford it; returning GI's were eager to obtain an education; and, finally, the GI Bill of Rights established a precedent by which the Federal government proved that it should and could effectively participate in offering higher education to young Americans. Finally, Sputnik dramatized the already existing U.S.-U.S.S.R. competition to seek technological superiority in specific areas and set off a new wave of Federal interest in education.

In all these cases, education was ill prepared to meet the changes it could have anticipated and planned for.

With these *ex post* examples in mind, let us consider the distant future. The day might come when medicine will succeed in allowing man to remain in full vigor for many more decades than he does today. If life expectancy should double, the traditional age-specific role structure in society would be torn to pieces. In a society in which everyone lives to be seventy, children up to adolescence can make up about a quarter of the total population. In a society in which everybody lives to be 140, the proportion of such children would fall to slightly above a tenth of the population.

Knowledge tends to grow at a rapid rate, and even today a professor often finds himself obsolete in his fifties. Certainly the Ph.D. degree could not be regarded as a "union card" for university teaching over a period of a hundred years. Even assuming that intellectual vigor is unimpaired by age, the contrast between distinguished and undistinguished teaching could be enormously accentuated. Most likely, formal education of the kind we know today would become a very small part of human activity.

An increase in longevity would tend to result in the need to prepare the individual for great environmental changes which would occur during his productive life. At the same time, the percentage of old-age voters would increase, probably leading to a concomitant increase in the "acceptance lag," i.e., the time it takes for basic change in public attitude.[6] In a sense, this would make a society more conservative in outlook than it otherwise would be. Longevity might bring other kinds of shifts in curricula. For example, recent history has demonstrated that youth does well in advancing knowledge in mathematics and sciences, but such subjects as law and philosophy are more tied to long worldly experience. Education may attempt to compensate for this imbalance. In response to these and other conditions, we might want to shift toward a system of continuous education, concentrating on different mixes of curricula through different periods of a person's lifetime; perhaps we may wish to merge formal education more closely with working activities. This might lead to a complete reorganization of our formal education and institutions.

Let us turn to one further possible future development that would be of great interest to education. There are reasons to believe that the proportion of high-intelligence students may increase.[7] Marriages among parents of high intelligence tend to produce intelligent children. The proportion of such high-intelligence-matched marriages has been on the increase during recent years because of the growing university and research communities.

Or one may wish to consider the possibility that induced changes could result from breakthroughs in molecular and developmental biology. Even now, such research suggests at least the possibility of artificially increasing an individual's problem-solving capacity. For example, it has been suggested that administration of growth hormones to the fetus during the period of neuron reproduction might increase the number of neurons by 20 to 50 percent.[8] Since

---

6. Werner Z. Hirsch, "About Tomorrow's Urban America," *UCLA Law Review*, XII, No. 3 (March, 1965), 880-896.

7. John R. Platt, "The Coming Generation of Genius," *Horizon*, Vol. IV, No. 4, March, 1962.

8. Examples of work going on in this field are described in *Control of the Mind*, *Part I*, New York: Seymour M. Farber and Roger H. L. Wilson (Eds.), McGraw-Hill Book Company, 1961; and F. R. Babich, A. L. Jacobson, F. Bubash and A. Jacobson, *Science*, 149, 656 (1965), and *Science*, 150, 636 (1965).

problem-solving capacities in mammals appears to be the function of the number of neurons available in the brain, children with extraordinary learning capacity might be produced. How we could best nurture the student of very high intelligence is something we have yet to understand, even with today's student population. Perhaps radical shifts in teacher requirements, teacher-pupil matching, educational technology, and curriculum might be indicated.

These are merely examples of issues with which Metropolitan Education Outlook Stations might concern themselves. They would want to investigate the probability of such events to occur, their general implications, and particularly their specific implications for the education of a particular metropolitan area.

Near-Term Opportunities

Let us turn from the distant future to the one that appears to be just around the corner. This may be the result of innovations in educational technology, new planning and organizing methods, or administrative rearrangements.

Many potential innovations of the near future are related to electronic computers and mechanized information systems: the computer-assisted learning machine, automated student counseling, instant-retrieval libraries, and so on. Such devices greatly enhance our ability to match students' capabilities and interests with efficient teaching means, and so promise greatly improved performance.

Such technological innovations require that computers store and retrieve very complete personal information about a person, his behavior, his opinions, etc. While this can be highly valuable for planning and administering education as well as for other areas of our lives, it also poses serious problems. The computer can take away our privacy, individualism, and anonymity. If such strategic information systems were to fall under the manipulation of malevolent parties, they could bring havoc to democracy and freedom.

Thus, one of the great challenges of this age is to develop safeguards against computerized information systems. The need for multi-access storage and retrieval facilities, based on efficiency, may make it very difficult to prevent crucial information from reaching the hands of those who could misuse it.

Perhaps we should create within the United States a semi-autonomous Federal agency (not unlike the Federal Reserve Board) which would have complete jurisdiction over information storage files and retrieval facilities. One of the basic tasks here would be to establish criteria which would determine which type of information would be made available to which persons or agencies for which purposes.

One type of computer-assisted learning machine which seems to offer both practical and early opportunities to education is the simulator-trainer. It uses program learning to integrate displays for animated schematics, prerecorded lecture and tutor sessions, text, and the building and manipulation of both theoretical and physical models of equipment.

The simulator-trainer appears to offer an effective tool for initial vocational training in high schools, particularly of problem children. The training period can be shorter and may help provide predictions of the rate at which the trainee will learn his technical skill and the ultimate level he will attain. This permits trainees to be channeled into curriculum specialities most suited to them.

The simulator-trainer also offers important advantages for the retraining of persons. This may become increasingly important in the face of growing automation. It appears to eliminate "classroom psychosis" (i.e., fear of people in their thirties, forties, and fifties of returning to the environment of the classroom), and reduce training time and costs. On the other hand, the extensive use of simulator-trainers will require heavy capital outlays compared with conventional classroom methods. Before educational officials rationally decide the extent to which such capital outlays are justified, they should have an idea of current trends, future problems and opportunities, the goals and objectives of various types of vocational training, costs and benefits of both trainer and conventional approaches, and they should examine alternative integrated programs for meeting these goals. Thus, it is here that the previously described Metropolitan Education Outlook Station and the analytical method would be essential.

There are a number of other aspects of vocational training which the urban education planner should face. Urban America needs persons with good vocational training, not only in commerce and industry but also in the government sector. Most vocational training in the United States has been furnished by employers. On the other hand, one can rationally argue that vocational training should take place in the school rather than on the job, when much theoretical knowledge and understanding is needed and when the equipment required is not expensive.

Vocational training which brings employment opportunities within the range of minority groups is particularly important. But these groups live for the most part in ghettos, which suffer from poor public transportation to places of potential employment (and adequate vocational training). In these cases, it might be valuable for urban school boards to seek the aid of industry and develop "train-mobiles"—mobile classrooms to bring vocational training into these areas. For example, it appears that such a train-mobile could help solve many of the education and employment problems of the Watts area in Los Angeles. Moreover, on-job training tends to work against Negroes, Puerto Ricans, and Mexican-Americans, because members of these minority groups often do not hold skilled jobs and are also subject to a high level of unemployment. Thus, if we are interested in improving jobs and income for minority members, we would advocate more vocational training in public institutions.

As a final example of near-future problems to be faced by urban school authorities, consider the often complete separation between the municipal government on the one hand and the local school district on the other. This separation, while having certain advantages, will impose increasingly severe difficulties in the future. Some of the planning, zoning, and industrial development decisions that a municipal government might make in its own interests may impose severe burdens on the school district. For example, many cities are taking steps to attract industries into their boundaries. If these industries are labor intensive, they are likely to confront schools with a large number of students to accommodate. If, for example, leather goods or textile industries were attracted into a city, the costs of providing education for the children of these workers can exceed by far the taxes paid by them to the school district and even the state and Federal subsidy payments likely to accrue to the school district.

If a city government decides to redevelop parts of its downtown area, new demands will be made on the schools. Thus, there have been cases where cities redeveloped areas for middle-income groups without providing schools for their children. As a result, the new apartments could not be rented, at least not to those persons for whom they were initially intended.

But perhaps the most important reason for close cooperation between the city and the school district is the fact that the lot of the culturally and economically deprived cannot be improved unless there is a coordinated and concerted effort which includes education, housing, and social services.

The Metropolitan Education Outlook Station can play a significant role here too in developing data and evaluating alternatives to be considered by officials responsible for decisions. It would thus furnish one basic link toward formalizing and coordinating city and school district planning without either unit's losing its identity and independence. Given this basic link, it should not be difficult to develop others, in the form of appropriate committees, etc.

Conclusion

In summary, it seems abundantly clear that urban education officials will continue to face an enormous range of problems and opportunities over the future. Many are already upon us. A host of innovations are already at hand; many more are on the horizon. But if we are to take advantage of these—if we are to turn problems into opportunities instead of the other way around—the present must be examined, the future must be scanned, plans must be laid, and institutions must be modified and put in motion. Resources are limited; choices must be made. Our problem is to make them to the best of our ability.

I have briefly discussed three major responsibilities of urban education officials: policy consideration, program formulation, and program administration. I have noted a number of examples of near-term and far-future issues to be faced in carrying out these tasks, and I have suggested several approaches intended to help us get under way. The Metropolitan Education Outlook Station as a means for scanning the future, for evaluating alternatives as an aid to local decision-makers, and for facilitating cooperation among administrative units should be particularly valuable. Cost-benefit evaluation and program-budgeting should play a role in this type of new institution and should be valuable when incorporated into the several appropriate functions of current organization.

Certainly these and the other measures I have suggested are no panacea, nor are they so intended. They do, however, offer a first step which will head urban education toward a dream rather than a nightmare.

RICHARD L. DERR

The author is presently Associate Professor of Education at Western Reserve University. His major fields of interest are social foundations of education and educational philosophy. For several years an elementary school teacher, Dr. Derr is the author of re-cent articles in Educational Theory *and* The Educational Forum.

URBAN

EDUCATIONAL

PROBLEMS:

Models and Strategies

A CRITICAL ASPECT of the contemporary attack on urban educational problems is that it has been organized largely in terms of theoretical models which direct ameliorative efforts at the individual student rather than at the community. The most popular theoretical models are those of "the culturally deprived child" and "the socially disadvantaged child."[1] Such models explain the problems of urban schools in terms of the deprivations and disadvantages experienced by many urban children. Accordingly, efforts to deal with these problems have focused on the individual student under the strategy of compensatory education.[2] The task of the school is that of trying to compensate for

AUTHOR'S NOTE: *The assistance of Peter Haiman, a doctoral candidate in Social and Historical Foundations at Western Reserve University, in the preparation of this manuscript is gratefully acknowledged.*

1. Benjamin S. Bloom, et al., *Compensatory Education for Cultural Deprivation,* New York: Holt, Rinehart, and Winston, Inc., 1965. *School Programs for the Disadvantaged,* Educational Research Service Service Circular, National Education Association, 1201 Sixteenth Street, N.W., Washington, D.C., January, 1965, pp. 7-74. Also see Robert D. Hess, *Inventory of Compensatory Education Projects,* Chicago: The Urban Child Center, School of Education, University of Chicago, 1965. Edmund W. Gordon (Ed.), *IRCD Bulletin,* New York: Project Beacon, Ferkauf Graduate School, Yeshiva University, March, 1965, Vol. 1, No. 2, pp. 1-2.

2. Bloom. et al., *op. cit.,* p. 20. Hess, *Ibid.*

the failure of the home and neighborhood to develop needed skills and attitudes. Models which center the attention of educators on interinstitutional relationships, i.e., those which obtain between the school and conditions in the community, rarely have been utilized.[3] Hence, the possibility of organizing the school's ameliorative efforts by strategies which are directed at community conditions is generally not entertained.

The wisdom of entertaining interinstitutional models is suggested by the fact that compensatory education programs have not yet demonstrated conclusive educational gains.[4] In part this may simply reflect a failure to organize the evaluation of such programs so that the gains which had been made could be shown. The use of control groups in a carefully designed evaluative program would help to clarify this question.[5] But there is also reason to believe that compensatory education programs are combating the symptoms rather than the roots of many of the problems which burden urban schools. It has been established that academic and behavior problems occur more frequently among lower-class students than among middle-class students.[6] Thus, schools in the central city of metropolitan areas can expect a high proportion of students with such problems unless the social class composition of central cities changes radically or the relationship between the social class position of parents and the educational problems of students is modified. Educational programs which seek to compensate for the shortcomings of the home and neighborhood will do neither. But social class is not the only community condition

3. Two exceptions are papers by Austin and Miller. See Ernest H. Austin, Jr., "Cultural Deprivation—A Few Questions," *Phi Delta Kappan* (October, 1965) Vol. 47, No. 2, pp. 67-70, 75-76 and S. M. Miller, "Dropouts—A Political Problem" in Daniel Schrieber (Ed.), *The School Dropout*, Project: School Dropouts, National Education Association, 1201 Sixteenth Street, N.W., Washington, D.C., 1964, pp. 11-24.

4. J. Wayne Wrightstone, et al., *Evaluation of the Higher Horizons Program for Underprivileged Children*, Cooperative Research Project No. 1124, New York: Board of Education of the City of New York, Bureau of Educational Research, 1964, pp. 243-244. For a comprehensive review see Doxey A. Wilkerson, "Programs and Practices in Compensatory Education for Disadvantaged Children," *Review of Educational Research* (December, 1965) Vo. XXXV, No. 5, pp. 426-440.

5. *Ibid.*, pp. 438-439.

6. W. W. Charters, Jr., "The Social Background of Teaching," in N. L. Gage (Ed.), *Handbook of Research on Teaching*, Chicago: Rand McNally, 1963, pp. 739-740.

which has been correlated with academic and behavioral problems of students. Poverty,[7] slum housing residence,[8] unemployment,[9] cultural deprivation of parents,[10] racial discrimination,[11] and father absence[12] have been shown to be related to school attendance, academic achievement, IQ scores, pupil retention, and other educational outcomes. The high incidence of such social problems in the urban community is undoubtedly an important contributing factor to the problems which plague urban schools. In recognition of this some educators have predicted that the proportion of students in urban schools with academic and behavioral problems will increase, rather than decrease in the next decade, despite the establishment of numerous compensatory education programs.[13] This is based on an interpretation of current demographic trends related to the increase of multiproblem families in the central city. If this prediction is sound, then the urban school can anticipate a constant supply of "problem" students unless some effective action is taken toward the source itself.

The popularity of the cultural deprivation model and other individualistic models may hinge partly on the assumption that the educational institution is virtually powerless to alter conditions

7. Patricia Gayo Sexton, *Education and Income*, New York: The Viking Press, 1961.

8. Daniel M. Wilner, et al., *The Housing Environment and Family Life*, Baltimore: The Johns Hopkins Press, 1962.

9. Vera C. Perrella and Forrest A. Bogan, "Out of School Youth," *Monthly Labor Review*, 1964, Vol. 87, pp. 1260-1268.

10. Martin Deustch, "Minority Group and Class Status as Related to Social and Personality Factors in Scholastic Achievement," *Society for Applied Anthropology Monograph*, No. 2, 1960. Also see Vera P. John, "The Intellectual Development of Slum Children: Some Preliminary Findings," *American Journal of Orthopsychiatry*, 1963, Vol. 33, pp. 813-822, and Basil Bernstein, "Language and Social Class," *British Journal of Sociology*, 1960, Vol. 11, pp. 271-276.

11. Helen H. Davidson, et al., "Characteristics of Successful School Achievers from a Severely Deprived Environment," unpublished research report, New York: The School of Education, City University of New York, 1962, 18 p. I. Katz and L. Benjamin, "Effects of White Authoritarianism in Biracial Work Groups," *Journal of Abnormal and Social Psychology*, 1960, Vol. 61, pp. 448-456.

12. David P. Ausubel and Pearl Ausubel, "Ego Development Among Segregated Negro Children," in A. Harry Passow (Ed.), *Education in Depressed Areas*, New York: Bureau of Publications, Teachers College, 1963, pp. 109-141. Martin Deustch and Bert Brown, "Social Influences in Negro-White Intelligence Differences," *Journal of Social Issues*, 1964, Vol. 20, pp. 24-35.

13. *School Programs for the Disadvantaged, op. cit.*, p. 2. Also see Austin, Jr., *op. cit.*, p. 67.

in the community. For the sake of argument, let us grant this assumption. But does it follow that school officials and teachers should therefore ignore these conditions and their effects on the school's operation? Are there no strategies available which would give policy-makers in the schools viable alternatives to the extreme position that if the school itself is not sufficiently powerful to solve social problems, then it is powerless to have any impact on them? There are such strategies but they are not made readily apparent by individualistic models. Interinstitutional models which formulate the problems of urban schools in terms of the latter's relationship to certain external conditions in the community are needed. One such model will be proposed here.

"Institutional Dependence"

This model may be termed the model of "institutional dependence." Such problems as absenteeism, scholastic failure, and school dropout are viewed, under this model, as symptoms of a far more fundamental problem of schools; namely, that they are dependent upon supportive and reinforcing conditions in the home, neighborhood, and community for the successful attainment of their own goals. This condition of dependence is not limited to central city schools — for it derives from the very nature of the educational institution as it is presently defined and organized in our society. The problem is that the central city system typically fails to receive adequate reinforcement; on the other hand, the suburban system typically does receive it.

In social scientific terms, the major task of the educational institution is socialization. It is to influence the behavior of the individual in such a way that those skills, attitudes, and understandings which will enable him to live a productive life as a member of the community and the larger society are developed.[14] The de-

---

14. Talcott Parsons, "The School Class as a Social System: Some of its Functions in American Society," *Harvard Educational Review*, 1959, Vol. 29, p. 298. Robert J. Havighurst and Bernice Neugarten, *Society and Education*, Second edition, Boston: Allyn and Bacon, Inc., 1962, pp. 74-75.

pendence of the school arises from the fact that the behavior of the student has been influenced by individuals and groups in the home, neighborhood, and community prior to his entrance into school and continues to be influenced as the school seeks to achieve its particular socializing tasks with the student. If other agencies of socialization intentionally or unintentionally reinforce the efforts of the school to develop particular skills, attitudes, and understandings, then the likelihood that the school will succeed is substantially higher than if it fails to receive this reinforcement. Differences between suburban schools and urban schools in the attainment of such educational objectives as scholastic achievement, low absenteeism, and active participation in school activities, can (at least in part) be explained by major differences in the extent of reinforcement afforded the two types of school by informal socializing influences on the individual.[15] In turn these differences can be partly explained by important differences between the sub-cultures of the middle class and the lower class.[16] In addition to this, the central city is often afflicted with numerous and severe social problems whereas the suburban community generally is not.[17] In many cities, informal socialization occurs within a setting of major social disorganization. In such a setting, the school is likely to receive only a modicum of reinforcement. Indeed, youngsters are likely to acquire habits and attitudes which are inimical to their achievement in the formalized socializing situation of the school. Hence social problems in the urban community have greatly complicated the problem of obtaining adequate external reinforcement that any school serving a predominantly lower-class population is likely to have. The current plight of the large city school system dramatically reveals the vulnerability of the school as an institution to the vicissitudes of its external environment.

Here is a model which focuses the attention of school administrators and boards of education on the dependency of the school, as a formal agency of socialization, upon the manner in which ex-

---

15. James Bryant Conant, *Slums and Suburbs*, New York: McGraw-Hill Book Company, 1961, p. 1. Also see Sexton, *op. cit.* and Alan Wilson, "Social Stratification and Educational Achievement," in Passow, *op. cit.*, pp. 217-235.

16. Wilson, *Ibid.* See also Charters, Jr., *Ibid.*

ternal forces influence the development of the student. The school, the family, and the neighborhood are treated as parts of the system of socialization.[18] This relationship between the school and other parts of the system is the unit of analysis in the institutional dependence model. Unlike the models of cultural deprivation and socially disadvantaged youth, which both use the individual student as the unit of analysis, this model deals with a unit which is sufficiently broad to direct attention to the sources of educational problems in the community.

Moreover a model which views the urban school as holding a weak position in a competitive situation with other agencies of socialization is heuristic as a source of strategies school officials could employ in an attack on educational problems. Two fundamentally different strategies come readily to mind.[19]

The Strategy of Integration

One of these strategies is for the school system to encourage and participate in efforts to solve urban social problems and thereby create home and neighborhood conditions which are more likely to support and reinforce the school, much as the middle-class suburbs now seemingly do. This can be labelled as the *Strategy of Integration* for its ultimate aim is to bring about closer integration of formal and informal socializing influences on the youngster's development. It is reflected — although probably not intentionally so — in certain aspects of large scale educational programs such as Higher Horizons and the Great Cities Project as well as by action programs such as Cleveland's Community Action for Youth and New York's Mobilization for Youth. In the former, various efforts have been made by teachers and school officials to enlist greater

---

17. Bernard Berelson and Gary Steiner, *Human Behavior: An Inventory of Scientific Findings*, New York: Harcourt, Brace and World, Inc., 1964, p. 608.

18. The concept of system is central to sociological analysis. The work of Gouldner has been particularly suggestive for this paper. See Alvin Gouldner, "Reciprocity and Autonomy in Functional Theory," in Llewellyn Gross (Ed.), *Symposium on Sociological Theory*, New York: Harper & Row, Publishers, 1959, pp. 241-270.

19. *Ibid.*, pp. 259-261.

cooperation from parents, to aid the latter in the solution of such problems as adjustment to urban life, and generally to modify parental behavior so that it would be more supportive for the school. The above mentioned community action programs are aimed toward the prevention and treatment of juvenile delinquency. School systems have been involved in this effort in various ways, with the apparent expectation that the realization of their objectives would be facilitated if delinquency in the community were to be controlled.

The Strategy of Functional Autonomy

A basically different approach to urban educational problems is to attempt to expand the functions and to increase the effectiveness of the school to such an extent that it depends only minimally upon reinforcement from home and neighborhood conditions for the achievement of its goals. Here the school would not seek to eliminate slum conditions in the community but rather minimize their importance to its own success by enlarging its role in the socialization of the individual. This strategy can be labelled as the *Strategy of Functional Autonomy*, for its ultimate aim is to enable the school to function in a state of near autonomy or independence from other influences on the individual. This strategy is reflected — again, not intentionally so, in all probability — in the pre-school program which has received its fullest impetus from the federally sponsored "Operation Head Start." In this program the school assumes a function which was formerly the primary responsibility of the home and, in so doing, presumably increases the likelihood of greater eventual success in achieving its own objectives with such youngsters by virtue of its earlier intervention in the socializing process. Proposals to increase the length of the school day and the school year also are consistent with this strategy since they would increase the exposure of children to the influence of teachers and correspondingly decrease exposure to informal socializing agencies.

The Strategy of Integration implies the belief that the most effective solution to the problem which the urban school has in securing adequate community reinforcement is to aid other public

279

and private agencies in the reconstruction of the community so that such reinforcement will be forthcoming.[20] A large part of the current ameliorative efforts of boards of education, school administrators, and teachers would be directed at changing the community and in facilitating the efforts of private foundations and local, state, and Federal governments in this regard. Whatever changes are made in the school would generally be made with the intention of modifying external conditions so that they would better reinforce the goals of the school. So a school system might expand its college preparatory program in order to attract middle-class families back to the central city or it might alter school district lines in order to modify residential housing patterns. The basic premise is that it would be futile for a community to make large investments in an effort to upgrade its schools as long as poverty, crime, cultural deprivation, family instability, and racial discrimination pervade the community.

The Strategy of Functional Autonomy suggests the alternative view; that the school can be aided better by changing its status as a dependent institution in the community. A major effort would be to provide schools with the facilities, opportunities, and skilled personnel they would need to realize whatever educational objectives they have been given the mandate to achieve by the community. The basic premise is that the means are at hand for transforming the school into a dominant source of socializing influence. Such a task would be a more manageable one, in which educators could engage, than the attempt to transform the entire community.

These two strategies differ fundamentally from the strategy of compensatory education. The latter encourages school officials to adjust the school passively to conditions in the community, in that the school would be obliged to institute programs to develop whatever skills and attitudes informal socializing agencies happened not to develop at any given time. No action — direct or indirect — is taken toward the community. On the other hand the Strategy

---

20. In many respects this strategy is congruent with the philosophy of education which is often labelled Social Reconstructionism. For a recent treatment by one of its strongest proponents, see Theodore Brameld, *Education as Power*, New York: Holt, Rinehart and Winston, Inc., 1965.

of Integration would involve schools in direct action on the community, action designed to change it in fundamental ways. The Strategy of Functional Autonomy would involve schools in indirect action toward community conditions in that an effort would be made to break the circuit between these conditions and the effectiveness of the school in achieving its objectives. Integration would seek to create a community which would help develop particular skills and attitudes. Functional Autonomy would seek to create a school which could develop skills and attitudes whether or not community influences helped.

Questions of Public Policy

It may be argued that the school should not consider the adoption of either strategy since it traditionally has taken a passive role in relation to community conditions. Such an argument no longer seems tenable since these conditions and educational problems are inextricably related. Furthermore, it is becoming increasingly clearer that the school is under heavy pressure from numerous groups, including the Federal government, to take a more active role in such community problems as poverty and racial segregation. The role of the school in the community has become blurred and it should become a subject of public concern and discussion. Numerous questions of public policy and of the capabilities of the school are involved in current local and Federal attempts to deal with the problems of urban schools. Their explicit consideration by laymen and educators would enable these questions to be resolved in ways which are consistent with dominant social values and the best available research evidence. Many of these questions are embedded in the Strategies of Integration and Functional Autonomy as assumptions and implications. Consider some of them.

The Strategy of Integration commits its user to the view that such social problems as proverty, family instability, and racial segregation can be eliminated or controlled. It further assumes that these conditions of social disorganization would necessarily be replaced with ones which will provide the urban school with needed types and amount of reinforcement. Closely related to this is the assumption that if present social problems were solved, then other kinds of social problems would not arise in their wake. For if they did, then the problem of securing reinforcement would remain. This strategy implies the view that it is proper and desirable for the school system to perform welfare functions like parental guidance and delinquency prevention. It is consistent with the conception that the school is a community institution, meaning that it should strive to meet whatever needs the community has at any given time. Moreover, there is the implication in this strategy that it is desirable to maintain the dependent status of the school in the system of socialization.

Conversely, the Strategy of Functional Autonomy contains the implication that it is undesirable for the public, on the one hand, to hold high expectations for the school, and on the other, to organize it in such a way that its success depends upon the chances of fortune in its environment. This strategy assumes that the public would sanction whatever reorganization would be required in the educational institution to increase its independence. Such a reorganization would include a reduction of lay control over the curriculum (but not over the objectives of the school) since the effectiveness of the school would depend partly upon trained experts determining how educational objectives could be best achieved in the school setting. Hence questions of lay versus professional control of the schools are involved. The strategy also assumes that our knowledge of human behavior and of the instructional process is such that the school can be reorganized so that it can successfully neutralize or counteract negative environmental influences, and provide positive influences which are lacking in that environment. The strategy carries the implication that parental influence over the development of children may be sharply weakened in the interest of having the school, following the dictates of the public, achieve its objectives. Finally, this strategy is consistent with the view that school systems should limit themselves to the preparation of young people for adulthood in our society and should allow other institutions to assume responsibility for making modifications in that society.

These are only some of the important implications and assumptions of these two strategies. Perhaps a sufficient number has been enumerated to reveal that they rest on quite different views as to the role which the public school should and is able to perform in the community. Hence, the strategies provide educators and laymen with two distinct approaches for dealing with the many theoretical questions and issues of public policy which generally remain submerged in current efforts to meet the needs of culturally deprived children. It is difficult to avoid consideration of these questions and issues when the model of institutional dependence is used to formulate the problems of urban schools. Individualistic models obscure these matters and by that very fact hold little promise for generating a successful resolution of the problems of urban schools.

GORDON J. KLOPF and GARDA W. BOWMAN

Gordon J. Klopf and Garda W. Bow-man are at the Educational Resources Center of the Bank Street College of Education, where Dr. Klopf is Associate to the President. Both are actively involved in the development of programs to improve the quality of urban educators, educational administrators, and supporting personnel.

PREPARATION OF SCHOOL PERSONNEL TO WORK IN AN URBAN SETTING

"HUMAN LIFE SWINGS BETWEEN two poles: movement and settlement."[1] The pattern of the movement of peoples throughout history has been toward the concentration of population into organized units for purposes of security, social intercourse, and economic productivity. Lewis Mumford points out that:

> Before the city there was the hamlet and the shrine and the village; before the village, the camp, the cache, the cave, the cairn; and before all these there was a disposition to social life that man plainly shares with many other animal species.[2]

Industrialization has heightened the pace of this natural tendency and the density of population concentration, since workers have gravitated toward factories and plants, which are located primarily in urban centers. The gigantic proportions of this "urban revolution" may be gleaned from the fact that in 1800 there was not one city in the Western world with as many as a million people.

---

1. Lewis Mumford, "The City in History: Its Origins, Its Transformations, and Its Prospects," New York: Harcourt, Brace & World, Inc., 1961, p. 5.
2. *Ibid.*

A century later, there were eleven such cities and by the midpoint of the twentieth century, the figure had nearly tripled—twenty-eight cities in Western Europe and in North and South America. Worldwide, there were sixty-one urban areas with a population of 1 million or more.[3] Within the United States alone, the 1960 Census reveals that there were 113 million people (more than 60 percent of the total population) living in 212 metropolitan centers throughout the nation.

However, as the migration from rural areas to the cities continued its overwhelming growth, the very density of the population drove out the industrial facilities which had served as magnets. Those who flocked to the city seeking job opportunities, freedom from racial restrictions, and a better life often found only overcrowded, rat-infested, strife-torn ghettos in which to settle. Two concurrent phenomena were basic causative factors in the urban crisis: the flight of industry from the inadequate space and high operating costs of an urban site, and the flight of the middle class to the surrounding suburbs. With the loss of these chief sources of tax revenue, inner cities throughout the nation were gripped by fiscal crisis. Two anomalies were evident: (1) a misfit of skills and available opportunities—that is, an increasingly blue-collar labor force in a primarily white-collar job market; and (2) an ever-increasing need for public services in a milieu of declining revenue.

A polarization ensued, with the very rich and the very poor living in close and frustrating juxtaposition. The very rich may look down from penthouses and from tiers of tiny balconies in towering luxury apartments upon the pockets of poverty below.

Richard Whalen epitomized the dilemma of the inner cities in the title of an article on New York City—the giant of them all. His title, "A City Destroying Itself," [4] synthesizes the problem very neatly.

However, although the city intensifies the destructive elements of civilization, it also intensifies the benefits to be derived from

---

3. Source: U.S. Bureau of Labor Statistics and United Nations Demographic Yearbook.

4. Richard Whalen, "A City Destroying Itself," *Fortune Magazine*, September, 1964.

communication and diversity. Those who perceive only the dirt, noise, congestion, violence, and incongruities of "megalopolis" fail to grasp the opportunities inherent in the broad scope and variety of human resources in close interaction. Mumford described the potential of urbanization as an "illumination of consciousness." :

> That magnification of all the dimensions of life, through emotional communion, rational communication, technological mastery, and above all dramatic representation, has been the supreme office of the city in history.[5]

Lindley and Chandler express the goals and the positive dynamics of the urban process in more specific terms:

> Those who look beyond the temporary traces that change and movement of people leave will see in urban developments opportunities for cultural, economic and educational attainments that are not possible in sparsely populated and poorly organized rural communities. . . . The diversity of human talents, itself, adds strength and enrichment to city life. In fact, the great metropolitan complexes are the only means of organizing life to provide maximum advantages of economic opportunity and cultural and educational resources to all the people.[6]

However, between these possible benefits of urban living and their attainment, an ominous gap persists and, in many respects, appears to be widening. The gap cannot be closed by any one segment of the institutional life of an urban society, but the institution which plays a central and catalytic role is education. The responsibility is tremendous.

It is the thesis of these authors that, to meet the challenge, educators—and particularly those in teacher education—must cease to equate urban education with education of the disadvantaged; instead, they must view the total spectrum of resources in an urban setting as well as realistically face up to the difficulties involved and

---

5. Mumford, *op. cit.*, p. 570.

6. Lindley J. Stiles and B. J. Chandler, "New Directions and Practices in City School," in Lindley J. Stiles, B. J. Chandler, and John I. Kitsuse (Eds.), *Education in Urban Society*, New York and Toronto: Dodd, Mead & Company, Inc., 1962, pp. 250-251.

accept the thesis that education is the cornerstone on which our cities must be built if our citizens are to achieve their potential. Teachers and administrators should look deeply into themselves to see if they are ready to accept the challenge. Those who are must prepare themselves for the task by reorientation and by in-service education. Administrators and teachers, as well as children, need remediation.

The pace and enormity of change require a deep and multi-faceted diagnosis of each situation, using all related disciplines and involving all levels of school personnel—superintendents, principals, supervisors, teachers, special services personnel, and auxiliary personnel such as aides and assistant-teachers. The education of teachers alone without the education of those who create the policies and set the tone within a school system is often frustrating, while the education of aides without the education of those who will orchestrate the teams in the classroom may be ineffective.

Before giving specificity to these comments, it is necessary to review the global goals of education and then to focus on those which are most crucial in the preparation of school personnel to work in an urban setting. Such goals are important to the learning of all children, but they are indispensable in a metropolitan complex.

The goal of education might be stated simply as the development of the individual in the context of all the implications of the society. In 1874 Herbert Spencer said, "To prepare us for complete living is the function which education has to discharge."

Although all of the child's environment "educates" him in one way or another, the school has been designated as the formal institution in our society with this assignment. The urban school has certain special responsibilities other than the conducting of programs. First, it must help the community decide what its objectives for education are. The school reflects the culture and concerns of the community, but its professional staff must share with the community leadership in determining what they want education to do and what part the school must serve in this process. If the home, the church, or the social agency is not having satisfactory influence on the institutional, social, and psychological develop-

287

ment of the child in terms of the kind of individual desired, does the school serve in a broader capacity, both as the sponsor of programs and the orchestrator of those aspects of a child's life which are most pertinent to learning? An illustration of this role might be the school system which is developing family and parent education and counseling programs, responding to the need for strong family life and for assisting parents with their role in the learning process of the child.

Basically, a school system in an urban area must recognize economic, cultural, and social diversity and develop its objectives and design its programs accordingly. To do so, the current pattern appears to be the organization of the so-called "comprehensive" school. Frequently, the ethos of the comprehensive school is a kind of "majoritorium" ideology. It is supposed to serve a cross section of children and aims to assimilate the minorities or the diversified groups in some "melting pot" fashion with various ability levels of the same curriculum.

The need would appear to be for diversified schools with varied objectives and programs as well as school personnel and facilities. Urban areas may need both neighborhood and area schools and new combinations of schools in park-like educational complexes. They may have to plan their curriculum, length of school day and year, school personnel, special services, facilities for instruction, recreation, and residence in consideration of the needs of the student population and of the system's overall goals for its youth. Secondary schools in particular will have a wide range of programs, learning facilities of all kinds, and rich and varied teaching and guidance staff, including vocational, social, and recreational workers. To assist the child in his development toward some degree of self-fulfillment, the staff, program, and facilities will have to be geared to the able *and* the not-so-able from all social and economic positions and family life patterns.

The teacher of the urban school must be a capable person. Edward Thorndike said, "A nation which lets its incapables teach it, while the capable men and women only feed, clothe, or amuse it, is committing intellectual suicide." However, a listing of traits.

characteristics, success factors, teaching styles, age, sex, race, or religion of teachers cannot be prescribed. A school system needs a range of individuals with different skills and approaches from wide and varied backgrounds. A few basic criteria would seem essential for effective teaching performance in most situations, particularly for teaching in an urban setting. Among these are the ego strength as a person to cope with the emotional strains of some urban school settings and situations.

The teacher has to see himself as a person, understand his strengths and weaknesses, and, as Arthur Coombs says, "be able to use himself as an effective instrument." The teacher needs to understand the role of education and appreciate the diversity of people. His perceptions of others need to be objective, honest, and accurate.

Another requirement of the urban teacher is the philosophical conviction that man is equal—given equal opportunity—and that the school is a central force in providing the equal opportunity.

The person who would be deemed capable to teach in urban schools needs a broad foundation in the liberal arts with study in the humanities and the physical and social sciences. These should help him achieve an understanding of man and society, the significance of culture and the arts, and the communication process. His learning environment should assist him in his development as a person with critical judgment, human values, and social sensitivity. He needs as well an academic program to give him the basic content for his field or level of teaching with some degree of depth in a single area of study.

The education of the teacher for the urban area as a distinctive program has been studied by numerous groups in the profession. Various designs and programs are recommended by organizations and institutions. Some institutions believe that there should be a different program for the urban teachers; others believe what is good training for the urban teacher is good for the rural or suburban teacher. The truly professional person adapts his basic preparation to the setting in which he is teaching. If he has a sound approach to the learning-teaching process, this is all he needs.

289

It is the thesis of this paper that some special focus is important for the preparation of the urban teacher. However, an excellent general program may meet all of these criteria.

It is important that the total professional program of teacher education include some work in research and scholarship, reality activity in actual urban school settings, and a meaningful relationship to the basic social, behavioral, and related academic areas. A model kind of school or a number of schools for experimental work with a functional control of conditions either as part of the teacher-education institution or preferably in an urban school system would appear most essential.

Because of the great range of student potential, the course sequence should have a heavy emphasis upon the diagnostic approach, i.e., the analysis of each student's individual behavior and learning needs and the possible causes of such behavior. In addition to basic courses in education, the professional sequence should include academic preparation in a social, economic, and cultural approach to society and the community. This needs to be done from a functional focus with an understanding of the city, its institutions, its people, and the family. Moreover, it should be integrated with field experiences including visits to social institutions, such as family courts and homes for children, as well as the varied cultural, industrial, and business activities of a city. A continuing relationship with one family in a helping capacity, such as home tutoring, provides a link between the institutional life of the city and the primary unit of socialization.

The development of a truly competent teacher for the urban school will depend upon intensive student-teaching experience in several urban school situations. Such experience needs a high quality of supervision with staff members who know urban schools, who are adept in teaching strategies, and who can serve as effective counselors and advisers.

If the professional preparation is preservice, the teaching institution needs to have a continuous relationship with the teacher for several years. The first year of teaching might really be thought of as an apprenticeship, for ideally the new teacher should not have complete and continuous responsibility for a class but should work with a master teacher who might be orienting several new staff members.

The teaching institution should have the teacher return for seminars, institutes, and some formal course work during a period of two to four years after completion of the basic program.

Since one important component—though not the only component—of educating the urban teacher is to prepare him for work with the environmentally disadvantaged, the needs of both students and teachers in such situations are listed below:

Special Needs of Environmentally Disadvantaged Children and Youth	*Understandings and Skills Needed by Teachers Who Work with Such Students*
(1) Individual attention and differentiated education	Understanding of developmental and learning theory
	Empathy and concern for individual students
	Skill in diagnosing a student's learning characteristics and needs
	A wide range of teaching strategies to meet these needs
(2) Opportunities for early success to strengthen self-concept	Understanding the life conditions, history, culture, and status of subgroups in this society and the damage that has been done to the self image of disadvantaged groups
	Skill in perceiving latent potential and devising ways of bringing it forth and rewarding its expression
(3) Specific, real, and relevant content	Understanding the real concerns as well as the interests of students
	Skill in expressing profound ideas in simple terms
	Ability to develop content vehicles which touch the lives of the pupils

Special Needs of Environmentally Disadvantaged Children and Youth	*Understandings and Skills Needed by Teachers Who Work with Such Students*
(4) Mobility in the classroom	Understanding the restlessness and pent-up energy of those who live under emotional stress
	Skill in use of small-group process in arranging classroom learning situations
	Ability to orchestrate auxiliary personnel and subject matter specialists in the classroom so as to develop variety and movement
	Knowledge and effective use of new programmatic devices
(5) Acceptance and respect as individuals	Understanding that other patterns of speech and behavior may be different but not inferior
	Understanding the causes of some aggressive, hostile, passive, or indifferent behavior and hence not take behavioral manifestations personally
	Skill in interpersonal relationships, combining necessary controls with warmth and informality in balance
	Skill in teaching English as a second language.

Finally, the preparation of school personnel to function in the highly complex, varied, and ever-changing milieu of the modern city is an unending process. The teacher, the counselor, the principal, the specialist, the supervisor, and the auxiliary personnel must see themselves as students in perpetuum. As John Dewey said, "Education is not training for life, it is life itself."

THOMAS F. PETTIGREW

Dr. Pettigrew is Associate Professor
of Social Psychology at Harvard University. The following paper was presented at the 1965 White House
Conference on Education and is re-
published here with the author's permission.

EXTENDING

EDUCATIONAL

OPPORTUNITIES:

School Desegregation

A MERICAN PUBLIC EDUCATION finds itself today in the eye of a racial revolution. But it is a revolution with a difference, for it aims to join, not uproot, the society it confronts. And public education is necessarily the prime vehicle for this process of joining the mainstream — just as it was for the assimilation of millions of immigrants at the turn of this century.

Thus, it is not suprising that the chief thrust of the Negro American revolution throughout the nation has centered upon education. The reasons for this are numerous. Racially balanced schools are commonly viewed by Negroes as the only form of public education which can adequately fulfill the American dream of equality for their children; they are convinced that only integrated living begun in the earliest years can ever eradicate racial bigotry. Furthermore, the United States Supreme Court's 1954 ruling against *de jure* school segregation bolstered these Negro attitudes. And, finally, the political realities of public education contributed to the selection of this realm for special attention by the revolution.

For 350 years, Negro Americans have learned that separate facilities for them almost always mean inferior facilities. Whether in the North or South, hard political realities mitigate against predominantly Negro schools receiving truly comparable instruction and facilities. Put forcefully, racially balanced schools are needed to insure the necessary political leverage; many whites, unfortunately, reveal a strong interest in the education of Negroes only when Negroes are found in the same schools with sufficiently large numbers of whites.

The basic question to be discussed at this session and to be answered in the events of the next few years concerns the response of public education to this revolutionary challenge. . . . Will public education as an institution typically resist the demands for change? Will educators and school boards so resent the picket lines and protest marches that they will refuse to rise innovatively to the new challenge? Or will public education, following U.S. Commissioner of Education Francis Keppel's strong recommendation, seize the initiative and utilize this time of change and transition to achieve a new standard of educational excellence?

If these sound like "loaded" questions, then they befit the explosive nature of this panel's topic. All of us who care deeply about public education, of course, hope that the institution will respond positively to the times and come out of this difficult period stronger than ever before. Yet we also know of many communities, North and South, where the current response of education to the Negro American revolution is, to put it mildly, quite negative. The reasons for such reactions and the problems inherent in the central issues of school desegregation and racial balance are varied and complex. This chapter briefly sketches out the problem and then raises five focal issues which often arise when school districts grapple with racial change.

The Problem

Without tracing the history of "Negro education," suffice it to say that the very need for the phrase — "Negro education" — signifies the long-term failure of American education to include the Negro American on fully equal terms. Even today, public education for Negroes, when compared with that for whites, remains in general "less available, less accessible, and especially less adequate."[1]

---

1. Eunice Newton and E. H. West, "The Progress of the Negro in Elementary and Secondary Education," *Journal of Negro Education*, 1963 Yearbook, 32(4), pp. 465-484.

In 1960, Negro college attendance was proportionately only about half that of whites;[2] the percentage of adult Negroes who had completed college was considerably less than half that of whites; and the percentage who had completed high school was precisely half that of whites.[3]

Worse, in some sectors of Negro America these nonwhite to white differences are actually widening. This is particularly the case with farm Negroes in the rural South — a segment that still comprises, despite heavy out-migration, over one-fifth of all Negroes in the United States. Thus, between 1950 and 1960, rural farm nonwhite to white differences in the completion of twelve or more years of formal education by the critical 25-to-29-year-old group widened in every one of the thirteen reporting southern states.[4]

Simply enumerating racial differences in years of schooling, of course, only begins to suggest the enormity of the educational hiatus now existing between Negro and white Americans. Sadly, the blunt truth is that "Negro education" is generally grossly inferior to "white education" in both the North and South; it typically involves less expenditure per child, less trained and experienced teachers, and less adequate facilities; and it often prepares Negro youth through both its explicit and implicit curricula to assume only low-skilled employment befitting "the Negro's place" as decreed by white supremacists. We can all think, of course, of notable exceptions to these harsh generalizations. But they spring to our minds because they are precisely that — notable exceptions. The

2. H. H. Doddy, "The Progress of the Negro in Higher Education, 1950-1960," *Journal of Negro Education,* 1963 Yearbook, *32* (4), pp. 485-492.

3. Metropolitan Life Insurance Company, "Nationwide Rise in Educational Level," *Statistical Bulletin,* July 1963, *44,* pp. 1-3.

4. J. D. Cowhig and C. L. Beale, "Relative Socioeconomic Status of Southern Whites and Nonwhites, 1950 and 1960," *The Southwestern Social Science Quarterly,* September 1964, *44,* pp. 113-124; and J. D. Cowhig and C. L. Beale, "Socioeconomic Differences Between White and Nonwhite Farm Populations of the South," *Social Forces,* March 1964, *42,* pp. 354-362. Note that the widening difference between nonwhite and white educational attainment in the farm South is strictly relative; the actual attainments for both groups rose throughout the South between 1950 and 1960. For example, in North Carolina in 1950, only 18.6 percent of the farm whites of twenty-five-to-twenty-nine-years-of-age had twelve or more years of school compared to a mere 6.5 percent of the farm Negroes; but by 1960, the percentages were 44.1 and 18.1 respectively. Yet the racial difference had more than doubled from 1950 (12.1 percent) to 1960 (26 percent).

most marked exceptions are found in truly integrated schools, where the concept of "Negro education" finally loses its meaning.

This situation would be alarming in any period of American history; but, it can only be described as desperate at this particular point in our national history. Apart from Negro American protests, automation and its attendant effects on the composition of the American labor force leave us no time for careful and deliberate solutions. Though there is considerable controversy as to whether automation does in fact decrease the size of the total labor force, there is complete agreement that it demands major occupational upgrading. The employment shifts are familiar: unskilled and even semi-skilled jobs are swiftly disappearing, while professional and technical jobs are rapidly expanding. Their serious educational deficiencies, together with employment discrimination, render Negro Americans especially vulnerable to these trends of automation. Already adult Negro rates of unemployment are roughly twice those of adult whites, and Negro youth rates of unemployment are almost twice those of white youth.

Nevertheless, Negro employment has been upgraded in recent years, though the pace of this progress has hardly been breathtaking. Thus, at the rate of nonwhite gains from 1950 to 1960, nonwhites would not attain equal proportional representation in the nation among clerical workers until 1992, among skilled workers until 2005, among professionals until 2017, among sales workers until 2114, and among business managers and proprietors until 2730 — eight centuries from now![5]

Obviously, massive Negro educational advances are required for the equally massive Negro employment upgrading that must be accomplished in the next two decades. Indeed, the Negro Ameri-

---

5. N. D. Glenn, "Some Changes in the Relative Status of American Non-whites, 1940 to 1960," *Phylon*, Summer 1964, 24, pp. 109-122. These projected dates for the nation do not just reflect southern conditions. At the 1950 to 1960 rates of relative gains in metropolitan Boston, for instance, employed nonwhites would not achieve proportional representation among clerical and skilled workers until the late 1980s, among professionals until the early 1990s and among business managers and sales workers until the 22nd and 23rd centuries respectively! T. F. Pettigrew, "Metropolitan Boston's race problem in perspective." In *Social Structure and Human Problems in the Boston Metropolitan Area*, Cambridge, Mass.: Joint Center for Urban Studies, 1965; pp. 33-51.

can finds himself on a fast-paced treadmill. Significant educational gains will be necessary just for the Negro to keep up occupationally — much less progress — in this automated age. And there are indications that education may prove to be a major bottleneck to the Negro's needed gains in employment. Hence, major corporations, motivated by the equal employment imperatives of Title VII of the 1964 Civil Rights Act, are already seeking many more technically skilled Negro college graduates than are currently being produced by our educational system.

To be sure, public education can hardly be held solely responsible for the restricted numbers and quality of trained Negro Americans. Limited educational opportunities are only a part — though a critical part — of the complexly interwoven "vicious circle" that narrows the Negro's life chances at every turn — low income, high unemployment, poor health care, inadequate housing, ghetto living, broken family life, etc.

This point is relevant to two related claims that obscure the real issues undergirding educational considerations of race. Ignoring the Negro's typically lean environment, racists have made a recent resurgence with their claims of innate Negro inferiority. Thirty years of solid evidence, however, make it possible to state that these claims certainly have no scientific validity.[6] A related claim also attempts to relieve the public schools of all responsibility for lowered Negro performance. It maintains that formal instruction is simply powerless to overcome the enormous deficits which many Negro children bring to the school situation — lowered motivation, poor speech patterns, broken family life, etc. This claim, too, is called into serious question as soon as one inspects the astonishing improvements in Negro performance made by truly imaginative school systems.

---

6. T. F. Pettigrew, *A Profile of the Negro American*. Princeton, N.J.: Van Nostrand, 1964. It should be noted, too, that racist notions of the innate inferiority of Negro Americans are accepted today by far fewer white Americans than twenty years ago. Thus, 80 percent of white Northerners and 59 percent of white Southerners in 1963 reported to survey interviewers that they believed the Negro to be as intelligent as the white, compared with only 50 percent of white Northerners and 21 percent of white Southerners in 1942. H. H. Hyman and P. B. Sheatsley, "Attitudes toward desegregation," *Scientific American*, July 1964, *211*, pp. 16-23.

297

To say this is not to deny or minimize the real deficits from which many Negro children of impoverished backgrounds do in fact suffer. The job *is* difficult for any school system, and most of the problems are certainly not the making of the schools. But American public education has often been called on to tackle difficult problems that were not of its making. And it appears that, when approached with good faith, rich imagination, and full willingness to rise innovatively to the challenge, the nation's schools can meet this vital educational problem successfully.

The first order of business is the elimination of the *de jure* segregation of southern and border schools. The first eleven years after the 1954 Supreme Court ruling against *du jure* segregation of public schools have witnessed slow, but fundamental, alterations. By the fall of 1964, 43 percent of biracial southern school districts had begun at least token desegregation programs that placed one out of every nine Negro Southern school children in schools with white Southerners.[7]

A disproportionate share of this progress, however, has occurred in the border South. While 93 percent of biracial school districts in the border South had desegregated, the figure for the ex-Confederate South was only 27 percent; and while three out of every five border state Negro children attended biracial schools, only one in forty-seven did so in the ex-Confederate South. Yet there are unmistakable signs that this pace is quickening. The average annual number of newly-desegregated school districts in the South has recently increased three-fold, with the threatened cut-off of Federal education funds under Title VI of the 1964 Civil Rights Act proving to be an effective stimulant. Thus, if the first decade after the 1954 Supreme Court desegregation ruling can be described as a slow-paced era of judicial orders, then the second decade after the ruling promises to be a somewhat faster-paced Civil Rights Act era.[8]

Ironically, however, as *de jure* segregation of schools slowly

---

7. *Southern School News*, December 1964, *11*, p. 1.

8. T. F. Pettigrew, "Continuing Barriers to Desegregated Education in the South," *Sociology of Education*, 1965, *38*, pp. 99-111.

recedes, *de facto* segregation is rapidly increasing. In literally every standard metropolitan area in the United States racial segregation of housing increased from 1940 to 1960.[9] Consequently, the ever-growing Negro ghettoes combine with the neighborhood school principle to establish an increasingly entrenched pattern of racially-separate education throughout the urban North and South. The *de facto* segregation problem is particularly serious at the locally-based elementary level. Even in Boston, where the nonwhite population in 1960 constituted only 9 percent, there are seventeen elementary and two junior high schools with 90 percent or more Negro pupils.[10]

If anything, the shift from *de jure* to *de facto* school segregation complicates the issue further — though at least the shift frees the school system from virtually a legal mandate to discriminate. The judicial and legislative status of *de facto* segregated education is only now taking shape. Moreover, many Southern cities are presently openly striving to emulate the Northern *de facto* segregation pattern.[11] Indeed, the normal processes of urban development — continuing in-migration of Negroes to the central city and out-migration of whites to the suburbs — lead to much the same situation without conscious planning for such racially separate patterns. In short, the *de facto* school segregation controversy now raging in the North and West will soon erupt in the nominally "desegregated" cities of the South.

In summary, the problem involves the need for a swift and massive expansion of educational opportunities for Negro Americans. The fact is, unless such an expansion occurs soon throughout the nation, educational deficiencies will seriously impair the Negro American's ability to keep up with, much less gain on, the employment upgrading required by automation. Not all of this problem

---

9. K. E. Taeuber, "Negro Residential Segregation, 1940 to 1960: Changing Trends in the Large Cities of the United States." Unpublished paper read at the Annual Meetings of the American Sociological Association, 1962.

10. Massachusetts State Advisory Committee to the U.S. Commission on Civil Rights, *Report on Racial Imbalance in the Boston Public Schools* January 1965, p. 49.

11. T. F. Pettigrew, "*De facto* Segregation, Southern Style," *Integrated Education*, 1963, *1*(5), pp. 15-18; and Pettigrew, "Continuing Barriers to Desegregated Education in the South," *op. cit.*

can be attributed to public education; much of it is a result of poverty, poor health, broken homes, and all the other special marks of oppression borne by Negro Americans. But much of the problem *is* attributable to separate schools in the North as well as the South. And the problem of racially separate schools is growing more, not less, complex as it evolves from *de jure* to *de facto* segregation. Within this problem context, five focal issues worthy of panel attention can be identified.

Five Focal Issues

1. *Political pressures.* The desegregating school system, and especially the school board, typically becomes the target of at least three distinct sets of political pressures: integrationist demands of committed Negro and white liberals; the fears of the less-committed, generally upper-status whites (who often mislabel themselves as "moderates"[12]); and the resistant demands of committed segregationists (who, depending upon regional euphemisms, may call themselves anything from the Citizens' Council to Parents and Taxpayers). Thus, the basic question here becomes *how does a school system utilize these conflicting pressures to achieve racial desegregation and educational excellence?*

The precise answer to this query will vary, naturally, according to the particular community situation. But it should be possible to generate certain broadly applicable principles in this session's discussion. Toward that end, a number of relevant considerations can be proffered.

First, integrationist pressures are not likely to recede. In fact, it is highly probable that the Negro American revolution will expand further — in terms of size, intensity, and the scope of its demands.[13] This process has already posed a dilemma for school officials. On the one hand, refusal to deal with Negro demands for

---

12. T. F. Pettigrew, "The Myth of the Moderates," Christian Century, May 24, 1961, 78, pp. 649-651.

13. Pettigrew, *A Profile of the Negro American, op. cit.*

integrated education usually leads to community crisis. On the other hand, changes made in direct response to sharp Negro protest often act to encourage further Negro pressure and to intensify white fears and resistance. The not-so-easy-to-accomplish ideal is to stay ahead of the issue, thereby averting crisis and the necessity to meet eyeball-to-eyeball demands.

Second, white opinions on school desegregation have undergone extremely significant alterations throughout the country in recent years — far greater alterations than commonly recognized. Table 1 provides relevant data. Note the sharp shifts in both the North and South from 1942 to 1963, and the remarkable reversal in opinion toward token desegregation in the South from 1963 to 1965.

TABLE 1

Changing White Attitudes Toward School Desegregation

"Do you think white students and Negro students should go to the same schools or to separate schools?"*

	Percentage Answering "Same Schools"		
	1942	1956	1963
White Northerners	40	61	73
White Southerners	2	14	34
Total Whites	30	49	63

"Would you, yourself, have any objection to sending your children to a school *where a few of the children are colored?*"**

	Percentage Answering "No, would not object"	
	1963	1965
White Northern Parents	87	91
White Southern Parents	38	62

". . . *where half of the children are colored?*"

White Northern Parents	56	65
White Southern Parents	17	27

". . . *where more than half of the children are colored?*"

White Northern Parents	31	37
White Southern Parents	6	16

*Studies conducted by National Opinion Research Center and reported in: H. H. Hyman and P. B. Sheatsley, "Attitudes toward desegregation," *Scientific American,* July 1964, *211,* 16-23.

**Studies conducted by the American Institute of Public Opinion and reported in: G. Gallup's press release of May 22, 1965.

Finally, we should not overlook the vital "off-the-hook" functions that Federal desegregation pressures often provide for local school systems. Federal court orders and threatened withdrawal of Federal monies furnish many embattled school boards, North and South, with the publicly-announced rationale they needed to desegregate. Indeed, one large northern city has allowed a *de facto* segregation school suit to remain in the federal courts long after it could have been dismissed, for the specific purpose of utilizing the suit as an "off-the-hook" excuse to carry forward its program of desegregation and educational upgrading.

2. *The focus of responsibility.* Mention of the effects of forces external to the local community introduces the next major question: *where precisely is the focus of responsibility for expanding educational opportunities for Negro Americans?* This, too, is a difficult query, for it immediately involves us in such thorny issues as the limits of local school control, urban annexation, and the needed suburban contribution to inner city education.

The greatest strength of American public education — local school district autonomy and control — is also often its greatest weakness. Racial desegregation and massive compensatory educational programs are examples of efforts that often need external support — political as well as economic. Recent Federal legislation has certainly recognized this fact. Yet large outside aid complicates further an already complex and delicate relationship between Federal, state, metropolitan area, and local district responsibility.

The focus of responsibility for racial issues, as with other educational issues, necessarily, then, becomes more involved. One point however, is becoming increasingly clear: that is, urban desegregation and educational upgrading cannot long remain the sole responsibility of inner city school systems, even when bolstered by Federal and state subsidies. In some cases, the central city is beginning to run out of white children in its public schools — as seen now in Washington, D.C. Central city enlargement through annexation, even when politically possible (as in Nashville, Tennessee and Richmond, Virginia), presents Negro leadership with a perplexing dilemma; for the same annexation process that brings white children into the school system dilutes Negro political power. Educators need not be surprised, then, if Negro leadership in their communities proves ambivalent at best in its attitudes toward annexation.

Suburban cooperation with central city desegregation and upgrading programs provides a more promising possibility than annexation. The so-called "white noose around the Negro's neck" must become a more positive force in racial change. But there are serious political and economic problems raised by such schemes, too; the urgent need for suburban involvement in inner city desegregation plans, however, commends this issue for special attention.

3. *Problems of how to do it.* Much of the debate surrounding school desegregation has revolved around the practical nuts-and-bolts question: *how can racially balanced education actually be implemented?*

Again the precise answer must vary greatly with the particular community. But there is now a wide variety of devices from which a combination plan can be custom-styled for each school system. These devices include: (1) the district-wide redrawing of school lines to maximize racial balance (positive gerrymandering); (2) the pairing of predominantly white and Negro schools along the borders of the Negro ghetto (the Princeton Plan); (3) the alteration of "feeder" arrangements from elementary grades to junior highs and from junior highs to senior highs in order to maximize racial balance (the balanced feeder plan); (4) a priority for and careful placement of new and typically larger schools near but not within the ghetto (the rebuilding plan); (5) the conversion of more schools into district-wide specialized institutions (the differentiation of teaching functions); (6) the establishment of broad

303

educational centers covering many levels and programs (campus parks); and (7) the subsidized transportation of students (busing). Considerable controversy has resulted from the use of this final device; indeed, much of the public seems unaware of the significant amount of desegregation that can be achieved by the first six devices without resorting to subsidized transportation. Only in the largest metropolitan cities will extensive subsidized transportation be necessary to achieve significant desegregation.

Any combination plan adopted by a community could benefit from several additional features. First, as mentioned previously, any urban plan should ideally involve the cooperation of suburban school districts. Second, predominantly white schools which, under the plan, would be receiving a sizable number of new Negro students should be bolstered with specialty courses of genuine appeal to white children and parents as well as Negro.

These should include not just the latest in remedial techniques, but also classes in "prestige" subjects of obvious value that are not normally taught in public schools.

Third, the plan should include the racial balancing of teacher staffs as well as student bodies, for Negro children need models of authority and achievement with whom they can readily identify. Generally, the desegregation of teachers lags far behind the desegregation of pupils — especially in Southern systems still shaking off the traditions of *de jure* segregation. For example, after a decade of pupil desegregation in the 133 elementary schools of St. Louis, only 19 had staffs during the 1964-65 year with at least 10 percent of the minority race, 42 had less than 10 percent of the minority race, and 72 had entirely Negro or white staffs.

A number of problems are involved here: the need for the upgrading of standards for many Negro teachers; the tendency to "cream-off" the conspicuously talented Negro teachers for predominantly white schools; and the operation of teacher seniority privileges. At least, a beginning can be made through the random assignment of all new teachers entering the system, though even this technique conflicts with seniority placements.

Fourth, it is a useful, if unfortunate, rule of thumb that those children who most need racially balanced education are the hardest

304

to desegregate in any plan. For a variety of reasons, lower-status Negroes (who generally live deepest within the ghetto) and elementary school children (whose schools are traditionally most tied to the neighborhood) have the greatest need for racially balanced training.[14] This means that balance plans which look adequate in terms of gross numbers of children affected at the higher grade levels may be including only higher-status Negroes and not significantly reaching the critical early years. Careful checks by social class and grade level are thus in order.

Mention of the difficulty of desegregating elementary schools raises one of the key issues to be discussed by the panel — *the concept of the neighborhood school.* Growing out of the "multiple communities" ideal of city planning at the turn of the century, the neighborhood school concept has assumed for many the aura of a sacrosanct shibboleth, a concept not to be questioned. Instead, we need considerable research, thinking, and open discussion on the subject. What are the real advantages of the neighborhood school? What are its disadvantages? How can it best be modified and blended with racial desegregation plans?

Finally, any implementation plan must be based on *a reasonable definition of just what constitutes meaningful "racial desegregation" and "racial balance."* Here there are at least two major alternatives to be compared in the session's discussion. One possibility is to peg the definition to the nonwhite percentage of the area's overall school population; thus if 12 percent of a system's students are nonwhite, then ideally each school in the system would approach a non-white student composition of 12 percent. There are at least two criticisms of this definition: it is often impractical in all but reasonably small areas; and it treats the individual school as a simple reflection of the community, rather than as an integumented institution with its own dynamics and requirements.

A second definition of a racially balanced school attempts to meet these criticisms with a relatively fixed, rather than variable,

14. T. F. Pettigrew and Patricia Pajonis, "Social Psychological Considerations of Racially-Balanced Schools." An appendix to: *Because It Is Right — Educationally — Report of the Advisory Committee on Racial Imbalance and Education.* Boston: Mass. State Board of Education, April 1965; pp. 87-108.

gauge. On the basis of several social psychological considerations (including the Gallup survey data shown in Table 1), the ideally balanced school is one whose student body includes from roughly 20 to 45 percent nonwhites.[15] The disadvantage here is that uniracial schools must result in systems with fewer than 20 percent or more than 45 percent nonwhite children.

4. *Racial balance and compensatory efforts.* Another focal issue boils down to the query: *how can a school system judiciously blend racial balance and massive compensatory training?*

The question arises because it is apparent that one without the other will not be enough. Merely balancing the schools without attention to the lower standards and achievement typically found in predominantly Negro schools is obviously fraught with serious difficulties.

Racial balance is one among many requirements of a first-rate public education in a multiracial society and world, but it alone does not guarantee educational excellence. Likewise, compensatory measures and the upgrading of standards in predominantly Negro schools are not enough either without also correcting the basic conditions which help to create the need for these compensatory measures in the first place. High on the list of factors contributing to the present situation, of course, is racial separation and discrimination. Thus, it makes no sense to correct past educational damage while allowing further damage to occur.

Granted then, the need for both, the session needs to discuss ideas for inter-meshing the two processes.

5. *Problems of the desegregated school and classroom.* A desegregated school does not guarantee an integrated environment, nor does it guarantee a good learning environment. Therefore, a final focal question becomes: *how can educators achieve interracial school and classroom environments which maximize intergroup acceptance and learning for all children?*

Social psychological research has specified the conditions toward which educators must strive. Desegregated situations achieve max-

---

15. *Ibid.*

imal intergroup acceptance when the groups are treated as complete equals, have common goals, do not directly compete against one another, and interact with the full support of authorities.[16] Moreover, desegregated situations provide an effective learning environment when they heighten the probability of success, reduce to a minimum both "social" and "failure threat," and exploit the social facilitation effect achieved by interracial acceptance.[17] Discussion by the panel and further research is needed, however, on the methods which educators might employ to achieve these desirable conditions.

In summary, five focal issues and an array of more detailed questions can be identified as relevant to the desegregation of America's public schools: political pressures, the focus of responsibility, problems of how to do it (including questions concerning the neighborhood school concept and a workable definition of "school desegregation" and "racial balance"), racial balance and compensatory efforts, and, finally, problems of the desegregated school and classroom.

If this session of the White House Conference on Education is to clarify effectively the critical problem of school desegregation, these five plus related issues must be dealt with forthrightly by all of us.

---

16. G. W. Allport, *The Nature of Prejudice*. Cambridge, Mass.: Addison-Wesley, 1954; Chapter 16.

17. I. Katz, "Review of Evidence Relating to Effects of Desegregation on the Intellectual Performance of Negroes," *American Psychologist*, June 1964, 19, pp. 381-399.

DAVID W. MINAR

Dr. Minar, a political scientist at
Northwestern University, is currently
serving as Acting Director of Northwestern's Center for Metropolitan
Studies (during the sabbatical absence of the center's director, Scott
Greer).

THE POLITICS

OF EDUCATION

IN LARGE CITIES

T HIS IS NOT THE place to attempt an urban sociology
or to rehearse the familiar generalizations about what
today's city life is like. There are, however, a few central features
of the picture that have a direct bearing on our purpose, and we
should be reminded of these. Perhaps we might begin by suggesting that there are two broad types of big cities in America now:
those that are still on the rise and those that are on the decline.[1]
Roughly speaking, the former are young and located in the South-
west, the latter are old and Eastern or Midwestern. The former
are the products of the automobile age; the latter, the products of
the age of waterways, railroads, and streetcars. The former are geo-

---

AUTHOR'S NOTE: A slightly different version of this paper was originally
presented at the Research Seminar on Racial and Other Issues Affecting
School Administration in the Great Cities of America, in Chicago, August 1-5,
1965. The seminar was sponsored by Northwestern University and supported
by the Cooperative Research Program, Office of Education, U.S. Department
of Health, Education, and Welfare. The paper presented there is included in
the Report of that project (No. G-028) edited by Michael D. Usdan.

1. Taken strictly in terms of the 1950-1960 population change, ten of the largest cities
lost ground (Baltimore, Boston, Chicago, Cleveland, Detroit, New York, Philadelphia, St.
Louis, San Francisco, Washington) and five gained (Dallas, Houston, Los Angeles, Milwaukee, New Orleans). From U.S. Bureau of Census, City and County Data Book, 1962
(a statistical abstract supplement), Washington, D.C.: U.S. Government Printing Office,
1962, Table 6.

graphically, economically, and culturally dispersed, while the latter are much more confined and concentrated.[2]

In sheer numbers, the older cities still dominate the overall American urban picture. As we will have reason to suggest later, however, the newer cities may tell us more about our urban future. There is much that differentiates the two types, including much that bears heavily on styles of life, political problems, and political processes.[3] At the same time, the two types have a great deal in common, including some overriding social characteristics that tend to heavily influence the educational system. For the most part, what follows will be concerned with the common features and their consequences, though perhaps our discussion will lean in some degree toward the more widespread phenomena of the older urban area.

The Sociopolitical Shape of Today's Big Cities

For several generations, large American cities have served as staging areas for the national culture, as ports of entry through which candidates for assimilation passed. With the legislated decline in immigration of the mid-1920s this process did not cease, for internal shifts of population have sustained the flow of the uninitiated unto urban areas. In recent years this flow has consisted mostly of members of "visible" minority groups: Negroes, Puerto Ricans, and American Indians, along with rural whites.[4] At the same time, the cities have seen a steady outward flow, particularly of middle- and lower-middle income families, to their suburban hinterlands. Thus, the members of visible minorities have made up increasing proportions of large city populations. While ten of the fifteen largest cities declined in population between 1950 and

---

2. Compare, for example, the following population densities (per square mile): New York, 24,705; Philadelphia, 15,768; Chicago, 15,850; Boston, 14,525; Los Angeles, 5,448; Houston, 2,860; Dallas, 2,027. Compiled from U.S. Bureau of Census, *ibid.*

3. See Scott Greer, *Governing the Metropolis*, New York: John Wiley & Sons, Inc., 1962, pp. 9-21.

4. Cf. Raymond W. Mack, "The Changing Ethnic Fabric of the Metropolis," in B. J. Chandler et al. (Eds.), *Education in Urban Society*, New York: Dodd, Mead & Company, Inc., 1962, pp. 54-69.

1960, every one of the fifteen saw an increase in proportion of non-whites. Only five had fewer than 20 percent nonwhites by 1960, and these proportions have doubtlessly grown in the intervening period.[5]

This means that the cities have continued to occupy the role of socializing agencies; the city has been and will be for some time to come a great teaching machine, introducing people to the larger flow of metropolitan life and its ways. The job must now be done, however, under somewhat more difficult circumstances than it was done in years past. The reasons for its greater difficulty apply differentially from place to place. The main factors, however, would seem to be these: (1) Because of long-standing cultural prejudices that affect the receptivity of society, the visible minorities per se are harder to "process" to assimilation. (2) Because of the changing shape of demands for labor and locational shifts in economic enterprise, the numbers of urban minorities find it difficult to sustain themselves and improve their occupational status. (3) The physical plant of the city, both public and private, is deteriorating and obsolete. (4) The resource (i.e., revenue) base of the city is contracting as a result of the shifts in population and economic characteristics and the physical obsolescence mentioned above. (5) These shifts have also robbed the central city of many of its traditional leadership resources. (6) The mounting thrust for equality of treatment for minorities has raised the level of consciousness of the city's socializational function.

The consequences of these conditions for the urban body politic are many, and perhaps the most acute of them have direct bearing on public education. When we speak of the city's major problem being socialization, we highlight both the centrality and the difficulty of today's city school system — for socialization is inherently a teaching process. While we do not know with any precision the relative contributions of family, school, other institutions, and the life routine itself to the socialization of new urbanites, we do know that we expect much of the school. Thus, educators are, whether realistically or not, supposed to lead the society in its

---

5. U.S. Bureau of Census, *op. cit.*

efforts to deal with its biggest job. In a limited way, it is not unfair to say that the schools are being called upon to solve the city's problems. From the standpoint of demands, or what we might call "social inputs," the situation of the big city school system has changed in three fundamental ways: First, the quality of demands has changed, i.e., new qualities are expected of the services the schools render; second, new groups, organized and unorganized, have entered the urban and hence the educational picture;[6] and, third, the support base for the educational function has changed with respect to revenue and leadership.

The Political Structure of the Great City

At the same time that these things are going on in urban political society, other developments have been under way in the city's political structure. Some loose historical reconstruction may help us to understand the character of the political system called upon to respond to today's demands on the city.

It is no longer widely supposed that city politics is the politics of the boss and his machine. Whether or not vestiges of the machine remain, its main features have disappeared, and most cities have come one or two steps beyond it. During the age of the urban machine, the city was dominated by those who held office and reaped the benefits that went with it — the "spoils" of patronage. The medium of exchange in the machine city was votes, and the machine flourished because of the presence of a large number of "vulnerables" in urban society who needed "small" favors for which their votes could be traded. These vulnerables were particularly the poor, the recently-arrived, and the small businessmen.[7] In structure, the machine was usually a hierarchy of go-betweens connecting those who delivered the votes and those who controlled the distribution of rewards.

---

6. See the comments of Sayre and Kaufman in their "Introduction to the Paperbound Edition" of *Governing New York City*, New York: W. W. Norton & Company, Inc., p. xlii.

7. See the analysis of Robert Merton in *Social Theory and Social Structure* (rev. ed.), New York: The Free Press, 1957, pp. 72-82.

As the social character of the city changed, so did the social foundation on which the machine had rested. This shift came about gradually, of course, and at different times in different places. Analyses of the decline of the machine tend to emphasize the critical importance of the decrease in immigration and the inception of public, particularly Federal, welfare programs. These factors doubtlessly reduced the number and the vulnerability of urban vulnerables. Another factor working in the same direction, perhaps with even greater force, was the change in the structure of economic enterprise. With the expansion and stabilization of the corporation, the small business began to give way, at least in proportionate influence, to the big one. The latter, being big and often national in scope, had greater powers of resistance and less particularized interests and was thus less dependent on the machine's favors.[8]

What succeeded the machine as the "typical" urban form is not so clear. In many cases it may have been a "power elite" of economic notables.[9] This type of structure is based not on control of votes and office but on ability to impress those who do make authoritative policy, (or refuse to make it). Those who hold this power are people of achieved or inherited position who work behind the scenes to pull the strings that make the policy process go. Their participation in the process may be self-interested or it may be based on a sense of civic obligation, a political *noblesse oblige*. In any case, they eschew public office and, often, the public eye.

Many words have been spent in social science over whether these monolithic power elites actually do exist and how to find out if they do. It would not serve our purpose to review the literature of this dispute here.[10] Speculation and impression suggest strongly

---

8. Greer, *op. cit.*, pp. 66-68.

9. The most important early uses of this model are Robert and Helen Lynd, *Middletown*, New York: Harcourt, Brace & World, Inc., 1929, and Floyd Hunter, *Community Power Structure*, Chapel Hill, N.C.: University of North Carolina Press, 1953.

10. See especially Robert A. Dahl, "A Critique of the Ruling Elite Model," *American Political Science Review*, LII (June, 1958), 463-469; Nelson Polsby, *Community Power and Political Theory*, New Haven: Yale University Press, 1963; Thomas J. Anton, "Power, Pluralism, and Local Politics," *Administrative Science Quarterly*, VII (March, 1963), 425-457.

that some cities were controlled this way during the period when the machine was dwindling away, particularly where the pace and distribution of economic growth facilitated the influence of the few.

Impression and some evidence also suggest, however, that the era of the power elite may have been a passing phase that the city has now transcended. The power-conspiracy version of the urban world is temptingly simple but probably too simple to describe accurately the great city of today. It seems likely that most contemporary cities are much more loosely governed from many more dispersed centers of power than the elite model supposes. The complexity of the urban social structure and such economic changes as the growth of the national (and metropolitan) corporation have made the city increasingly difficult to manage through any integrated privately based structure.

A more typical form today is probably pluralistic, a set of smaller and shifting centers of power that take shape around specific clusters of policy interests.[11] Thus, city politics is what Norton Long has called an "ecology of games," a flexible, shifting interplay of forces whose actors vary as the problems at issue vary.[12] Influence in such a city is not confined to economic dominants; indeed, in many cases the economic elite seems to have abdicated its role of civic responsibility except where its obvious self-interest is at stake. The particular shape of a given game is determined by the stakes of that game, though with certain interests having a semipermanent advantage.

It would appear that in cities of the pluralistic type, a special and important part may often be played by those with political authority, especially, for example, by the big city mayor. What a pluralistic system is most likely to lack is overall coordination and perspective. This the mayor can supply. He can become an identifier of proposals, a go-between, a negotiator among the forces, public and private, that play in the urban game. In playing this part, the mayor can be the most visible point in the system, for his

---

11. Robert A. Dahl, *Who Governs?*, New Haven: Yale University Press, 1961.

12. Norton E. Long, "The Local Community as an Ecology of Games," *American Journal of Sociology*, LXIV (November, 1958), 251-261.

is the point of convergence of all major civic efforts. Thus, he may seem to be a leader, even if his role is substantially that of broker of power and programs. The central function of big city politics is this function of brokerage among a multiplicity of interests.[13]

Contemporary city politics show one other feature that must be emphasized: the considerable and growing influence of bureaucratic technical expertise. The importance of the hired expert is more visible and doubtless proportionately greater in the smaller community than in the large city. It is most prominently apparent in many places where the city manager clearly has the upper hand, in policy initiative as well as in administrative control. Although the manager plan has not been used in large cities, these places have certainly felt the growing need for technical leadership. In a variety of such fields as health, welfare, planning, and policing, the city must call on the experts, and the advancing complexity of urban life pushes toward more, not less, such reliance in the future. The age of municipal technology is with us, and while political forms may ordinarily lag behind social realities, we may expect that in the next stage of urban political development the technical expert will play a predominant role. What shape the technician-dominated system will take and how the expert is to be controlled may be the vital questions for our urban future.[14]

The Peculiar Place of Education in the Politics of Today's Big City

Having reviewed the social situation and political structure of the city in general terms, we may now turn to the place of public education in the urban picture. At the level of gross description such terms as "ambiguous" and "problematic" obviously seem apropos. What can we say that takes us beyond this level? As an earlier section of this chapter suggested, the demands on the urban

---

13. Although phrased somewhat differently, this seems to be the theme of the interpretation of Chicago politics advanced in Edward C. Banfield, *Political Influence*, New York: The Free Press of Glencoe, 1961, and that of New York politics found in Sayre and Kaufman, *op. cit.*

14. This, of course, is a manifestation of the classic problem of bureaucracy.

educational system have not grown less, while the conditions under which they are to be satisfied grow ever more complex. What of the decision-making system through which these particular demands are to be met?

Traditionally, American educational organization has been heavily influenced by the push toward separation from the other functions of the community. The overarching political importance of education as a means to social progress has virtually been a part of the American credo, but it has been thought best to shelter the process of education itself from the world of political action. This isolation reflects, perhaps, a societal urge to protect the young from the influence of politics, a sphere of activity that Americans have tended to regard as unsavory. In recent years too, as society generally has undergone greater functional specialization, the educational process has been professionalized and therefore regarded as a process to be understood and controlled by expertise.

The effects, of course, are mixed. Formal authority over the schools has been retained in lay hands and the schools have not always been insulated from municipal politics. Particularly in the past, many school systems have been dominated or exploited by bosses and power elites, often for quite uneducational purposes. The thrust, however, has been otherwise. The interference of politicians has notably declined in most places, even where formal appointive powers remain with them. Through legislative change and the evolution of usage, school government has moved closer to separation and professional control.[15]

The current dilemma of the schools may arise from just this situation. The school men of the large cities, in other words, may have become technical experts before their time. It is interesting to compare the use of expertise in general management with its use in school administration in big municipalities. The manager plan as such has not been employed in the big cities to any signifi-

---

15. For a discussion of separation from a political scientist's perspective, see Roscoe C. Martin, *Government and the Suburban School* ("The Economics and Politics of Public Education, 2,") Syracuse, N.Y.: Syracuse University Press, 1963; also Edward M. Tuttle, *School Board Leadership in America*, Danville, Ill.: Interstate Printers and Publishers, 1958.

cant extent.[16] Presumably, it has not been thought adaptable to and has not been acceptable within the political framework that holds the large community together. As the conditions of government have changed, the big city has responded to the need for technical-professional leadership on a specialist basis, rather than by hiring an overall administrative manager. In a few cities, general management leadership has been instituted through the person of a "chief administrative officer."[17] His functions, however, have been more restricted than those of the manager under the orthodox manager plan, and, more importantly, this chief administrative officer has been seen as the principal administrative aide of an explicitly political mayor. Thus, in the big city the technicians have been sheltered by political leadership that can effectively exercise the political "brokerage" function.

The situation of school government has typically been quite different. For reasons noted above, the school administrators have been role-defined as technical leaders and set off from the conventional channels of political activity. Boards of education, which formally link the schools to the authority system, tend not to develop strong, cohesive leadership patterns, and their members are not likely to be political insiders. In the smaller and relatively homogeneous place, professional educators are able to operate in their own spheres much like city managers. They build trust and exhibit capacities that enable them to administer with a relatively free hand and in the nature of things they also assume a great deal of policy leadership. In the big and heterogeneous city, however, professional municipal administrators ordinarily have had a kind of political protection (or direction, depending on how one wants to see it) that educational administrators no longer have.

---

16. Only one (Dallas) of the largest fifteen cities uses the council-manager form; only three other cities of more than 500,000 (San Antonio, San Diego, Cincinnati) use it. Of thirty cities in the 250,000-500,000 category, only twelve have managers. See International City Managers' Association, *Recent Council-Manager Developments and Directory of Council-Manager Cities*, Chicago: International City Managers' Association, 1961. Note that these large cities have been mostly places of rapid population growth in recent years and that they adopted the plan when much smaller in size.

17. See Wallace S. Sayre, "The General Manager Idea for Large Cities," *Public Administration Review*, XIV (Autumn, 1954), 253-258.

The effects of this arrangement vary with local political circumstances. In places and times of social placidity, the educational system takes its guidelines from standards of professional excellence. While its objective quality is conditioned by the abilities of those in control and the resources available, it is free from the distraction and plunder of politics. On the other hand, when the social seas get rough, the system may founder, for its commanders know how to keep the decks clean but not how to trim the sails. The educational administrators tend not to be oriented toward performing the political function and not to have others at hand to do it for them.

Today is not a time of placidity in the big cities; it is a time of troubles. It is, as we pointed out above, a time when extraordinary demands are made on the schools and when resources are on the decline. The very success of American society, symbolized in affluence, has made it impatient of imperfection in important enterprises. Easily the biggest specific source of trouble for the schools is, of course, the demand for equal opportunity for minority children, which is being stated in ever more intense and pervasive terms.

All of these major issues for urban education have overriding political dimensions, and they are the subject of new forces and tactics on the political scene. Perhaps the important point, however, is that they have developed at the juncture in time when the educational sector of the political system is ill-equipped to handle them. They call for skillful performance of the political brokerage function. But those who are responsible are not used to being brokers, and those who are brokers are not responsible. While the school system has achieved protection from politics, politicians have also achieved some protection from the issues that plague the schools. Neither protection, of course, is complete, as the recent experiences of some big city mayors have forceably demonstrated. The place of education in the system, however, is such that there are few smooth relationships and accustomed routines through which the political leadership and the educational leadership together can be brought to confront urban problems. The dilemma is inherent in the shape of the system.

The solution of school problems is further handicapped by the political, social, and economic facts of metropolitan fragmentation. Because of the flight to the suburbs, the political leaders of the central city do not have a balanced social situation with which to work. The metropolitan relationship tends to seal the city's problems in, to confine them to a part of the larger "natural" city, the entire metropolis. Thus, the central city gets little help in financial or leadership contributions from the suburbs; and for the social groups most acutely affected, the suburb does not even serve as an escape hatch. In the absence of any serious prospect for "metro" government in most places, this multidimensional segregation probably will have the effect of compelling the central city to look to the state and national governments for ever-increasing support and guidance. Whether this will have good consequences for policy and policy-making in the city may very much be doubted.

From a political scientist's point of view, then, the problem for big city schools would seem to be to give them political means for solving their political problems. Neither the problems nor the democratic processes can be wished away. For the time being, school policy will have to respond to social demands as well as to standards of professional performance. School policy, like the policy of the entire municipality, will feel the pressures of new groups with new expectations. These already include not only the racial minorities but also better organized teachers, social workers, and other personnel. In the future, they might even include the most downtrodden minority of all, the students, if recent developments in colleges and universities make their way down through the grades.

How is this alteration in educational government to come about? One thing is sure: If there is a simple answer, it is not an obvious one. Some standard prescriptions may readily be recommended: imagination, creativity, boldness, openness to change, communication, better training, and, above all, research. Beyond these, the going gets harder. One suggestion does seem to result from what we have been saying: Much more attention should be paid to the processes and structures of school government, and these need to be seen in their relation to the entire flow of community political

318

life. The discussion of school issues tends to concentrate on policies, on what to do about curriculum, what to do about integration, what to do about teaching the disadvantaged, etc. These are worthy points of focus, but without distracting resources from these efforts, we should put more into examination of how policies are made, into the study of decision-making processes. Processes are the channels through which the cues to socially satisfying policies are understood and translated into action. Old consensus-building routines may be doing more harm than good; the only way we can find out is to open our minds to the evidence, hopefully evidence that has been systematically gathered and evaluated. Failures in the city's efforts to deal with its problems may be rooted in failures in institutional decision-making behavior.

Two other general lines of action may be suggested. Both are familiar, neither is easy, both are somewhat unpalatable. One is to induce school men to act more like politicians, to induce them to accept and act out their roles as brokers of political interest, as some few clearly do now. Even when educational administrators begin to behave this way, they must also continue to serve their functions as technical experts. No doubt we can train future generations of school administrators to do both. The dispiriting fact, of course, is that today's problems will not wait for a new generation.

The second path of action, rather more complementary than contradictory to the first, leads toward pulling education into the main flow of city politics. To be sure, the municipal mechanisms often seem to have little to recommend them. But if political problems require political solutions, today's urban educational problems may best be treated through the community's recognized political institutions. On behalf of this position, it can also be argued that the city's various problems need to be handled as a whole, through coordinated policy rather than in little lumps as though they were unrelated to each other. The close interconnections among education, housing, welfare, health, and the maintenance of order illustrate the point in an obvious way.

The situation that confronts urban education poses a cruel dilemma. In the short and middle run, it seems to require political invigoration, however that invigoration can be accomplished. On

319

the other hand, in the long run, it may require less of political leadership and more of technical expertise. The social stresses that now plague our cities will not last forever; if, as we may suppose, the assimilation processes continue as they have in the past, the future city of the long run will be a place of fewer intergroup conflicts. The assimilation of visible minorities may be more difficult than assimilation has been before, but the society has never before been so self-conscious about assimilation. Nor has it been so affluent, a factor that should facilitate assimilation a good deal. Predictions about the time required to "settle" racial problems would be foolhardy, but these problems are not insoluble and may not take as long for solution as pessimism leads many to believe.

Social experience suggests, of course, that as old problems disappear new ones take their place. But it seems unlikely that the urban problems of tomorrow will require the same political treatment as those of today. Technological innovation will probably push the city in the direction of greater physical dispersion and higher levels of service. The old cities of today, as they replace physical plant, may come to look more and more like our "new" cities of the twentieth century. This trend, like others operating on today's world, will push toward greater reliance on technical expertise, and hence greater power in the hands of the technical expert. In the coming era, the educator, like his professional counterpart in other fields of community service, may well find himself with a freer hand and a heavier responsibility than ever before. Meanwhile, his problem is twofold: how to deal with a political today and how to get ready in a political today for a technical tomorrow.